TWELVE SERMONS.

TWELVE

SERMONS:

DELIVERED AT ANTIOCH COLLEGE

BY

HORACE MANN.

BOSTON:
TICKNOR AND FIELDS.
M DCCC LXI.

CAMBRIDGE:
THURSTON & MILES,
Stereotypers and Printers.

PREFACE.

The Twelve Sermons constituting this volume, were written and delivered while Mr. Mann was President of Antioch College. The Faculty of the College retained the privilege of preaching in their own hands, and either officiated alternately, or agreed upon inviting other clergymen, or perchance laymen, from abroad, to take their places.

The Editor has added to the Sermons the Meditations that were found in the manuscripts, and which, though not read, undoubtedly formed the basis of the prayers accompanying the Sermons.

The careful revising hand of the Author would doubtless have given these Sermons to the world, if he had ever published them, in a more perfect form, and with the addition of much that was spoken extemporaneously when delivered; but they will be valuable as they are, it is hoped, to those who loved to listen to his teachings.

CONTENTS.

GOD'S BEING THE FOUNDATION OF HUMAN DUTY.

SERMONS.

I.

GOD'S BEING THE FOUNDATION OF HUMAN DUTY.

In the new and almost parental relation in which I stand to young men and young women, I propose to deliver a series of Discourses on various subjects pertaining to Human Duty, and particularly designed to show that the realization of Happiness can alone come from the performance of Duty.

These Discourses will not be theological, though they will have something to say respecting the existence, character, and attributes of God, and much to say respecting his laws and government on earth. They will not be strictly scientific ; though they will welcome and solicit the aid of all those departments of systematized knowledge which we dignify with the name of science ; — all our natural and moral sciences being but expressions of God's will as manifested in nature and man. Least of all will they be devoted to mere questions of political economy, or profit and loss, in a mercantile or worldly sense ; though even here, they will avail themselves of every opportunity to demonstrate that, as "godliness is great gain," so there can be no great gain, or gain of any kind, in despite or in defiance of godliness.

Not being an ordained minister of the Gospel, I may conform to the almost universal custom of such persons, in not speaking from a text; and yet I may be allowed to cite the text which an ordained minister would preach upon.

In regard to Duty, I believe not only in the Ten Commandments, but in ten thousand. God lives and rules by law; and, therefore, wherever He lives, and wherever He rules, there is law, and a law of God is a command. All the kingdoms of nature around us — the inorganic which exists, and the organic which lives, and the sentient which feels — are pervaded by God's laws. We also, in all our powers, faculties, and susceptibilities, are the subjects of God's laws. Our limbs and our body, our stomach and our brain, not less than our heart, each is the subject of God's laws. That is, there is a right way, and there are wrong ways for them all; and God commands the right way. There is, therefore, not only a Decalogue, but a Mirialogue.

Of course, among all these commands, there must be the first ten. But having learned these, we ought to go on and learn the rest as fast as we can; and, as we learn, we ought to obey; otherwise, the learning is but the unprofitable hoard of the miser.

But if I discourse on Duty, I must have a foundation for my discourse. I must have proof of the solidity and validity of that foundation. No man should affirm anything, or deny anything, without proof, that is, without reason. With all rational minds, it is in vain for me to build the most magnificent superstructure of argument, and leave the four corners hanging in the air.

I find the foundation of Duty in the being and attributes of God. There are secondary and incidental arguments, but this is the primary and original one. There are collateral arguments; but this is fundamental. Even on the atheistic hypothesis of no God, it could be shown that Duty is expedient; but on the theistic hypothesis of a God, it can be demonstrated that the knowledge and the performance of Duty are the highest moral necessities for every human being.

It may be a very easy matter to adduce such evidence of the existence of God as shall be acceptable and satisfactory to one who believes it already. Such a one is only to be moved down the inclined plane of argument, and goes easily. But I wish to adduce such evidence as shall be imperative and constraining to those minds which do not derive their evidence from their belief, but their belief from their evidence. Such minds are to be moved up the inclined plane of argument, and so both friction and weight are to be overcome.

First, then, I would reverently attempt to prove the existence of a God, by the same kind of evidence as proves the existence of the external and material world. Do you believe in the existence of rivers and forests, of mountains and oceans, of sun, moon, and a firmament of stars? Do you believe in the existence of men, and of the various zoological races, whether they walk or fly, or creep or swim? Do you believe in the existence of anything outside of yourself, or in anything that is not yourself?

People who do not believe in the existence of anything outside of themselves, or in the existence of anything which is not themselves, are commonly considered the subjects of medical treatment, before they become the subjects of syllogistic or argumentative treatment. And this medical treatment, in well-ordered states, is administered inside a lunatic or insane asylum. When, therefore, we see a man outside of an asylum for the insane, we are entitled to presume that he does believe in the existence of a material world. As to those who are inside of the insane hospital, let them first go through with a course of medicine, and afterwards, if necessary, with a course of logic.

But on what evidence do we believe in the existence of a material universe outside of ourselves? I answer, on the evidence of the senses, and of reason.

On the evidence of the senses. There is an ancient proverb, that "seeing is believing." By our eyes, we see that things exist around us. And we see the greatest differences between these things, in color, shape, size, &c. If all of them, taken together, are not something, then they are nothing; and it seems to me that Nothing would look more alike, — that is, if it could *look* at all. The external world gives out its myriad varieties, of sounds to our ear, of odors to our smell, of tastes to our palate, and of tactual sensations. The mountain top does not appear like the mountain cave; the shriek of a drowning man does not sound like an infant's laugh; water new-born from a pure fountain does not taste nor smell like the drunkard's foul beverage; and the thorn-tree does not feel like the pigeon's plumy breast. If *Nothing* could be seen or heard, or smelt, or tasted, or felt, would it not be more alike? When Nothing can blast the eye-balls in the lightning's flash, or solace the diseased vision in the verdure of spring; when Nothing can stun in the whirlwind's roar, or whisper a welcome to its sweets as its comes o'erladen from spicy groves; when Nothing can congeal us with arctic colds, or dissolve us with tropic heats; when

Nothing can tear us in pieces by the tiger's fangs, or bind up our wounds with Æsculapian skill; when Nothing can consume our bodies and scatter the ashes to the winds, or, with Egyptian unguents can preserve these same bodies for thousands of years; — when Nothing can do all these things, and ten times ten million more like them, and repeat them forever, then it will be time to alter its name, and call it Something. Now, that is the Something, which is not you, but is outside of you, whose existence I am demonstrating. But, if you say that the thing which you call Nothing has the power to put on all this myriad of forms and to do all this myriad of things, then you mean by Nothing, what I mean by Something, and we will not dispute about words.

Now I think it can be shown that there is as high a kind of evidence to our spirits of what we call the Spiritual World, as there is to our bodily senses of what we call the Material World.

I think it can be as convincingly proved that Arkwright and Fulton had mechanical talent; that Lord Chatham and Dr. Franklin had statesmanship; that Shakspeare and Milton had poetic genius; and that Howard and Oberlin had philanthropy; as that they had bodies, lived in houses, breathed air, and ate food. My mind or spirit has proof of the existence of mind or spirit in others, — proof of affection, talent, genius, virtue, devotion, just as my bodily senses have of the existence of what we call the material universe, — seas, plains, fish, beast, bird, man, stars, galaxies. The spirit has powers of perception for spiritual qualities outside of itself, just as the body has organs for the perception of material properties outside of itself. What is this, which we call love or hate, which we call philanthropy or misanthropy, which we call fidelity or perfidy, which we call saintliness or sin, devotion or impiety; — are all these the attributes and qualities of Nothing also? The Levite and the Samaritan, Napoleon and Washington, Judas and Jesus, were they all the same, too; or rather, were they all Nothing? I say, as I said before, that I think we should find Nothing less variously diversified; or, if you say that Nothing does put on this multiplicity and diversity of forms, then you affirm that it is no longer Nothing, but Something. Rational beings, then, who believe in the existence of what we call Matter, cannot escape from a belief in what we call Mind.

But perhaps an objector will say, that a proof of the existence of mind does not prove the existence of a Supreme Mind, — of a creative, intelligent, sovereign, first cause. But here, too, it seems to me that the evidence is overwhelming. It is the same in nature, or in kind, as the evidence before referred to, — the evidence of the existence of matter, and of the existence of mind, — the same in kind, though infinitely greater in amount and in demonstrativeness.

Whether unaided human reason would ever have conceived or originated the idea of a God, has been questioned, and is perhaps questionable. But this I deem to be a fact not questionable; that there is a sentiment in man, something instinctive, though infinitely higher and wider in its functions than mere animal instinct, which does suggest, intimate, nay, which would originate the conception of a Supreme Being. And if any pestilence of atheism could suppress or abolish all expression and belief of the existence of a God in a whole generation, the next generation would originate the same idea for itself. Extinguish it in the parent, and it would blaze up anew in his children. Just as perfect arms and perfect feet will come to children, though born through a father whose own limbs have all been amputated, so an inborn sentiment and apprehension of a God will come to a child whose father has striven to smother and stifle that sentiment in himself. All nations and tribes which have ever been discovered, and into whose condition any adequate scrutiny has been made, have been found to possess the idea of a Supreme Being. The polished Athenians erect a temple to the Unknown God. The Persians worship the sun. The degraded African has his Fetich. And thus, I say, we have inward faculties of veneration and wonder, which of their own mere action suggest the existence, evolve the idea of a great Spiritual Being above us, just as we have outward senses that excite the idea of material objects around us. To any one who could perfectly comprehend our structure, a knowledge of the eye, even before birth, would communicate the fact of the existence of light; a knowledge of the structure of the ear would show that it was made for sound; and an inspection of lungs and blood would prove the existence of the air. Just so the religious sentiments of veneration and wonder, which are natural to us and born in us, suggest or originate the conception of a God. Now we may call this Being by any one of a thousand names, — with the Hebrews, *Eloi;* with the Greeks, *Theos;* with the Romans, *Deus;* with the French, *Dieu;* with the Germans, *Gott;* or with the English, *God;* or we may call Him the Unknown or the Unnamed God; or we may call Him by the sublime appellation "I am." That is another matter. We are now speaking of the sentiment in the human mind, and not of its name in a human language.

After these strong religious sentiments of veneration and wonder have excited the idea of a God, just as thirst or hunger excite the idea of water and food, then the reason or understanding takes up that idea, and gives it shape and qualities. And here two things are certain ; that, in forming its idea of God, the mind can attribute to Him no quality or attribute of which it has itself no conception, and that it will attribute to God such qualities and attributes as most abound in itself. You may hear a thousand men expatiate upon the character of God, and no two of them will apportion His perfections alike. The austere man always attributes to Him more of a stern justice ; the benevolent man more mercy ; the lover of grandeur and sublimity regales himself and exults in God's wonder-working Omnipotence ; while the self-esteeming man thinks God loves him and his friends better than the whole world besides. How can it be otherwise ? How can man build up the idea of God in his own mind out of conceptions or thoughts which he never had in that mind ? If he has no science, no idea of the laws of nature and of mind, how can he conceive of a God, who works eternally by law ; or if he be supremely selfish, how can he conceive of a God of love ?

After our religious instincts, then, have given us the conception of a God, or after we have been taught by our parents or otherwise, to form this conception in conformity with our religious instincts, then our own appetites and passions, hopes and fears, reason or unreason, humility or pride, go to work to think out a God for themselves, or to find one in the Bible, or in the Koran, or in the events of Providence; and they put into their conception or picture of God, more or less of this quality or that, just as they have more or less of this quality or that in their own minds. The contrary would be to say that a man could in his theology attribute ideas and qualities to God of which he himself had no conception; that a painter can put colors into a picture, when he neither has any such colors on his pallet, or any idea of them in his mind.

Here, then, we arrive at two great conclusions; first, that the natural powers of man do suggest the idea or conception of God, so that we find the most savage and barbarous nations in possession of the belief; and second, that human passions and reason modify this belief. All men, then, are alike in having the conception of a Deity; but they are amazingly unlike in the Deity they conceive of. I suppose there are no two men in the world, nor ever were, whose conceptions of the Deity were precisely alike. One man is a cannibal, another is a Christian; one man has vast knowledge of the works of God, another has ignorance vaster still; one man has fervid religious sentiments, another is cold and phlegmatic. Now, if such different men should agree to repeat the same stereotyped phrases respecting the Deity, and should repeat them ten thousand times, the ideas and emotions attached to them and excited by them in their minds, would be as different as the men. The iron or the chalk, the ivory or the fungus, will show in the fabric that is made from them. Are there any two persons in all the British realms who have precisely the same idea of Queen Victoria? nay, could they all see her, what different views they would carry away!

Not only so, but each man's own ideas of God undergo the greatest changes, nay, revolutions. John's idea is not only different from Peter's, but John's idea, when a man, is vastly different from John's idea when a child. How different is the geologist's idea of a God, when he sees in the great strata of the earth an illuminated volume, all pictorial with proofs of power, wisdom and goodness, — how different, I say, is his idea of God, from that of a President of a certain Southern College, who professes to believe that the bones of the mastodon, shells, sharks' teeth, trilobites, and other fossil remains of preadamitic ages, were scattered about by God at the time of the creation, only as a puzzle for the human race, and to see how much nonsense men would believe for His glory! How different the idea of God which an astronomer has, who comprehends the sublime laws of the solar and the stellar system, and who can foretell every eclipse that will happen for ten thousand years to come, and when the comets will return from their unutterable distances — how different is his idea of God from that of the barbarian — who believes the heavens to be only a few miles above our heads, and that the stars are nothing but spangles made for show. Indeed, all sects and theologies are founded on the differences of idea which men entertain of a God.

And there is another consideration far grander and more important than this. Variant, conflicting, irreconcilable as are men's ideas, when compared with one another, respecting the character and attributes of God; yet the very extremes of them do not differ from each other one ten thousandth part so much as they must all differ from the truth, — from a true, adequate and absolutely correct conception of what God is. Can your finite mind comprehend and embrace the infinite God? If not, then what is that almost infinite part of Him which lies outside of your comprehension? So impossible is it for finite natures to understand the whole of God's infinite nature, that we may say with reverence, that even He, the Infinite himself, cannot make us wholly understand it. How can His infinite knowledge of Himself be transferred to our finite faculties? As well might His infinite power be incorporated in our mortal arm, or His all-seeing wisdom be matched by our dim faculties, or He make us infinite like Himself. He can hold the ocean in the hollow of His hand; but with us, in our present state of development at least, to do this is a natural impossibility. Now that part of God's nature which we do not understand, may be vastly different from the part of which we think we have some just conception: not contradictory to it, but different phases of it, as the colors of the rainbow differ from one another. God loves variety; and He may have constituted other worlds different from ours. How different the forms of life He has created upon earth! How different the fish from the bird, and both from the quadruped, and all from man! The ærolites that fall upon the earth have elementary combinations differing from any found on the earth. The moon is supposed by philosophers to be without an atmosphere. If so, no breathing thing can live there, and lungs would be a supernumerary organ. But does it follow that the moon is a great waste or desert, in which is no life, no happiness; but everywhere silent, melancholy desolation? It may have inhabitants differently constituted from us, physically; and why not differently constituted from us morally? — that is, inhabitants to whom God makes known some other glorious part of His infinite nature? The stars that fill the firmament are of such different colors, that if they could be thrown together in a mass, as we throw glass beads into a cup, they would be as variegated with colors of red, blue, yellow, &c., as a cup full of parti-colored beads. What right have we to say that the inhabitants of these starry realms are not as differently constituted from each other, as are the shining robes of light that adorn them? What right have we to say that God has not revealed to them other attributes of His infinite nature, and manifested Himself to them in other forms, which shall appeal to their natures, as His goodness, power and wisdom appeal to ours?

The light of our sun pours out on all sides. A beam of that light strikes the earth, another beam strikes the planet Venus, another Mars, and so on: but what a vast proportion of that light passes through the inter-planetary spaces, and seems to go off into immensity and be lost! But if we really believe in an immensity, and believe that immensity to be full of God's worlds, then not a particle of light is lost. Some of that which passes through the inter-planetary spaces strikes the stars, and is seen by them, and that which passes through the inter-stellar spaces, strikes the constellations and systems beyond, until somewhere in the vast concave around us every particle of light that radiates from our sun shall, in the immensity of God's universe, help illuminate a world, and none of it go off into uninhabited space to be lost. Why may it not be so — nay, have we not reason to believe it is so — in regard to the infinity of God's spiritual attributes, as well as to His natural light, and that in different worlds there are different beings, and that He apportions some part of His infinite perfections to each, so that it requires the knowledge of all of them to know something of all of Him, and that it will be a part of the work of the endless ages of eternity to read the lesson in this volume of God, which, for want of a better name, I must call an Infinity of Infinities.

We, therefore, on this narrow earth of ours, can no more tell what new powers and wonders, what other exquisite senses, and what other enrapturing objects of sense, what other glorious faculties, and what other magnificent theatres for the exercise of those faculties, God may have created in other parts of His boundless universe, than the aborigines who once inhabited this beautiful neighborhood could tell, from its climate, its vegetable growths, and its animals, what other climate, what other vegetation and animal life would be found in the torrid or arctic zones, or among their antipodes. And it would have been an incomparably less folly in them to pretend to know all about the richness and variety of God's works throughout the four quarters of our globe, from what they saw in this vicinity of ten miles square, than for us to pretend to know through what perfections God manifests Himself in stars and constellations outside of Sirius and Orion and the Pleiades, because we know something of His providence in this sublunary world.

Did I not say then truly, that, much as theologians or sectarists may differ from each other in their belief of the attributes of God,—the Trinitarian from the Unitarian, the Partialist from the Universalist, the Necessitarian from the believer in Free Agency, the Catholic from the Protestant,—their distance from each other is almost infinitely less than the distance of all of them from the truth. Oh, would to Heaven that those who condemn and doom their fellow men because of certain metaphysical differences of belief respecting God's character and attributes, would for one moment reflect what would be their own fate if God should condemn and doom them because of the difference between their best conceptions of Him, and His consciousness of Himself. How would they stand appalled and overwhelmed if the rude picture of God in their minds were exhibited by the side of the Divine Original, and they were held punishable because the mortal limner had not correctly imitated the Immortal Prototype!

Now, this view of our subject leads to several conclusions.

First, it shows us that the learned man and the illiterate man, the scientific man and the ignorant man, not only do not, but they cannot, while remaining as they are, have the same conception of God, any more than they can have the same idea of Paradise Lost, or the liad; any more than they can have the same idea of the Principia of Newton, or the Mecanique Celeste of La Place. The philosopher cannot expunge from his mind his knowledge of the works of God, and receive back into it the crude conceptions, or caricatures, which infested it when he was a child. Nor is this difference confined to intellectual conceptions of the Creator. The same is true of all our moral perceptions of the character of God. How can a man, who, during his previous life, has been accustomed to the brutality and abomination of Cannibalism, or to the gross and foul rites of Fetichism, ever have those immaculate conceptions of God's nature which the prophet Habakkuk felt when he described him to be of "purer eyes than to look on iniquity"? How can a child or young man who has wallowed along, for twenty years, through the filth and loathsomeness of Wapping or St. Giles; or who has swam for twenty years, as a fish swims in water, amid the squalor and beastliness of the wynds of Edinburgh, or the Five Points of New York, cleanse his mind from the fetor it has contracted, and come out fresh and fragrant as a June morning, full of the perfume of flowers and the songs of birds? Though his general conceptions of God's character may be changed, though a new set of resolves and desires may supplant the old ones, yet, as the pot will smell of the ointment it has held, so will the odors of sanctity and even the incense of praise that come from him, be adulterated by the foul emanations of his previous life. This is the way that Christianity became corrupted with the doctrines of Paganism. The Pagans who became Christians did not leave all their Paganism behind. And this we all know to be the case, when men of low life and manners, of vulgar and beastly associations, become Christians now. As the crooked spine sticks to the hunchback, so the old moral tang inheres in all the savor of their lives.

But secondly, if men, in this state of existence, with their unequal faculties, unequal attainments, and unequal opportunities, are not alike, and never can be alike in their intellectual or metaphysical conceptions of the Deity, how can they be alike in worshipping the same living and true God? I answer, that with the greatest diversity of thought, they can be alike in their affections. Love must be the same in all worlds. The love that trembles and flickers in the bosom of the lowliest worshipper upon earth, is precisely the same, in nature and in substance, with that which blazes forth from the loftiest and most adoring seraph, and makes the wide heavens resound with its celestial anthems. There are some things which must be the same wherever they exist. They are incapable of alteration ; for, if altered, their very nature is abolished and lost. Arithmetic and mathematics must be the same in all worlds. Nowhere can two and two be more than four, or less than four. Everywhere the three angles of a plane triangle are equal to two right angles. So love must be the same in saint or seraph ; just as hate is the same in murderer or fiend. The altar may be mean or magnificent ; the censer, where we burn our incense, may be large or small, of gold or of clay, but the flame of devotion that ascends from it is the same in all. Alike it aspires to heaven. We can be alike in spirit, however great or small we may be in thought ; " for, thus saith the high and lofty One that inhabiteth eternity, whose name is Holy ; I dwell in the high and holy place ; with him also that is of a contrite and humble spirit ; " but nowhere is it said that God dwelleth with the great intellect ; or with the intellect that can form the grandest conceptions of Him.

Here, then, is a point of conformity, of uniformity, of identity even, among men in other respects antagonistic and antipodal. No two men can picture out God in thoughts that shall exactly match each other, as a cubic foot of space is like another cubic foot of space, or as a right angle is like another right angle ; but all can love the God whom they conceive. They may and must have somewhat different ideas of His perfections ; but alike they can adore the perfections they know. They have various hypotheses about His modes of government; but alike they can have the resolve of obedience to His laws. They may have different beliefs in articles respecting His purposes and plans, but all can have that trust in His wisdom, and that confidence in His justice and goodness, which will enable them to say, "Not my will, O Father, but thine be done."

The only unity, then, which there can be among the worshippers of God, is a unity of spirit. Even in the world of the blessed, while the archangel has a less inadequate conception of the Supreme, while he can comprehend a larger segment of the great circle of all perfection than you or I, his idea of the Being whom he worships must be different from ours; but let us thank God that our humble tribute of devotion, though poured from the nut-shell capacity of our hearts, will be as acceptable to Him as though its copious floods came from the hollow of the ocean, or the concave of the sky. The bond of love engirdles the universe; it is the oneness of Creator and created; so that, as Christ said to his disciples, "ye shall know that I am in my Father, and ye in me, and I in you."

MEDITATION.

Our Father who art in heaven, hallowed be Thy name. We acknowledge Thy infinite perfections in the hope of elevating our own characters by a contemplation of Thine. We acknowledge Thy power which in the past eternity did create the earth and the heavens, and in the fulness of time did prepare this world to become a fitting place for the habitations of men. We acknowledge Thy omniscience which doth see through all the immensity of Thy works, and dost so order the events of Thy providence, that all which follows is in grand and glorious harmony with all that preceded. We acknowledge Thy justice which will never do us wrong; and oh, most devoutly would we acknowledge Thy love, which sees all our inward wants and makes provision for them. Oh, Heavenly Father, may we enlarge our knowledge, may we expand our minds, may we stretch out our conceptions, so as to form a less narrow, a less limited, a less imperfect conception of Thee, and when our faculties have exerted all their powers to comprehend Thy works and Thy glorious nature, may we say with Job; "Lo, these are parts of His ways, but how little a portion is heard of Him."

We thank Thee that when the world was sunk in iniquity and corruption, when tyrants governed nations, and selfish passions governed men; when pride and vanity and appetite reigned through social life; when the strong oppressed the weak, and the cunning overreached the simple; and the worship of Thee had degenerated into idolatry in some nations, and into proud Phariseeism in others, — that Thou didst send Thy Son Jesus Christ to be an example to the world, of perfect purity and goodness; to show men what they must do to secure salvation from evil. May we study his character profoundly, and imitate the beauty of his life. Was he obedient to his parents? so may children now be! As he never defrauded his neighbors, may we practise honesty in all our dealings! As he never owned a bondman, may we see how opposite to his life and example is the ownership of bondsmen! As he went about doing good, may we also go about, giving bread to the hungry, knowledge to the ignorant, and showing the way of salvation to those who sit in the region of the shadow of death; and may we, like him, though nailed to a cross of public odium and calumny, never feel one revengeful impulse towards our enemies, but be ready, as he was ready, to carry the malefactors upon the cross in his arms to Paradise. And may we aspire to that sublime and godlike sentiment which prompted him, in the midst of his agonies, to say, "Father, forgive them, they know not what they do!"

Heavenly Father, may we ask of Thee aright; may we not ask Thee to give what Thou hast enabled us to obtain — and made it our duty to obtain — for ourselves. May we not ask Thee for harvests, while we will not sow; may we not ask Thee for learning, while we will not study; may we not ask Thee for wisdom, while we disdain to meditate upon Thy laws; may we not ask Thee for strength and health, while we are indulgent to our appetites; may we not ask Thee for happiness, while we refuse to love; may we not ask Thee for heaven, while we neglect to learn and obey Thy laws here.

GOD'S CHARACTER THE LAW OF HUMAN DUTY.

II.

GOD'S CHARACTER THE LAW OF HUMAN DUTY.

I INTRODUCED my last discourse, by telling you, my young friends, that I meant to address you, from time to time, on subjects pertaining to Human Duty. First, however, I desired to establish a foundation for Human duty; else when I had reared the most comely and imposing superstructure in my power, its four corners should be left hanging in the air. I took the position that the foundation of human duty is to be found in the being and attributes of God: and that as we have a group of bodily senses, — sight, hearing, taste, smell, and touch, — by which we recognize material objects; so we have a group of mental faculties, which develop within us the conception of a God. And as no nation or tribe, however barbarous, was ever found, who did not believe in the existence of the earth, and of sun, moon and stars, so no nation or tribe was ever known to exist who did not believe in the existence of a God.

This led me to consider how, or in what manner, after having first obtained the idea of a God, different minds fashion that idea into such an infinite variety of forms, and accumulate upon it, one after another, the attributes which they suppose it to possess. How almost infinitely different is the Hottentot's or the Esquimaux's God from the God of Dr. Chalmers or of Dr. Channing; and if the ideas of God entertained by Dr.

Chalmers and Dr. Channing were brought together, and laid side by side, how different from each other would they also be!

How come men to have such conflicting ideas of the Supreme Being, and of His attributes? It is because they build up their ideas of Him out of ideas previously existing in their own minds. And how else can they do it? How can a man form a conception of any being, or of any thing, but out of ideas already possessed? Can the dramatist put sentiments into the mouths of his characters, or an orator put arguments into his speech, of which sentiments and of which arguments neither of them ever before had any possession, or any conception even? As Solomon could not have built the temple of the Lord out of the cedars of Lebanon, and made doors of the olive-trees, and overlaid the floors with gold, if he had had no cedars, nor olive-trees, nor gold, to do it with, so he could form no conception of that Lord, but out of ideas already in his possession. Hence the universal truth that men's conceptions of God, and the attributes they ascribe to Him, are gathered and fashioned after their own ideas, sentiments and characters. Is it said that God made man in His own image? It is no less true that man makes God in his own image. Hence that ascending scale in the attributes of God, as they are conceived by the lowest savage, by the enlightened heathen, or by the Christian philosopher. As you begin at one end of this scale, you find the gods of the African or Asiatic tribes, mean and contemptible idols; or malignant divinities, not fit to have the control of apes or baboons. Rising from these, you have the gods of the sensual nations, who have prepared a paradise of immortal beauty, where the passions are to be forever fresh and forever gratified. And at the higher end of the scale you have one only living and true God, — a Being of infinite power, wisdom, love and holiness. The gods of the Greeks were beautiful, because the predominating idea of that people was the idea of beauty. The gods of the Romans were proud and bloody divinities, because the Romans were a proud and bloody nation. It is impossible for the selfish man to have the same ideas of God as the benevolent man; impossible for the ignorant man to have the same ideas as the learned man; and as impossible for the grown-up man of educational culture to return to the crude and unworthy conceptions which he had of God when he was a child, as it is for the oak to go back into the acorn, or for the bird to return to its shell. Had every individual who has ever lived daguerreotyped his ideas of God, to be arranged in a gallery as pictures are arranged, there would be millions and millions more of such pictures than of all the human beings who have ever lived. And if God does not expect impossibilities, then He never expected, in this state of the world, uniform conceptions of His nature and attributes.

And furthermore, no mortal man ever had or can have an adequate idea of the one living and true God. It would be as easy to put your arms around immensity and clasp your hands on the opposite side, as to comprehend adequately, with any faculties which we possess, the infinite attributes of the Omnipotent, Omniscient, All-holy and Everlasting God. After enumerating all parts of His nature which we do know, we must have algebraic signs to indicate those still greater parts of Him which we do not know. Nay, is it not impious for feeble and ignorant man, who cannot take larva or chrysalis, and by dissection foretell the properties of the insect it shall produce, to speak with flippancy and arrogance, as we often hear, of the most secret counsels and the most remote purposes of the Eternal Jehovah?

Is it said we have a revelation in the Scriptures, and therefore we may affirm what He is? I answer that there are many points which the Scriptures do settle, and concerning which there is no dispute; but there are also many concerning which, in our present state of knowledge, the wisest and the most pious of men are at variance; and this should teach us diffidence and modesty, and not presumption or dogmatism.

After all, however, what a wonder of wonders it is, that amidst the almost infinite diversities of conception in the human mind, respecting the Deity, there is one point of absolute uniformity among all his true worshippers! In ideas they conflict, but in love they all harmonize. Love is the same in all worlds, and in all natures. If a hundred stringed instruments, all in chord, are placed in a single apartment, and any one of them be touched by a master's hand, the strings of all the others will vibrate in unison with it, and will give out strains of accordant music. So all the hearts that love God are in sweet accord, and when one of them is touched, it thrills hallelujahs through all the moral universe. The music of the planetary spheres is at least a beautiful imagination, but the music of the spheres of love is no fiction.

At this point let me pause for a moment, to make a single reflection. If men necessarily build up their ideas or conceptions of God and of His attributes from their own previous ideas, from the resources of knowledge and of affection which they previously had in their own minds, then every step in education, the inculcation of every new idea, the acquisition of every new scientific principle, the development and training of each intellectual and moral faculty, furnishes precious materials out of which a more adequate and glorious idea of God can be formed. As out of richer paints and purer marble, the artist can make a better picture or statue, so, out of grander and nobler thoughts and out of diviner affections, can we form sublimer and more *God-like* conceptions of our Father in Heaven. Cannot the geologist, who looks backwards into the myriads of ages that were spent in bringing the world into a habitable condition for man; and the astronomer, who knows that the whole solar system is wheeling on around a centre so remote, and through an orbit so wonderfully vast, that, during the six thousand years since the creation of Adam, it has moved through only about one degree, or made only one three hundred and sixtieth part of the first revolution; cannot these, I say, have an idea of the everlastingness and infinitude of God, such as is impossible for the blind mole of a man who moves for a few feet to and fro, in darkness, underground, along a groove, which some other blind mole of a man cut for him? Have not the mathematician and the natural philosopher an idea of the exactness and inevitableness of God's laws, such as a man who was cast on the waves of ignorance at his birth, and has been floating hither and thither on those waves ever since his birth, can never have? Cannot the profound judge, accustomed all his life to discern between the right and the wrong, form a truer idea of

Divine justice, and of righteous laws and measures of retribution, than one whose hand never so much as tried to poise the balances of equity? Cannot the benevolent person, — a Howard, an Oberlin, a Wilberforce, a Mrs. Fry or a Miss Dix, — rise to more vivid and glorious conceptions of God's goodness and love, — to conceptions more impulsive to good, than a cannibal who feeds on human flesh, or a kidnapper who feeds on human hearts, — better than a man whose brain and muscular system are as non-electric, as great non-conductors of sympathy as a statue carved out of chalk, while his heart is only a nodule in the middle of it? And cannot the mind that has been trained to logical and coherent thought, that can lay its foundations of everlasting principles, that can build up systems of jurisprudence, of ethics and of government, and radiate over the whole, the celestial sentiments of philanthropy and reverence, — cannot such a man delineate portraitures and flash out conceptions more true, more radiant, more honoring to God, than the moral idiot, or the butterflies of fashionable life? I repeat, then, that every lesson of sound science or knowledge, of whatever kind, which the teacher gives or the student learns; every energy which the student rouses or the teacher directs, supplies materials and means in our minds for a nobler idea of the God we worship. Knowledge, then, enters largely and essentially into the true idea of a Christian, and the highest type of a Christian cannot exist without it.

Having now taken a view of God from the human side of the question, I shall endeavor to take a view of him from the Divine side, — from a contemplation of those attributes which the wisest and best men concur in ascribing to Him.

First, let us consider the eternity of this existence. Was there ever a time, a first period when God did not exist? If so, then, how came He into being? He could not create Himself, for that would be to suppose Him in existence as a Maker, before He was in existence as a Being made. If created by another, who was that other; and could he have made him different from what he is? And how came that precedent Being into existence? If created, then again, by whom? and so backwards and backwards forever. No, our faculties can find no resting-place, save in the conclusion that God was not created, but is Uncreate. And if our finite minds cannot fully embrace and comprehend the idea that God is self-existent and eternal, they are still driven back to this conclusion from every other attempt at solving the difficulties of the question. The magnificent language of the Psalmist, that He is "*from* everlasting *to* everlasting," affords the only scope for our knowledge, and the only solace for our ignorance.

Of God's attribute of power, how feeble and pale are our most high-wrought and vivid conceptions. How little we comprehend the significance of the tremendous words, Almighty, All-powerful, Omnipresent, — words that should strike the soul as successive thunder-claps would strike the ear. We catch a feeble glimmer of God's power from the lightning, which so sweeps all vitality out of the man whom it strikes, that the process of putrefaction begins in a moment; in the tornado, whose swiftness turns the fluid and voluble air into wide-reaching, iron-headed solidity, so that it strikes cities and forests like a battering-ram; in the ocean storm, that tosses proud navies upon its surface like bubbles; in the earthquake, which shakes cities as though they were toys in its hand; in the volcano, the mere reflection of whose terrors seems to fill the sky with demon shapes of fire, and whose fathomless cauldron up-boils as a fountain of desolation. Yet these occasional manifestations no more represent God's resistless forces working through all the frame of nature, than the leakage of a few drops of water, or a little jet of steam, or a feeble hiss of imprisoned air represents the driving, cleaving, or crushing force of the fiery and ponderous machines of human workmanship. Animal fear sees God's power with the senses, — in noise, in tumult, in flame; but reason sees it in silence, in order, in its still yet eternal activities. Reflect, for a moment, what this power is constantly doing, in the inanimate, insentient world. Who, from the surface of the earth and of the sea, lifts up those particles of water that form the clouds, that descend in rain, that sustain all vegetable and animal life, that fill the channels of the rivers and brim the ocean; who impels the winds in their variable or their periodic courses, and who sends the ceaseless currents of electricity around the globe?

But the thought is too vast, and in attempting to grasp too much, we lose all. Let us divide the great theme, and look at it in parts. Take the first warm day in spring; go out into the cultivated fields; walk through the solemn woods, or by the streams. What millions of millions of roots are now waking from their wintry slumber; how in all their veins they tingle with new life, as, through all their myriad pores they suck in the water that lies by their side! How many seeds beneath your feet are alive; what gases are in fermentation within them to swell, and burst, and send out the new germ! The air is populous with insects that perform their mystic dances in the sunbeam. The migratory birds rise in such flocks as darken the air, to go northwards on their heaven-appointed course, and the migratory fishes make a wave swell up in the sea as they journey southward, to fulfil the great economy of life. Yesterday, the branch of every tree as it stood out against the sun was naked ; to-day, his light is obscured by its myriad leaflets. Each one of all those insect swarms, of those flocks of birds, of those shoals of fish, has its bones and muscles, its lungs and brain ; and an instinct that guides them to their destination burns in them all, as though each one were a king or a queen, and. gloried in his royal blood. What varied, what amazing, what incalculable life ! Who fashioneth these countless forms ? From whose capacious urn are they filled with life and joy ? Who metes out the span of all their days, and upholds the order of their generations ?

Take a day in summer ; the winds are astir, the waters flow, the light descends. Can you count the spires of grass in all the fields, or number the flowers in garden, and copse, and dell ? Every stalk of grain is higher and larger at night than in the morning, and with what motions, and selections, and adaptations, its growth has been accomplished. Take a single tree that has been cut down, and count its pores, multiply these by all the trees of all the forests in all the earth, and multiply these again by all the particles of sap that have travelled up and down in them all. Who supplies these countless growths with the peculiar nourishment that each one needs ? Who winnows light, air, and the gases, that the sour and the sweet, the nutritious and the medicative, may receive according to their affinities ?

Who superintends this vast laboratory, and keeps it from lapsing into chaos ?

Take a day in autumn, when the infinite grains of corn are ripening; when orchard-trees, and forest-trees, and the vines that cling and festoon upon them, are preparing their innumerable fruits and seeds, and when the bulbs beneath the ground are finishing the work of their year and their life. Who is the Sculptor that moulds their forms? Who is the Limner that paints them with such exquisite tints? Who is the great Chemist that fills them with such delicious and infinitely varied savors and flavors, for the nutrition, the health, and the gratification of man; — some for the young and some for the old; some for the strong, and some for the invalid?

Now somewhere, on this globe of ours, and at all times, there is spring; somewhere there is summer; somewhere there is autumn; and all the varied processes of spring, summer, and autumn, are going on together.

Look at the higher life of man. It is supposed there are nine hundred millions of human beings on this globe. Who opens and closes their ever-beating hearts? Who heaves and contracts their restless lungs? Who, through artery and vein circulates their ever-flowing blood? Who kindles in the brain the steady light of truth, or coruscates across its dome the auroral light of sentiment and love? Who spreads the table at which these multitudes are fed? Who spreads out the beautiful drapery of twilight before drawing the curtain of darkness around their bed; and who, when the morning sun comes rolling westward with its broad wave of light, wakens them to joy and activity again?

What I have now referred to is obvious and open to the naked eye. But take a microscope, and what infinite wonders are revealed, — vast populations, not merely like drops of water, but *in* drops of water, — so minute, that were they to assemble in World's Conventions, in the London of a drop of water, they would not alter its balance, any more than our World's Conventions, in our London, changes the equilibrium of the earth. Who gave them their gladsome life, their winged motions, their ecstatic loves?

But let us spring from this to the opposite extreme, — from the microscopic to the telescopic, — to the infinite worlds above us and around us, compared with which our earth is but a drop of water or a grain of sand. And all these worlds, too, are they not as full of elemental forces, as swift in their velocities, and as resistless in their strength, as is our own? Are they not, also, full of some form of glorious life? Who is it that burnishes the heavens every night with those glorious orbs, and upholds them and keeps them from sinking back into chaos?

Go out at midnight; look up into that dread yet glorious concave, and ask your soul whose arm it is that upholds those unpillared chambers of the sky: who fills that vast domain with organized, and sentient, and doubtless with rational and spiritual life; and then reflect that all the galaxies and constellations which you can behold with the unassisted eye, are only the frontispiece, not to the mighty volumes of God's works, but only to the index of the mighty volumes? Beyond Sirius, beyond Orion, beyond the Pleiades, the azure fields of immensity are all filled with worlds, system beyond system, and rank behind rank, whom God in

His mercy has removed to those immense distances from us, lest our mortal vision should be blasted by their overwhelming effulgence. And as you cannot find one inch of our lower earth where God is not at work, so there is not one inch in all those boundless upper realms where God is not at work.

My children, against such a God, as with feeble words and inadequate thoughts I have attempted to describe, — against such a God, do you wish to lift, or do you dare to lift, your pigmy arm? His resistless laws that cleave a pathway wherever they are sent, and punish the transgressor wherever they are transgressed, — these laws do you dare to break? If you would hesitate to violate a father's command, when he stands over you with a rod; if you would shrink from resisting the authority of a sovereign, who has judges, and officers, and armies, and navies, in his control, then, oh how can you ever dare, how can you ever wish to dare to confront the power and majesty of the Eternal One; — of that One who can enwrap the heavens with His thunder-clouds, and make you the mark of all their volleyed lightnings; who can array His volcanoes in battalions, and bury you beneath their molten lavas; who can sink you in the earth's central fires, to lie, without consuming, in that seething cauldron, or imprison you in the eternal solitudes of polar ice; or — unspeakably more terrible than all this, — can turn your own soul inwards in retrospection upon its past life, to read its own history of voluntary wrong, in its self-recorded Book of Judgment? Nor can you find refuge in non-existence. You may call upon the seas to drown you, but there is not water enough in all the seas. You may call upon the fires to consume, but the fires will say, we cannot consume remorse. You may call upon arctic frosts to congeal the currents of life, but they will say, we have no power over the currents of thought, or the pulses of *the immortal life.* You may *call* upon *the universe* to annihilate you, but the universe will respond, "God alone can annihilate, and God will say, live forever."

I do not address you, my young friends, as members of this or that religious denomination, into which the world is so unhappily divided; I do not appeal to you merely as Christians, acquainted with the blessed life and character of Jesus Christ. You might be Mahometans, you might be Pagans, you might be savages, and still I would say, do you dare encounter and confront the great Ruler of heaven and earth? Oh, that I could so thunder in your ears, that the sound would never cease to vibrate in your hearts, that word which God has written in letters of flame over every avenue to temptation,— which he has inscribed on the lintels and door-posts of the gate-ways of sin, which is blazoned on the hither side of every seducement to wrong.

BEWARE! IF YOU TREAD THERE, OR LOOK THERE, OR THINK THERE, YOU ENCOUNTER OMNIPOTENCE.

God is Omniscient. Must not He who made every-thing, know how every thing is made? Must not He who can regulate the beating of an animalcules pulse, who can touch with exquisite life the nerves in the antennæ of a microscopic insect; — must not He know what is going on in your mind and in your heart? In your widest reaches of thought, how infinitely beyond you He thinks; in your furthest scope of knowledge, how infinitely beyond you He knows. On all sides, He is outside of you. Is there any deepest cavern, or blackest midnight, where you go to contrive alone, or to conspire with others, where He is not present? Think, then, of this, my young friends, that God not only knows of your most secret desires and purposes, but knows the mental and moral habits and forces out of which they come. What is there, then, that you would refrain from doing before the friend you love, or the master you fear, that you would dare to do before the God who knows it all?

Among God's other attributes is that of justice. The most just men upon earth, — those in every nation who are worthy to be called its Aristides, may do wrong. Limited knowledge may vitiate the best of purposes, and finite beings may make mistakes that will condemn the innocent or save the guilty. But an Omniscient Being is safe from all errors; and therefore, of one thing we may be certain, that in His dealings with us, and in His administration of the universe, He will never do wrong.

Of the fact of God's attribute of Justice, no truly religious man doubts; but in regard to the manner in which that attribute is exercised, the Christian world holds opposite opinions. One party maintains that every voluntary departure from God's laws, whether more or less heinous, deserves an eternity of punishment, and hence that such eternal retribution must be suffered by the offender himself; or that a third person must suffer vicariously for him. The other party maintains that when a sinner leaves off sinning, he does, to a great extent, leave off suffering. They explain God's laws in regard to moral evil, by the analogy of His laws in regard to natural or intellectual evil; that, as when the drunkard leaves off drinking his liquid fire, he quenches the Tophet which he had kindled in his stomach, and stops the scorching flame from ascending into his throat; and, as when the man who has sought to gather grapes of thorns, or figs of thistles, finds that they will not grow thereon, he plants another stalk, and gets his fruit; so, when the man who has lived without God in the world, turns to God in obedience and adoration, he leaves behind him with his atheism, the blankness and solitariness of his atheistic life. The one party paints the consequences of sin as so vast and terrible, that a third person must be called in to lift off the burden of those consequences; while the other party, though they paint the consequences of sin just as terrible, while the sin lasts, yet maintain that when the sin ceases, the consequences mainly cease. I say, *mainly cease*, for all admit that the mortification and shame of the old sin, like the scar of some dishonorable wound, remain forever. Both, too, acknowledge the efficacious intervention of a third person; but the one maintains that the mediator bears off the penalties from themselves, while the other maintains that the mediator only helps the sinner to escape from the sin, and then the penalties stop, of course, as fiery thirst stops, when slaked with water. The latter say, that the order of the Divine government is, "the soul that sinneth, it shall die." "But if the wicked man will turn from all his sins that he hath committed, and keep all my statutes, and do that which is lawful and right, he shall surely live, he shall not die."

Now, on this contested point, I give no opinion. I here intimate no opinion. Let it be to you as though I had no opinion. Sufficient for our present purpose is it, that either view vindicates God's *glorious attribute* of Justice; for how glorious it is — glorious in both views, glorious on both sides of it. How admirable for the innocent man always to be able to say, I know that my judge is just; I know that where I am innocent I never shall be condemned. And what a noble government is that, where the tempted man must say, I know that if I sin, I cannot escape from suffering. Protected in innocence, sure of punishment for offences, how can the rational man, in the exercise of his reason; — mark me, in the exercise of his reason, — how can the rational man ever dare to commit a sin?

I can now mention but one more of the Creator's attributes. "God is Love." How striking this expression of the Evangelist, not only once affirmed, but repeated. God is declared in the Scriptures, times almost without number, to be holy and just and true, but nowhere is it said that God is holiness, or is justice, or is truth. The adjective is used, indicative of a quality inhering in some being, but not the substantive noun, in which the qualities inhere. We can conceive of each one of all God's attributes, as being a vacuum to all the others; so that they can co-exist without interference and act without obstruction. But of no attribute save this of love, is there such intense and vehement expression, to signify that this is the sublime, paramount, crowning fact of the Godhead; as though this were His whole nature, and all other qualities were absorbed and swallowed up in this perfection. God is Love.

And does not all that we know of God's works confirm this sacred declaration? What more beautiful than this wonderful world which He has spread out around us? What more perfect than the unerring laws, by which it is governed, and which the sciences have just begun to reveal to us? Not only how morally, but how mathematically true it is, that "all things work together for good to them that love God," — that is, to them that learn His laws and obey them; for knowledge and obedience are the only true manifestations of our love to Him. How beneficent, that when we have gone astray, we can be restored!

I said before, how can any of you, finite and feeble as you are, dare to brave the terrors of the Omnipotent; how can any of you dare to violate the law of one who is All-knowing to know, and All-just to judge your offences? But here, the key-note changes; my expostulations turn from alarm to entreaty; from fear to gratitude; and if I could, I would say to you all, in tones of sweetness and affection, deep and tender as those which angels use, how can you ever do with your hands, or speak with your lips, or conceive in your hearts, anything that is blasphemous, or defiant, or dishonoring, or unpleasing, to that Being of perfect Love?

MEDITATION.

Our Father, we adore Thee as that Being whose power extends over all worlds, whose wisdom and skill have been incorporated, and are now and evermore indwelling in all created things; whose love pours forth over the universe and through all the ages — that love, one drop of which fills the ocean of immensity and still leaves the infinite of Thy nature full. We render Thee thanksgiving that in the far off ages of past eternity, Thou didst make provision for the natural wants of man in the fertility and exuberance of the earth, in the riches of the forest and the mine, in the variety and abundance of tropical and temperate zones, in the fulness of rivers and seas. We thank Thee for the beauty Thou hast showered down on all terrestrial scenes, for the green and flowery earth, and for the azure sky; for the effulgence of the rising sun and the many-colored drapery of his setting hour; for rainbows and auroras, for the varied beauties of seasons, of island and continent; for all that can tend to excite the ardor of our devotion, by showing Thee to be so excellent. We thank Thee for those glorious faculties of intellect with which Thou hast endowed man, and for those laws and principles, uniform and eternal, blended with each created thing, which are the objects of those faculties; some, capable of being known by a child, simple as the alphabet, easy as its mother's name, yet, rising in complications and profundities, to such as task, such as surpass an archangel's power. Oh, our Heavenly Father, we thank Thee that we have the prospect of studying these wonderful truths in the ages of eternity, — an exhaustless source of knowledge of the grandeur and the glory of Thy nature. We thank Thee for the men of talent, of skill, and of genius, who have risen up, from time to time, and, by deep study and long vigils, have sought out these laws, and have thereby helped to save mankind from idolatry; have swept away ten thousand superstitions that tormented the race, and have supplanted the folly and vagary, the senseless dreams and caprices of ignorance with the eternal principles of knowledge, systematized in science, and made transmissible to all our descendants. But above all, for that moral part of our nature which dominates all the rest, and for the seers and prophets, men wise in holy things, who have illustrated it. If in the majesty and robustness of the intellectual powers, Thou hast shown the paternal character; in the sweetness, the tenderness, the delicacy and purity of our affectional nature, Thou hast shown the maternal character. If one class of these gifts is such as an Infinite Father would give us, the other is such as an Infinite Mother would give.

Heavenly Father, may we seek the love of truth; — truth in outward act, in inward thought, ay, in the innermost thoughts of the heart, at all times, in the market-place, and in the forum; in solitude, and at midnight; in business, in pleasure, in study, and especially in investigating Thy nature and laws. May no preconceived opinions ever chain us, ever deter us from this search, though instilled into us by a father whom we revered, though we drank them in on a mother's breast, sweetened with a mother's caresses. If our right eye offend Thee, may we pluck it out; if our right hand lead us to do wrong, may we cut it off.

When assembled together for improvement in health and strength, in knowledge and virtue, may the earthly teachers teach youth to go to Thee who can teach them more than all earthly intelligences. If tempted to do wrong, may they remember the friends who have sent them away to be taught; may they see the paternal eye, feel the maternal hand, hear the maternal voice, saying, My son, my daughter, if sinners entice thee, give not heed unto them. May they help one another, and feel it impious to ask Thy help while they do not regard each fellow being as a brother, or stand as stumbling-blocks in each other's way.

LAW—THE FIRST PRINCIPLE OF SPIRITUAL LIBERTY.

III.

LAW—THE FIRST PRINCIPLE OF SPIRITUAL LIBERTY.

In former Discourses, I have endeavored to give some proofs of the Being or Attributes of God. But all this would be nothing but mere curious speculation, if we did not hold the closest personal relations to that Being, and if our nature and destiny did not primarily depend upon His attributes. If accident should cast us upon the shores of an unknown country, our first and most anxious inquiry would be, what kind of men and government lived and reigned within its borders; whether man-lovers or man-eaters; whether an arbitrary, tyrannical, and cruel king, or a beneficent and parental one. So when we are cast upon the shores of time, and see this outspread universe around us, the most momentous question we can ask is, what kind of a Being governs it, and what we must do to adjust ourselves to our new condition. If God be the Creator and Governor of all existences, then He is our Creator and Governor. If He be All-powerful, then it is useless, nay, it is madness, for us to defy or resist Him. If He be Omnipresent, then we cannot escape out of His jurisdiction, as guilty men sometimes flee from the rod of the civil magistrate. If He be Omniscient, then no omissions or technicalities of an imperfect criminal code, no craft of counsel, nor suborning of witnesses, could save us; and it would be of no use to plead "Not

Guilty," when we were guilty. If He be just and good, then we know that in order to have any sympathy or communion with Him, we, too, must be just and good. What He loves, we must love; what His holy nature repels, we must repel; or else we array ourselves in perpetual warfare against Him, and such a warfare must be fatal to the weaker party, that is, to us.

Since, then, there must be the most intimate relation, — a relation at all points between God and ourselves, no fact can be more important for us to know than what that relation is. In what relation, then, do we stand to our Creator, Governor, and Final Disposer? and in what correlative relation does He stand to us?

The grand and paramount relation in which God stands, not only to the whole human race, but to all creatures that have life, and to all things that have no life, is that of Law-giver. He has made laws for whatever He has created. There is not a constellation so vast, nor an atom so small; there is not an archangel so exalted, nor an animalcule so insignificant, that is not all penetrated and encompassed, bound in and bound down, by the law which God has impressed upon its being. In us, no thought nor desire rises into the light of consciousness, no muscle contracts, no nerve vibrates, no drop of blood flows in our veins, or hair grows upon our heads, but in accordance with the laws which God has severally impressed upon them.

But before going further, let us understand the meaning of this superb and majestic word, LAW.

"Law," says Mr. Justice Blackstone, "in its most general and comprehensive sense, signifies a rule of action; and is applied indiscriminately to all kinds of action, whether animate or inanimate, rational or irrational. Thus we say the laws of motion, of gravitation, of optics, or mechanics, as well as the law of nature and of nations." "Thus, when the Supreme Being formed the universe, and created matter out of nothing, He impressed certain *principles* upon that matter, from which it can never depart, and without which it would cease to be. When He put that matter into motion, He established *certain laws of motion*, to which all movable bodies must conform." — If we further advance from mere inactive matter, to vegetable and animal life, we shall find them still governed by laws; more numerous, indeed, but equally fixed and invariable. — "This, then, is the general signification of law, a rule of action dictated by some superior being."

"The word *law*," says Mr. Erskine, "is frequently made use of, both by divines and philosophers, in a large acceptation, to express the settled method of God's providence by which He preserves the order of the material world in such a manner, that nothing in it may deviate from that uniform course which He has appointed for it."

"Laws," says Montesquieu, "in their most general signification, are the necessary relations derived from the nature of things. In this sense, all beings have their laws; the Deity has His laws; the material world its laws; the intelligences superior to man have their laws; the beasts, their laws; man, his laws." — "God is related to the universe as Creator and Preserver; the laws by which He created all things, are those by which He preserves them. He acts according to these rules, because He knows them; He knows them because He has made them; and He made them because they are related to His wisdom and power." If all things, then, have their law, you see what infinite number and variety of laws there must be. There are not only ten Commandments, but ten thousand times ten thousand. Parents make laws for their families, schools and colleges are governed by laws. All societies and associations; all states and nations have their laws; and there are international laws, designed to regulate the intercourse of nations with each other, whether they are in peace or at war. We speak of the Mosaic law, meaning the institutions of Moses, as distinguished from the Gospel. We speak of the Ceremonial law, also, which commanded certain external rites and observances for specific cases, and for a limited time, as distinct from moral precepts, which are of perpetual obligation. Written laws are laws written out and enacted by the supreme legislative power of a country; and unwritten laws are those which derive their binding force from established usage or long custom. and they are expounded and defined by the courts. Each of the organs of our Physical system has its laws. If, during the process of digestion, we take iced-water, or any other cold substance into the stomach, in sufficient quantity to reduce its temperature below 98°, digestion, forthwith, ceases; and if that temperature be not raised, digestion will not re-commence, and sickness must ensue. If the brain be over tasked, inflammation, and at last, insanity ensues. If the lungs are stinted for air, or are filled with bad air, the blood cannot be oxygenated or vitalized; black blood is sent into the head, and then all the capacities of the mind, its joy and its genius, must suffer. Each of all the myriad varieties of vegetable growths has its law. Some plants demand the tropical and some the arctic zone. Some aspire to the skies, and stand up with independent strength; some creep along the ground, or parasitically cling to a self-sustaining trunk; like a toddling child who can walk only as he holds up by a stronger hand. Thus weak minds toddle.

Did you ever observe the law by which each leaf of the deciduous tree has a joint near the stalk where it is attached, and by means of which joint it is making preparation, all the time it is growing, for dropping off as soon as its functions as a living organ are performed? Did you ever observe the wonderful arrangement of the leaves of trees by which their attachment to different sides of the tree can be expressed arithmetically? Thus, if you mark the point at which one leaf starts out from the trunk or branch of certain kinds of trees, you will see that the next leaf above it is exactly on the opposite side, so that the third one is over the first, the fourth over the second, and so on, — each two leaves being equal to one turn round the tree as you ascend. This is arithmetically expressed by the fraction of one-half; because each new leaf makes half a turn round the tree. In the plant called succory, it takes three leaves to make this spiral turn round the stalk; so that the fourth leaf comes perpendicularly over the first, and begins a new turn. As it takes three leaves here to make one turn, we denote this by the fraction of one-third. In the apple tree, five leaves or buds make two turns round the tree, so that this fact is expressed by the fraction two-fifths. In the currant bush, eight leaves make three turns, so that the ratio here is three-eighths. In the plant called shepherd's purse, it is five-thirteenths; and in another still, twenty-one successive leaves, as you ascend spirally around the tree, require thirteen turns. And here another most curious fact is observed, that these several numbers form an ascending series in which the denominator of the preceding fraction is the numerator of the succeeding one; and the denominator of the succeeding one is the sum of the two preceding denominators. Thus, starting with 1-2 and 1-3, we then have 2-5, 5-8, 8-13, 13-21sts, and so on. Here, as you will see, the denominator of the 2-5ths is the numerator of the 5-8ths, the denominator of the 5-8ths is the numerator of the 8-13ths, and the denominator of the 8-13ths the numerator of the 13-21sts. So you will see the other wonderful fact I mentioned, that the succeeding denominator is equal to the sum of the two preceding denominators. Thus, 1-2, 1-3, 2-5; $2+3=5$; 1-3, 2-5, 5-8; $3+5=8$; 3-5, 5-8, 8-13; $5+8=13$; 5-8, 8-13, 13-21; $8+13=21$. In this last statement, there is one apparent anomaly, too subtle for explanation on this occasion, though adding to the beauty of the result.

Now this exemplifies, in Botany, what I mean by a *law*. It applies to the rose-bud, the oak-leaf, the pine-cone; and though we can conceive of other methods of arranging the leaves, on plants and trees, yet such other methods are nowhere to be found in nature.

And it is a phenomenon hardly less worthy of note, that if, in the position to which leaves and petals belong, they find an obstruction to their development, such as a deficiency of light, for instance, they will strive to find some other way, and turn aside and avoid or surmount the obstacle. Do we do so, when we encounter obstacles in obeying God's moral laws? Like the little blind germs of the leaves, imbedded in darkness beneath the bark of the tree, do we strive to reach outward, and bask ourselves in God's moral light?

Now turn your attention for a moment to a field of nature as different from what we have been contemplating, as the planets above our heads are from the vegetation beneath our feet. The mean motion of each planet, as compared with its next interior planet, is uniformly represented, with great approximation to exactness, by one of the fractions of the same series I have given you in reference to the growth of leaves.

Look now into another department of nature, and behold the chemical law; — that law which determines the manner in which atoms shall combine with each other. For instance, water is composed of oxygen and hydrogen, and there are always *eight weights* of oxygen to one of hydrogen, and the oxygen and hydrogen will not combine in any other proportions. But when oxygen and sulphur unite to form hydrosulphurous acid, then eight *parts* of oxygen require *sixteen* parts of sulphur, or they will not unite. But if sulphur and hydrogen unite, it takes sixteen parts of sulphur to combine with one of hydrogen. So fourteen grains of nitrogen will unite with eight, or sixteen, or twenty-four, or thirty-two, or forty grains of oxygen, but in no other proportions. One grain of hydrogen will not unite with nine or with seven grains of oxygen, but only with eight. These are the laws of chemical combination; but when you come to mechanical admixtures, there you may mingle bodies together in almost any proportions you please; — as a pound of sugar or of salt with a gallon, or with a hogshead of water. To form the great constituent bodies of the physical world, nature's laws are peremptory and invariable, but to adapt those bodies to the common and variable uses of life, we have unbounded scope and discretion.

Look, for another law, at the analogy between man and the birds and fishes. A fish's fin, a bird's wing, and a man's arm, are only the same rudimentary organs differently developed, proving that they all had a common Author. After contemplating such facts of which all the kingdoms of nature are full, how much deeper the impression, — and the impressiveness too, with which we read such passages as these: "Hear, O Israel; the Lord our God is one Lord;" or, "I am the Lord thy God, which have brought thee out of the land of Egypt, out of the house of bondage. Thou shalt have no other gods before me." Not only the reason of man, but all nature, through all her organs, responds, "There is no other God but Thee."

I have spent all this time in illustrating the idea of law, because it is a fundamental idea. It is to all theology and ethics, what a definition or postulate is to geometry. You cannot take a second step without error, unless you understand this first step.

Now let us see what are some of the limitations and characteristics of the idea of Law.

1. Though we personify *Law* and speak of it as a separate existence or power, yet it is not a being of itself, and it has no power. In scientific strictness, God's law means simply the mode in which God acts, — in which He creates, upholds, commands, warns, rewards or punishes.

When the heathen nations looked out upon the universe, and saw the vast variety of God's works, and the boundless diversity of their modes of action; — the stars rolling, the tides heaving, the fountains gushing, the rivers flowing, the lightnings flashing, the winds blowing, and all vegetation springing into green life, with all the other activities which the full realms of nature reveal, they could account for the phenomena only on the supposition that a god presided over each class of activities, instead of supposing one God who acted in so many ways. And hence, when we speak of the goodness of God, the power of God, or the wisdom of God, we mean nothing separate or distinct from God, but only the benevolent, powerful, and wise manner in which He uniformly acts; — just as when we speak of the patriotism of Washington, or the philanthropy of Wilberforce, we do not mean to excite the idea of any existence separate from Washington or Wilberforce, but only to describe their love of country and of mankind.

2. Carrying this idea of the word *law* along with us, let me observe in the second place, that God's laws are resistless; — that is, *He* is resistless in whatever he does. Who shall measure strength with the Omnipotent? If He has attached pain and early decrepitude to gluttony and intemperance, can you detach them, so as to commit the offence and still escape the penalty? When He has enabled you to protect the eye against the sun's light, can you gaze with impunity upon its intolerable splendor? When He has made the air a necessity for the lungs, can you fill them with water and still live? When He has made your body out of combustible materials, can you leap into burning Etna and come forth unscathed? When He has culled the subtlest and choicest particles from all nature's elements, out of which to form that wonderful electric battery, your brain and nervous system, so that your lightning

thoughts and joyous emotions can leap and flash, like auroras over the whole; can you consume or corrode that brain or nervous system with alcohol, tobacco, or other narcotics, without impairing its native velocities and dimming its native splendors? — any more than you can pour tar and vinegar into the wheelwork of your watch, and still have a good time-keeper? Every one knows that in every human face there is an impalpable, immaterial something, which we call expression, which seems to be, as it were, *the soul made visible.* Where minds live in the region of pure thoughts and happy emotions, the felicities and sanctities of the inner temple shine out through the mortal tenement, and play over it like lambent flame; the incense makes the whole altar sweet; and we can understand what the poet means when he says, that

> "Beauty born of murmuring sound
> Shall pass into her face."

On the other hand, no man can live a gormandizing, sordid, or licentious life, and still wear a countenance hallowed and sanctified with a halo of peace and joy. Around such great manufacturing towns as Birmingham in England, or Pittsburg in this country, where bituminous coal is used, you will find the roses in the flower-bed and the strawberries and grapes on the vines, blackened and defiled by a foul deposit from a thousand chimnies. Thus do obscene, profane and irreverent men scatter their grime and stench upon the innocence and beauty around them; but most deeply and foully upon themselves. And since God has throned conscience in the human soul, no man can violate its dictates and still escape its scourge and sting without repentance and reformation.

3. In the third place, I believe the laws of God to be infinitely wise. Some learned and pious men have said they could not believe in the doctrine of *Optimism;* that is, that this world was constructed upon the best possible plan. In the infinite varieties of God's works, they think He has practically compared the adjective *good*, and having a good, a better, and a best, that this world can at most be called *good.* I am an Optimist. I believe the order of Providence to be the best possible order; and I have no faith in the criticisms which a blind mole may make on the range and height of the mountains under which he burrows. All the exceptions ever yet taken to the perfectness of God's works have turned out to be futile and presumptuous. Sir Isaac Newton thought there was a screw loose somewhere in our solar system. He supposed the moon to be gradually sliding out of its orbit, so that in process of time it would require to be set back into its path by miraculous interference. But La Grange, on revising Newton's calculations, found him, and not Jehovah, in error, and that the moon wheeled by a law that never erred, or rather, that in the way God's hand moved it, it is sure to come round to the true place at the true time.

4. God's laws exhibit infinite skill. When we use the word skill, in relation to an earthly contrivance, we mean that foresight which can adapt means to ends, and can predict effects from causes, and can do these things so as to secure successful results. In human works there are all degrees of skill, and of the want of it. A few years ago, the Emperor of Austria ordered a splendid barge to be made, in which the royal family might sail upon the grand canal. So the skill of the kingdom was put in requisition, and a

structure of immense costliness and splendor was made. When they launched it, it would sail very well on the canal, but was too wide to pass through one of the locks. Even the most ingenious inventors are obliged to modify their original plans, and often wholly to reconstruct their machines before they succeed. How long did Fulton experiment before he triumphed, and what vast improvements have been since made upon him! It is but about a year since Ericsson supposed he had invented a hot-air engine which would supersede the steam engine, and no inconsiderable part of the civilized world rung with acclamations at the astounding triumph. A trial trip to Washington forced him to take his whole machine to pieces, and it is doubtful whether a new one will lead to any better results. But look at God's works. Does the solar system ever get out of gear? Are not the three angles of any possible triangle always equal to two right angles? Does the law of specific gravities ever change; or that of chemical combinations? Will frost and snow, of themselves, make flower-beds and harvests? Or can a wicked man ever enjoy that peace of God which passeth understanding? No. Whatever you desire, or yearn for, or hope for, you must first find out the law of God which applies to that case, and then obey it. And when you understand that the universe is not a mere machine, which God, having first made, now "stands outside and sees it go;" but, on the other hand, that the universe is only the manifestation of God himself, upholding and moving the work of His hands, it becomes not only plain but inevitable, that everything pertaining to it must be infinitely skilful. He himself being the actor, He must act according to His own eternal attributes of Power, Wisdom, and Love.

5. In the next place, God's laws are uniform. If *His* laws merely define the manner in which *He* works, then, as there is no variableness nor shadow of turning in Him, there can be no failure in His laws. It follows from this that in the contemplation of God, or, looking at the subject from the divine side, there can be no such thing as a miracle. If God foresaw everything from the beginning, how can he be taken by surprise, or ever encounter an unexpected event? Babbage invented an extraordinary machine, called a Calculating Machine, which, by the turning of a crank, would perform the most wonderful mathematical problems. He said he could make his machine so that it would bring out the same result a million times, and then, the next time, bring out an exactly opposite result. Now, to a bystander, who had seen the same result a million of times, and should then, the next time, see a contrary result, this would seem a miracle, but it would be no miracle to Babbage himself, for he would expect it. A miracle, then, is, *to us*, a supernatural event. Even the deist admits the existence of miracles, in this sense, as when the sun was spoken into being, and when the invertebrate orders of animals, the fishes, the birds, the quadrupeds, and afterwards man, were called into life. None of the events which marked these mighty eras were contrary to the course of nature, they were only in further development of it. When, therefore, you can account for any event or phenomenon, on natural causes, that event or phenomenon is not a miracle. For a cork to swim, or for lead to sink, is not a miracle; but the contrary would be. For a man to get diseases and early decrepitude by a life of debauchery, is not a miracle. Debauchees without the diseases and the

decrepitude, would be the miracle, — a miracle which God will not work, and the devil cannot.

Many people seem to think that they honor God more, by supposing that He is constantly working miracles, constantly interfering and wresting the order of nature, to prevent some evil, or to effect some good, than by believing that He established an order of nature so perfect at first that it needs no interference. Suppose one clockmaker were to make you a clock that should keep such imperfect time as to require him to come to your house every day to set it and repair it. Suppose another to make you a clock so perfect that it would run for years without error, which of the two would be the best clockmaker?

Ignorance is one of the main causes of the belief that God is constantly wresting the order of nature. Before men understood astronomy, their only way to explain an eclipse was to suppose that God darkened the sun or the moon, instead of believing that the earth and the moon, in their accustomed revolutions, intercepted the sun's light. When people did not know that filth, intemperance, and other forms of bad living created contagious and fatal distempers, then they attributed pestilences to the direct act of God. Before the laws of electricity were understood, when any particular man or house was struck with lightning, it was supposed that God specially aimed at and hit that man or that house, just as a sportsman aims at a particular bird. And it is one of the most remarkable facts in all history, that, just in proportion as science has advanced, supposed miracles, or a belief in common miracles, has ceased. *I say, just in proportion as science has advanced, supposed miracles, or a belief in common miracles, has ceased.* This is true, not only of our predecessors, but of our contemporaries. Now, among barbarous nations, in Asia, Africa, or elsewhere, miracles are just as rife, just as much a thing of daily occurrence, as they were among the heathen nations of antiquity, or among the so-called Christian nations of the Middle Ages. This is so true, that in regard to the present age of the world, the universal fact may be expressed in this formula: — Knowledge has its boundary line, where it abuts on ignorance; on the outside of that boundary line are ignorance and miracles; on the inside of it, are science and no miracles. And what is very remarkable, is, that the same fact holds true, in regard to the same people, who are ignorant on one class of subjects, and learned on another. In the subjects which they understand, there are no miracles; in the one they do not understand, miracles abound.

Pride, or self-conceit, is another prolific cause of a belief in miracles. It is so grateful to a selfish man to believe that God loves him better than He loves others, that he riots, and wantons, and gloats over the idea with a conceitedness and self-flattery, which to a man of intelligent piety, is most offensive. When an epidemic prevails, and one man escapes; when a steam-boat explodes, and one man is saved; if he be a selfish or a vain man, he is sure to attribute his rescue to God's special interference in his behalf. When the terrible Norwalk tragedy happened last year, why was Elder Barr, a man so good, so pious, so devoted to the interests of education and religion; — why was he lost, while so many others who, as compared with him, were so worthless, useless, or contemptible, were saved? No. God acts by general laws; and when any one comes within the action of those laws, be he a President of the United States, or a Missionary carrying salvation to the heathen, he has no escape from their uniform and resistless force. Not one jot or tittle of the law shall pass away.

The next characteristic or quality of God's laws which I shall mention, is, that they are so comprehensive, so universal, that they absolutely exclude all chance. Strictly speaking, there is no such thing as chance in the universe, and when a philosopher uses the word *chance*, he does not mean to exclude the idea of law, but only to show that he is ignorant of the law. When we speak of probable storms at sea, or of winds on land, we do not mean to intimate that the event of which we doubt is not certain in itself; we only mean to declare our ignorance of the causes which will decide it. Even Chaos — a word we use to express the negation of all law — must have its law. If it be in motion, it must have its laws of motion; and if it be at rest, it must have its law of inertia.

In regard to these great classes of facts which science has not yet explored, and which, therefore, we call uncertain, we have demonstrative proof that they are certain, in themselves, because, when you take great numbers of individuals, or extensive periods of time, the results are uniform. If asked respecting any particular family, how many of its children are sons, and how many are daughters, we should have no rule to determine our conjecture. But if asked respecting a million of children who were born last year, how many of them were sons, and how many were daughters, we should immediately answer, with a certainty of being correct, that the number of each was nearly equal, — probably the daughters a little in excess. It is so in regard to crime in given states of society. The criminal statistician, in France or England, will tell you to-day, with but very little departure from exactness, how many crimes will be committed next year, in their respective countries, and not only so, but how many of each sort; — so many murders, so many burglaries, so many thefts, &c. So, though you cannot tell whether the children of Mr. A. B.'s family will be at school or not, next year, yet you can tell with great approximation to accuracy, how many children will be at school in the State of Ohio, and in the United States.

Now, my young friends, do not all these events incontestibly demonstrate a lawgiver? That lawgiver is God, the Creator of all things.

Some have contended that all this universe of events, and the laws by which they are governed, could have been the product of chance, — Lucretius, among the ancients, the French and German schools of atheists among the moderns. I mention this now, only to show that I do not think their arguments have been met with the right answer. Cicero encountered this hypothesis, but I do not think he met it with the right answer. In contesting the opinion of those who maintained that the universe was formed by a fortuitous concurrence of atoms, he says: * — "If any one thinks that this could be, I do not see why

* "Hoc qui existimat fieri potuisse, non intelligo, cur non idem putes, si innumerabilis unius et viginti formæ letterarum, vel auræ vel qualislibet, aliquo conjeciantur, posse ex his in terram excussis, annales Ennii ut deinceps legi possent effici; quod nescio, an, ne in uno quidem versu, possittantum valere fortunæ." (De Nat. Deorum, Lib. II., p. 509. Ernest, Lond. 1819.)

the same man should not suppose that if an innumerable quantity of letters of the alphabet were thrown promiscuously upon the ground, they would not fall so as to make the annals of Ennius; whereas it seems to me, it would be scarcely possible for them to make one verse." This argument of Cicero was reproduced in the time of the French revolution. To put down the atheists, it was said that no number of types, if shaken and thrown down together, could so fall as to produce the Iliad of Homer; and to this, the shrewdest and profoundest answer was made that ever was made in behalf of Atheism. I refer to the celebrated retort of a French Atheist, who replied, "Give me types enough, and shakes enough, and I will produce the Iliad of Homer." Now, regarding simply the doctrine of chances, I do not see how the correctness of this answer can be denied. Suppose one had a font of types, each letter and point of which should be so numerous, that it would fill all that immense sweep of stellar spaces that can now be seen by the largest telescope; and suppose all these types were put into an urn so vast that the very handles of it would let the Milky Way pass through them unbent; and suppose this urn were swung round and round until all the types were shaken together as dice are shaken in a dice-box, and then hurled out upon a plane so vast, and with such a centrifugal force that they would not lie but one deep; and suppose these throws could be repeated for great cycles of time, of which ages should be the seconds, I do not see why, somewhere at some time, they should not turn up the Iliad of Homer, — and Euclid's Elements to boot.

But this answer of the atheist, keen as it is, and profound as it may seem to be, — does it meet the difficulty? The problem is, with types enough, and shakes enough, to produce an Iliad. Well, Mr. Atheist, fill the void spaces of immensity with types, in order to supply one of your conditions of success, and then can your tiny arm lift, and rattle, and throw them? And if thrown, and you have waited your thousands of years for them to fly off into space, and spread themselves over your plane, then can your slow-footed steps traverse the illimitable fields of space in search of the much desired spot, where your Iliad of Homer might be? And if this space were once traversed, then can your shallow hands scoop up this sky-full of types and replace them in the box, preparatory to another throw? And if the lucky cast did not come until a period somewhat late in the flowing eternity, how much of the work would the threescore-and-ten years of your mortal life-time enable you to accomplish? And how, on your atheistic hypothesis, would you, Mr. Atheist, with your tiny arm and your tinier causality; with your shallow hand, and your shallower logic; with your short life, and your shorter vision; — how would you ever have been in existence yourself to try your ridiculous experiment; and in what type foundry would your font of types be cast? Even if the conditions were granted, none but a God could use them for the expected purpose, and so you have supposed a God in order to supply the conditions, — not of creating a universe, but of getting at an Iliad only. Such is the sublime folly of the grandest answer that Atheism ever made.

A profound writer has thus sarcastically presented the atheistic side of this question. "Talk of Providence! There is no such thing. I have been through the universe, and there is no God. God is a whim

6*

of man; nature is a fortuitous concourse of atoms; man is a fortuitous concourse of atoms; thought is a fortuitous function of matter, a fortuitous result of a fortuitous result, a chance-shot from the great wind-gun of the universe, — which itself is also a chance-shot from a chance-charge of a chance-gun, accidentally loaded, pointed at random, and fired off by chance."

The last characteristic of God's laws, which I shall mention, is the most wonderful of them all. It is that they are accompanied by a sanction. By the word *sanction*, I here mean the penalty that attends transgression. No human law can execute itself. But God's laws execute themselves. The human lawgiver has to provide a train of officers. When the judge passes sentence of death, the malefactor does not forthwith find himself dead. The executioner must be called in. If a criminal be condemned to imprisonment, the air does not immediately begin to shape itself into the four walls of a prison which draw together around him, and close him in their strong embrace; but a sheriff must take him and lock him in the cell. Not so with God's laws. They execute themselves, as lightning executes itself, even before you hear the thunder. By creating a natural incompatibility between them, God prohibits the stomach from taking arsenic, and when the stomach does take arsenic, He has to send no angel to afflict that organ with unspeakable and mortal agony. God forbids intemperance, and what a ghastly throng of woes comes to avenge it! God commands cleanliness; and if people will wallow in filth and imbibe foulness at every pore, what pestilences stalk forth to avenge his violated law! So when God prohibits men from doing wrong, and they will do wrong, remorse comes of itself, — sometimes earlier, sometimes later, but always it will come, and with more terrible avengings, the longer it delays.

From human penalties men sometimes escape; — they conceal the offence, they foil the prosecutor, they flee the country; but who can secrete anything from the All-seeing Eye; who can circumvent the All-knowing Mind; who can flee beyond the jurisdiction of the Omnipotent? For all conceivable, for all possible offences against God's laws, whether of the body or of the mind; whether committed in this life, or in the next, there is an inexorable, an irrepealable, an adamantine law, that the offenders must suffer until the offences cease.

And now, my young friends, it is not without a special purpose that I have labored thus long to give you an idea of the word *law*, and of the resistlessness and universality of the Divine law. There are two grand, fundamental truths to be drawn from what has been said. Though I have not time to enlarge upon them now, I hope to do so hereafter.

The first truth is, that if the whole universe, — nature and man, body and soul, — is pervaded by the laws of God, then, in order to do the will of God, we must know what His laws are. This is a universal truth. The navigator cannot cross the ocean in safety, unless he understands the laws of navigation; and the more perfectly he understands and obeys those laws, the more safely and rapidly can he sail the seas. The farmer must observe agricultural laws, and just in proportion as he does so, will be the abundance and the excellence of his harvests. The physician must understand both Physiology and Pathology, — the laws both of health and disease, — or he will kill instead of curing. Who would ever consult a lawyer, ignorant of the constitution and laws of the land? And so the perfect Christian must understand the laws of God, as well as resolve to obey them. He must supply his intellect with knowledge as well as fill his heart with love. And before all men in the world, the Christian Pastor, — the Feeder, — for that is the meaning of the word, should abound in knowledge. It is bad enough for our market-men to supply us with unhealthful food; but that injures our bodies only. It is bad enough for our lawyer to give us false counsel, but that can only put our worldly estate in peril. It is bad enough when our surgeon amputates the limb he should save, but that only mutilates our bodily frame. But when our spiritual provider feeds our souls with chaff and husks, with the superstitions of the Dark Ages, or the dogmas of men, instead of the bread of eternal life, he does a wrong which the ages of eternity can never fully repair. How can a man who is ignorant of God's laws be God's ambassador or representative? Get knowledge, then, my young friends, get wisdom, and with all thy gettings, get understanding. Get science (which is nothing but a knowledge of God's laws) as a religious duty. Before you can *obey*, you must *know*. Knowledge, then, is essential to a rational piety. And by this, I do not mean to lower one class of duties, but only to elevate the other.

The other truth deducible from this Discourse, is, if possible, still more important. It regards the quality or nature of the obedience we render to any law. When we obey from compulsion, from fear, from a dread of evil; that is, when we are frightened into obedience, or scolded into it, or scourged into it, such compulsory obedience is always attended with a sense of degradation, of shame, and of pain. It is a perversion of this feeling that leads some half-grown men to say, "I am willing to do it, but if commanded to, I won't." But, on the other hand, when we see that a law is useful, right, wise, beautiful; when our whole moral and intellectual nature approves it, and consents to it, and rejoices in it, then, in such obedience, there is a sense of dignity, of elevation, of everlasting joy, which is indescribably pure and glorious. The drunkard is a slave, — one of the meanest and miserablest of slaves. If some master stands over him with whip or bludgeon, and forbids his indulgence on pain of instant beating, then he may abstain; but how painful, how mean and contemptible are all his feelings. A brutish appetite contends with a brutish fear. Torture, rage, malice, are all his feelings. Tophet is in his bosom. He burns for the draught, and he cringes at the blow, and each kind of pain aggravates and maddens the other. But now, suppose that same intemperate man to rise out of his brutish nature, and to become a man in truth. Suppose him to stand erect, and say; "I will be a slave no longer!" Then, in every struggle which he wages with his accursed appetite, he goes into the battle like a hero. In the fiercest contest, he has a proud feeling that he is the superior; and so he bears himself loftily through every struggle, and comes out of it triumphantly, like a great conqueror, — like the noblest of conquerors, for he has subdued flesh and devil at once. Such a man, after such a contest, is transfigured. He has a new and nobler soul in him. He feels taller, and he is taller; for, in the consciousness of rectitude he stands more erect, and looks upon men and nature from a manlier brow and with a loftier glance. All the faculties within him, hail him and say to him; "Now thou art a man." And they crown him with conscious honor. It is so with him who dethrones any vice, and enthrones the correlative virtue in its stead. And what is the difference between this moral hero, this valiant conqueror in the noblest fields of conflict; — what is the difference between this man, and the craven, cringing, cowardly wretch, who abstained from the same indulgence through the dastard, brutish motive of fear? The difference is simply this. One obeyed from external and brute restraint; the other from an internal and voluntary one. Both alike abstained, but one was a beast and a slave while he abstained; the other, a hero and a conqueror. Now this, my young friends, is the liberty wherewith Christ makes men free. This is the escape from bondage into the glorious liberty of the children of God. What was before an outward and an imposed law, is now an inward and a spontaneous act. What was before a servitude, is now a sovereignty. In the one case, the obedience was slavish; in the other, it was Christ-like. In the one case it was torment, in the other it was bliss.

Study the laws of God, then, my young friends, in regard to your whole nature, — Body, Mind, Heart. Bring yourselves on the side of those laws which are wise, good, and holy, and which you cannot resist; adapt yourselves to your position in the universe; and never forget that such are the irrepealable ordinances of God, that the righteous martyr at his stake, enjoys more, and suffers less, than the sinner on a throne.

MEDITATION.

Our Father, Thou dost talk with us from heaven now not less than with Thy servants in days of old. Thou dost teach us in Thy providences and in the stupendous order of nature, not less impressively, not less intelligibly, than if Thy voice should peal into our natural ear from Sinai's awful Mount. Deep-piercing to our intelligence are Thy warnings and Thy threatenings to-day, as if they flashed visibly from mountain or cloud into our natural eye. Thy righteous laws promising reward; Thy no less righteous laws menacing punishment, are wrought into our very frames, into our organizations, into whatever organ we have for physical life, so that we have an ever-open book before us calling us to Thee by the most powerful of persuasions and entreaties, forbidding us to forsake and forget Thee, by admonitions to which the adder's ear could not be deaf. And in addition to all these appeals and expostulations in favor of the right; in addition to all these protests and deprecations against the wrong, revealed to us in the very constitution of our being, we have the words, the precepts, the example, the life, the character, of Jesus Christ, himself the glorious pattern of what we ought to be. When his public ministry began, he was first called to resist temptation, first beset, as all youth in all times are beset, by the appetite for food; yet, though he had fasted for forty days and forty nights, he would not yield to taste of what it was wrong for him to eat; then tempted by the inflations of pride and self-sufficiency, that snare by which so many youth are made an easy prey to ruin, the belief that they are sufficient for themselves, that they may violate law and duty, and still secure prosperity and honor; and then tempted by ambition, the love of power, of dominion, that beguiling seduction that draws so many away, that fills and crowds the broad road leading to the chambers of death. Oh, may the youth of this age, of all coming ages, first of all, strive to imitate his example in withstanding the temptations which lie in ambush along their path. Our Father, look upon us as thy children. We have needs. Thou hast the inexhaustible fulness from which they can be supplied. Thou who in Thy good providence dost give us our daily bread, give us that for which our souls are languishing and perishing, the bread and the waters of life. Thou who hast given us this mortal existence, wilt Thou prepare us for that immortal existence which lies beyond the grave. Thou by whom it has been ordained for all men that they once shall die, save, oh save us from that second death which consists in alienation from Thee, and voluntary disobedience to Thy high will. Thou dost give us pleasures of sense, pleasures of the body. Oh give us those purer and nobler satisfactions of the soul by which we shall be able rapturously to exclaim, like the Psalmist of old, "My delight is in the law of the Lord."

Oh, our Father, may we seek more and more to know Thy laws, that we may obey them better; for how can our weakness defy Thy Omnipotence, or our ignorance take counsel to defeat Thy knowledge? Oh

God, Thy laws are in the heavens above, and in the earth beneath, in every ray that streams from every star; in every leaf that hangs on every tree; in the structure of every living thing; in our bodies, and in our souls. The laws of the universe are but the thoughts of God. We live then in Thy presence, we are encompassed by Thy power. Thy knowledge shines like a sun in the inmost recesses of our hearts, and our most secret thoughts are known to Thee. In view of this, may we have sincerity towards Thee, may we imitate the example of Thy Son Jesus Christ. He came to a world sunk in ignorance, to a world that had never known, or that had forgotten Thy attributes, to a world that lived in defiance of Thy commandments. But he did not come as a conqueror, to subdue and enslave; he did not come as an avenger, to overwhelm or destroy; he did not come with lightnings and with thunderings, to terrify and to blast, but he was heralded by angels who proclaimed "Peace on Earth;" — he taught the doctrine of a Paternal Ruler of the Universe; and he went about doing good. May we imitate his example!

SIN—THE TRANSGRESSION OF THE LAW.

IV.

SIN — THE TRANSGRESSION OF THE LAW.

In my last Discourse, I endeavored to illustrate the great truth, that the relation between God and ourselves is not merely that of Creator and created, but that also of Lawgiver and the subjects of law. God being our rightful Lawgiver, we, as His subjects, owe Him allegiance.

I then defined the meaning of the word *law* — that it merely signifies the *manner* in which God acts — and I illustrated the idea of law by copious examples, selected from the different kingdoms of nature, — from the inanimate not less than from the animate world; from body and from spirit. I showed also that even within the narrow circumference of human knowledge, there is an immense variety in the works of creation, and that each order, each genus, each species, each individual and each organ and faculty of each individual, has its appropriate law. Strictly speaking, there is no such thing as chance. When the navigator says he is beyond soundings, he does not mean to imply that there is no bottom to the sea; but only that it is so deep that he cannot find it, &c. All classes of created existences have their laws, though as yet we may not have discovered them, the chemical, the botanical, the zoölogical, and these laws are uniform; that is, when you ascertain how they operate in one case, you know how they operate in all like cases. The astronomer, from his knowledge of planetary motions, can not only calculate the eclipses of this year, but, in his thoughts, he can wheel the heavenly machinery backwards, and tell the exact time of all the eclipses that have happened for six thousand years, and he can also wheel it forwards, and tell the exact time of all the eclipses that will happen while our present solar system lasts. This seems a vast duration to be penetrated by the foreknowledge of the astronomer; but the moralist can penetrate infinitely farther into futurity than this; for he can foretell, that, not only while the solar system lasts, but while God lives, the wicked soul, should it remain wicked, must be miserable: but the pious spirit, so long as it remains pious, must be happy. Such is the uniformity of God's laws, enabling us to predict future histories, from known facts.

In the natural world, even when we find what appears to be an anomaly, we do not find it to be any violation of law, but only the application of a new law to new circumstances: and that the new law also is uniform. It is the law of fluids, for instance, that they shall contract, or be reduced in bulk, as they grow cold. A gallon of water becomes less and less in size, as it grows colder; until just before it reaches the temperature of 32° of our common thermometer, — which is the freezing point, — when it suddenly expands. It expands just at the moment when it is to be turned into ice. Now this sudden expansion is not a violation of the law of contraction, but it is a new law applicable to a new state of facts, and established for the wisest of purposes. For, if a cubic foot of water should continue to grow more and more solid as it grows colder up to the time when it hardens into ice, then the cubic foot of ice would be heavier than the same bulk of water, and would sink to the bottom, of course. And thus, as soon as one layer of water should freeze and sink, the water that came to the surface in its place, would also freeze and sink, and so of the rest, layer after layer, until our ponds, our rivers, and even our great lakes might all be turned into ice in a single winter, and then a hundred summers might not be sufficient to thaw them. What a beautiful thing it would be, if the heart of a miser, as it grows harder and harder with avarice and griping, should, just before it solidifies into the miser petrifaction, suddenly begin to expand; and afterwards restore its hoards, as the water gives out its latent heat for the benefit of the world. The new law of loving our neighbor as ourselves, applied to him, would work this marvel.

Again; while any vegetable or animal organization retains the principle of life, it grows, or moves, or acts, in some way, according to the nature impressed upon it; but as soon as life departs, the chemical law takes possession again, and the vegetable or animal body, whatever it may be, decays, is decomposed, and returns to its original elements. Indeed, if life departs from any portion of our bodies, even for an hour, mortification commences, and the vital organization is reduced to insensate matter. Thus it is that the same materials may pass successively under the action of different laws; be mineral this year, vegetable next, and animal the third, and then return to its original condition, to pass through the same cycle again.

All the organs of our bodies, when we are in a state of health, have their laws of health, and these laws, when embodied in a science, we call Human Physiology and Hygiene; but if these laws are violated, so that the organs pass out of a healthy condition into a diseased one, then they become subject to a new set of laws, — to the laws of Disease, — the science of which is called Pathology.

So the moral nature of man has its laws, — laws by which any one and every one who chooses the path of duty and virtue and piety, and walks in it, will find himself constantly ascending the Mount of Blessedness, whose upper circles command all the benefits of this world, and whose summit is crowned with all the glories of Heaven. But any one and every one who chooses the path of disobedience and follows it, will find himself descending to misery and ruin. And the virtue and the happiness on the one hand, and the vice and the misery on the other, are not arbitrary or fortuitous connections, but each necessitates the other; neither can exist without the other; they are component parts of the same thing, just as oxygen and hydrogen, in certain proportions, are component parts of a drop of water, and you cannot have a drop of water without them, or them in that combination, without water.

So, as the word law simply expresses the method in which God acts, it follows that these laws, that is, His method of action, are irresistible; so that, if it be a proof of intellectual idiocy or insanity for a man to take red-hot iron in his hands, or to pour molten lava down his throat, or to feed on hellebore, or make his nightly couch in a furnace, it is a proof also of moral idiocy or insanity, to bid defiance to the laws of God.

But how can we say that God's laws are irresistible, and, at the same time speak of our resisting or violating those laws? How can we resist, or violate a resistless and inviolable law? A single word will explain this. When we speak of violating one of God's laws, we do not mean that we abolish, or annihilate it. Though the law may have been broken ten thousand times, it remains as binding and operative as before. It would be simply absurd for a man to say, "I have broken the commandment against theft, and therefore, there are now only nine commandments left." Though one may have broken every one of the commandments a hundred times, the Decalogue is as whole and as imperishable as before. While one obeys the laws of health, of virtue, or of religion, he is under the laws of health, virtue and religion; but when he violates those laws, then he comes under new sets of laws, — the laws of disease, vice, and irreligion. To a man who never committed murder, or robbery, the laws of murder and robbery do not apply; but the moment those crimes are committed, then the laws and their penalties instantaneously attach to the offender; — just as when water is above the temperature of 32°, the law of fluids applies to it; but when it sinks to 32°, then the law of congelation applies to it. This shows the propriety of our speaking of resistance and violation, by free agents, of irresistible and inviolable laws. If, then, God acts by laws, and makes us know, or enables us to know, what those laws are, we, as His subjects, are bound to obey them, by an allegiance which we cannot shake off. And, if bound to obey, then any wilful or conscious violation of them is guilt. Or, as John says in that part of his first Epistle which I read to you this morning, "Sin is a transgression of the law;" which, perhaps, might be more pithily rendered into our language by inverting the order of the words, and saying, "The transgression of the law is sin."

I have spoken to you of the grandeur and amplitude of the word LAW, how it reaches to the heights, and descends to the depths, and is commensurate with the extent of all being. But this correlative word SIN, — this wilful violation of law, — has a meaning too large and terrible ever to be described or conceived by mortal mind. Sin! think of it, look at it, tremble and flee! On the one side, is there not a God of Infinite Power; for what but Infinite Power could have created the stars and constellations above us; or the exquisite mechanisms of the vegetable and animal worlds around us, or our own frames so fearfully and wonderfully made, or our souls, whose thoughts "wander through eternity?" Is He not a Being, as wise as He is powerful, and as benevolent as He is wise? And was it not through good-will that He created us, encompassed us with an atmosphere of blessings, and made us capable of ascending forever along an infinite scale of excellence, of enlarging our natures with new accessions of wisdom and truth, of adorning ourselves with beauties which exist only in the Paradise of God, and of rejoicing from age to age with more intense and seraphic exultations?

On the other hand, think what it imports, that a creature of the dust, a being of yesterday, with but a hand's breadth of knowledge and the experience of an hour, should attempt to make laws for himself, instead of finding out and obeying the laws that God has made for him; that such a being should suppose that he has found out a path, by which he can reach happiness sooner, feel its thrills more deeply and enjoy it longer, than by following the counsels and commands of his infinitely wise and perfect Father; is it not amazing, and would it not be incredible, if our whole lives, full of observation and experience, did not make us see and feel its truth!

Milton has personified Sin, and described her as a hideous monster set to guard the gates of hell:

> "Before the gates there sat,
> On either side, a formidable shape,
> The one seemed woman to the waist, and fair,
> But ended foul in many a scaly fold,
> Voluminous and vast, a serpent armed
> With mortal sting. About her middle round
> A cry of hell-hounds, never ceasing, bark'd,
> With wide Cerberean mouths, full loud, and rung
> A hideous peal; yet, when they list, would creep,
> If aught disturbed their noise, into her womb,
> And kennel there, yet there still bark'd and howl'd
> Within unseen."

But no physical imagery, though gathering disgust upon disgust, and accumulating horror upon horror, can paint the dreadful reality of sin itself. Sin is not a fabled monster, but a real one. It is not an existence outside and apart from man's bosom, but within it. It is not a creature whom you must go to the gates of a material hell to see, — it is not a caged beast or fiend carried about in chains for a show, — but it is a resident of every guilty man's heart. Would to God that sin had no terrors worse than barking hell-hounds, fiercely rushing out from their ambush to seize unwary victims, and then dragging the prey to their loathsome kennel. But sin is a voluntary exiling of one's self from communion with God and all good beings; it is a forfeiture of all the heavenly peace of virtue, of the blissful harmonies which flow in, like music, upon the soul, after duties faithfully performed; it is haggard fear, blanching the face; it is convulsions of agony, crushing the heart; it is remorse, shrieking with intolerable torment, "Oh, would to God I had never been born;" and not unfrequently it drives its victim to madness, to despair, to suicide.

Do not look upon sin, then, as some frightful spectre conjured up by another, but as something created by yourself; not as a tormentor that will pursue your steps wherever you flee, but as a criminal force, which, wherever you may flee, you carry in your own bosom; not as an enemy that you may outlive, or that will grow weary in its besiegings or pursuit, and, at last, leave you to rest; but as a foe, which, if you do not exorcise and expel, will remain a part of you forever, and when its name is called, though in the presence of an assembled universe, you will be forced to answer, "It is I." Sin consists not in vultures tearing your heart with bloody talon and beak; not in wolves hounding your panting steps, across lonely wastes, in midnight darkness; not in serpents coiling themselves round bosom and throat, and strangling out your life; not in pirates torturing out the secret of your hidden wealth; not in bigots stretching you upon the limb-disjointing rack, or binding you to the fire-engirdled stake; all this could be borne, has been borne triumphantly, with shouts of exultation and joy; but sin consists in a false state of the mind and heart; in dishonest contrivances; in impure desires; in intemperance; in concupiscence; in profanity; in blasphemy against the good God; in those acts of wrong, which, whatever they may be, register themselves, as they are committed, upon the eternal tablets of the heart; and, unless repented of and forsaken, will remain the blackening autobiography of eternity. Sin is the weakness and disease of the moral faculties. You know what is meant by a withered limb, — an arm that you cannot raise up to your head, a foot you cannot move forward in your path. Sin, committed against our fellow-men, is such a paralysis of conscience or justice. You know what is meant by an idiot, — a blank, stark, brainless moonling, — one who dwells amid the beauties and glories of nature, yet finds no charm or splendor in them all; one who lives amid its harmonies, yet hears no music; one who walks among all the grandeurs and varieties of creation, but to whom they all seem tame and monotonous. Such is the loathsome idiot, having only the outward form, bereft of the inward majesty of a man. The sinner is the moral idiot. To his sightless eye, and his tuneless ear, all the brightness and joy of the moral world is blank and inane. Of that summit and crown of all mortal and immortal beauty, — the Beauty of Holiness, — he sees not a feature nor a gleam. To this idiot sinner, or sinner idiot, all the power and wisdom of this truth-compacted universe, is empty and formless as chaos itself; and, instead of dwelling in the beatific presence of God, and in communion with all good spirits, he roams a voluntary exile, fatherless, motherless, friendless, and forlorn, through the unanswering void of immensity. Such is sin; such it is to be a sinner.

But instead of these general views, let us look at the subject of sin with a little more particularity and individualizing, and make the domain of conscience and religion larger. Moral and religious teachers have confined their expositions, their rewards, and their penalties, to too few things.

The *transgression of the law* is sin. Before, then, there can be any sin, there must be a law. On this point I have before spoken to you at sufficient length. I have shown you that every created thing, animate, or inanimate; everything, organized, or unorganized, has its law. All the organs of your bodies, and all the faculties of your minds, have their law; and when these laws, or any one of them, is knowingly or wilfully transgressed, there is sin. This shows us what transgression is; let us now see who is capable of being a transgressor. The etymological meaning of the word *transgress* is, to pass over or beyond a prescribed limit. A wilful transgression, then, can be committed only by some one who knows, or was bound to know, and had opportunity to know, where the limit is. None but an intelligent and moral being can know this. Hence, none but an intelligent and moral being can be a transgressor, that is, a sinner. When a railroad locomotive runs beyond its station house, it has passed its limit or goal; but it is not a sinner. When fire escapes from furnace or chimney top, and burns down a house, or a city, it overleaps its boundary, but fire is not a sinner. When a stark idiot destroys property, or takes human life, he is not a sinner, for he knows no better. You might as well say that the moon is a sinner, when, in passing between the sun and the earth, it casts its shadow on the latter, and causes an eclipse. One of the conditions of sin, then, is that, there must be a law; and another condition is, that there must be a capacity for understanding the law. Every duty is a law, and, hence, as I have often told you, there are not only ten commandments, but ten thousand; and, therefore, transgression, or sin, may manifest itself in ten thousand different ways.

As conditions of sin, then, there must not only be a law, and a general ability in the subject, sufficient to understand the law, but the means of knowing or understanding it must be supplied. While a proposed law still remains in the lawgiver's bosom, or is only promulgated in an unknown tongue, the subject cannot transgress it, in a moral sense. The Roman Emperor, Caligula, is said to have caused his laws to be written in a handwriting so fine, and to be posted up on columns so high, that the people could not see to read them, and then he punished those by whom they were not obeyed. Who was the greater criminal in this case, the alleged law-breaker, or the law-maker? And when a man assures us that God acts by this rule, what does he make of God but another Caligula, only an infinitely worse one?

So an *ex post facto* law is always an iniquitous law. What, in the language of jurisprudence, is called an *ex post facto* law, is a law which looks backwards, instead of forwards, which declares it to be criminal to have performed an act, that was not criminal at the time when it was done. For instance there may be no law, at the present time, against making gunpowder; if, then, the Legislature should pass a law, declaring that every man who has made gunpowder during the past year, should be subject to fine and imprisonment, this would be an *ex post facto* law. I have heard theologians say, that all men, except, perhaps, the ancient Jews, who lived before the advent of Jesus Christ, must be forever lost; simply because they had never heard of, and therefore never believed on Him. Would such persons, or would they not, be judged by an *ex post facto* law?

You see, also, that, as men pass through the greatest variety of relations and circumstances, they become subject to the greatest variety of laws, and therefore may commit the greatest variety of sins. Every new relation, and every new set of circumstances, presents an occasion for the application of a new law. If one has a father, he is bound to that father by the filial law. If he should lose that father and have a guardian, then he is no longer bound by the law of the son to the father, but by the modified law of the ward to the guardian; and when he becomes twenty-one years of age, then he is absolved from all legal obligations to his guardian, but he takes on the responsibility of a citizen to the State; and if he should marry and have children, then he comes under the parental obligation, and is legally bound for the nurture, support, and education of those children, until they arrive at the age of twenty-one, at which time this new relation is modified, both on his part, and on theirs.

Then, there are laws applicable to all our appetites and propensities. There is a law which forbids our indulgence in food or drink, to a degree that would be injurious to health. We have no right to eat more because our food tastes good. We should eat in reference to the stomach, and not to the palate. No matter how sweet, and savory, and odorous, your food may be, — the more so the better; — it was intended that eating and drinking should give us pleasure. Btu what I insist upon is, that health, and not immediate pleasure, should be our law at the table; and whoever obeys this law, will obtain not only more health, but more pleasure, in the long run.

By applying this train of thought to other spheres of

action, you will readily perceive that there can be an almost infinite number of offences; and offences, too, of every variety and degree of heinousness. Some are peccadilloes, faults, defects, or blemishes in moral character. Others are of a graver nature, trespasses, misdemeanors, and crimes inferior to felonies; while others involve moral turpitude, belonging to what, in law, is called the *crimen falsi*, such as conspiracy to injure, perjury, subornation of perjury, &c.; and others are crimes against God himself, — profanity, blasphemy, impiety, sacrilege.

If, then, there are various grades of offences, there must be various degrees of guilt among offenders. Did not Christ say, it should be more tolerable for Tyre and Sidon, and even for Sodom and Gomorrah, than for the offenders in his day? Justice punishes according to the ill-desert of the offender. For the same outward act, it does not punish an ignorant, untutored child, as it would an intelligent adult. It surely will not punish the rulers of a nation who have been bred all their lives long in thoughts and sentiments of oppression, for committing acts of oppression, as it will punish, for similar acts of injustice and cruelty, those who have been bred all their lives long to a knowledge and an appreciation of the Rights of Man. "And that servant," says Jesus Christ, "who knew his Lord's will, and prepared not himself, neither did according to his will, shall be beaten with many stripes. But he that knew not, and did commit things worthy of stripes, shall be beaten with few stripes. For unto whomsoever much is given, of him shall much be required; and to whom men have committed much, of him they will ask the more."

Hence we see that God will punish the clear-headed,

strong-minded, far-seeing man; that He will punish those who have been illuminated by the glorious light of the Gospel, by a different standard from that by which He will punish weak and imbecile men, or the barbarian and heathen.

The same year that Prof. Webster was executed in Massachusetts, for the murder of Doctor Parkman, another man, named Washington Goode, was hung for another murder. The first was educated, learned, and, from his birth, had enjoyed all the advantages that refined society, schools, churches, colleges, could bestow. The latter was a colored man, born in obscurity, swaddled in ignorance, nursed by the griping of the iron arms of poverty, left to fall into intemperance, and besotted by vices, until he approached, at least, near the line of moral unaccountability. Petitions for the pardon of them both were signed and sent to the Governor. Now, what would you have said of the Governor, had he pardoned the man whom all the attendant circumstances of life had tended to rescue and to uplift; but had sent the man to the gallows, whose every faculty from his birth, had been loaded with some immoral gravitation that weighed him downward to ruin? What should we think of the Ruler of a State who could do this? What should we think of the Ruler of a Universe who could do this? I know that it is said that God, by right of His sovereignty, may do anything with the creatures of His own creation. The God I worship recognizes no right to be unjust! And there is no rule of reason or religion, which authorizes me to judge of his good attributes, in order to love and adore Him, which does not also authorize me to pronounce upon any evil attributes that are imputed to Him.

God punishes, also, for the offence committed, and not for any other offence. What should we think of the father of a family, the teacher of a school, the faculty of a college, or of the tribunals which administer the criminal laws of a State, if they had but one and the same punishment for all varieties of offenders? Has the Infinite God less justice, less discrimination, less primitive appliances to fit different degrees of wrong, than earthly father, teacher, faculty, or judge? He punishes physical sins, or transgressions of physical law, physically; and other sins according to their kind and aggravation. Does a man expose himself to sudden transitions from heat to cold? he is punished by rheumatism, inflammation, and consumption. High living aggravated by indolence, is punished by gout. Licentiousness rots men, until they become like rotten sheep. Intemperance demonizes the heart, maddens, and, at last, stultifies the brain, divides the limbs, and joints, and organs of the body, into a thousand parts, and sets a devil over each part to torment it. National crimes, — slavery, or any form of legalized oppression; forbidding popular education, or even neglecting to promote it, — are punished by wide-spread poverty, by ignorance, by long haltings in the march of civilization, and, in many cases, by pestilences, famine, and death. Crimes against the soul of man, — such as sectarianism, bigotry, intolerance of free thought, — are punished by a meanness, and narrowness, and cruelty of national character, and by the extinction of all manly, noble, and generous sentiments. Crimes against the moral laws of God, — such as profanity, blasphemy, sacrilege, &c., are punished by moral insensibility, or by remorse; and, until repented of and abandoned, — by exile from

God's holy presence, that is from those aspirations and communings, and exaltations of joy, which fill the life of good men, wherever they may be, with unspeakable ecstasy and rapture. We see by all this, that a man may obey some of God's commandments while he breaks others. Those which he obeys, he is rewarded for; but for all those which he breaks, he is punished. The civil magistrate punishes only for the crimes which men commit. If a màn be guilty of horse-stealing only, he is not punished for bigamy. If he be guilty only of theft, he is not punished for setting houses on fire. So we may be sure that God will only punish men for the offences which they commit. If the wickedest man that ever lived makes a perfect steam-engine of five hundred horse-power, it will work just as well as though it had been made by the best of saints. Being an engine of five hundred horse-power, it will not be cut down to an engine of four hundred, or three hundred, or one hundred horse-power, because its maker practised one, two, or three vices, or committed so many crimes of a hideous dye. The vices or crimes will be punished, according to their respective qualities, but not the steam-engine. For, wherever the man is guilty, there he is sure to be punished by the adamantine law of eternal rectitude, just as he is sure to be rewarded wherever he is meritorious. Hence, if a man loves God with all his heart, and soul, and mind, and strength, and his neighbor as himself; if he does justly, loves mercy, and walks humbly with his God; if he visits the fatherless and the widows in their affliction, and keeps himself unspotted from the world; then, there is only one sense in which it may be said that such a man cannot enter the kingdom of heaven, — that is, *because he is in it already.* So, if one's life and character are the reverse of all this, then, there is only one sense in which it can be said that such a man will not be doomed to perdition; — namely, that he was doomed there long ago, and the sentence is already in process of execution. Heaven and hell are not places, but states of mind; not regions for the geographer to explore and set out by metes and bounds; but conditions of the soul which we call remorse, hatred, and torment, or joy, beatitude, and ecstasy. For, as Milton says,

> "The mind is its own place, and in itself,
> Can make a heaven of hell, a hell of heaven."

I have time to set forth but one idea more on this immensely important theme. It is an idea of modern date, — first advanced by one of the most philosophic and wisest men of the age. As we have a thousand instances which show us how much philosophy has been aided by religion, this shows how much aid religion may borrow from philosophy.

The idea I am about to announce, takes the highest religious platform, to begin with. It assumes, in the first place, that man is bound, as far as it is possible for such a finite being to do, to *know* the will of God, and then he is bound to *obey* it. But I believe the opinion has always prevailed, and, until the idea to which I refer was first broached, the opinion was universal, that our obligation to obey God's commandments or laws was more sacred or less sacred, had more or less binding stringency, and was accompanied and enforced by higher penal sanctions or by lower penal sanctions, according to the manner in which those laws were made known to us. That is, that when an acknowledged truth or duty has been made known to the world by a man of a particular class or nation, or by a man not believed to be divinely inspired, it has less efficacy, less binding power upon our consciences and lives, than if it had been communicated to us by a Hebrew prophet, or by a man supposed to be divinely inspired. According to this theory, God's truths or commands are not worthy our homage and observance because of their intrinsic justice or holiness, because they are God's truths or commandments, but because of the channel through which they came to us; because of their accidents. Now the new and advanced idea which I wished to set forth is, that any duty, any obligation whatever, as soon as we are convinced that it is God's will, or God's law, has the same sovereign authority over us, and its violation will be accompanied by the same fearful penalties, as though the proclamation of that same will, or law of God, had been made amid the thunderings and lightnings of Sinai, or from the burning bush of Horeb.

There are immense differences, it is true, in regard to the importance of different truths or commandments, — some referring to the body and some to the soul, some pertaining to this life, and some to the next — and there are different degrees of faith or of conviction, according to which men believe duties or destinies to have been divinely revealed or philosophically discovered; but, when any one of God's truths is demonstrably made known to us, that truth is equally entitled to our homage and observance, and binds us by the same awful sanctions, whether revealed from the cloudy top of Sinai, or discovered by philosophic research, or even by accident. It is the duty, and not the mode of demonstrating it; it is the holy message, and not the chance messenger; it is the majesty and sanctity of God's commands, and not the red or black ink in which they may be printed; it is the holiness of the light dispensed, and not the direction from which it shines, which thunders and flashes its appeals on the soul, and says: Obey, for it is God's will. What matters it to me whether the telegraphic wire which brings me intelligence of my friend's death, or of his marvellous rescue from death, be made of iron wire, or of steel? It is the death or the life of my friend, and not the wire, that is vital to me. My young friends, what a solemn thought is this! How are all the common duties of life elevated into a higher region, and illuminated with a diviner light by the reflection, that the truths of Physiology which you learn in your class-rooms; that the truths of mental and moral science which you acquire in your course of college studies; that your duty through life to educate all people in all lands, to the highest practicable extent; that your duty to oppose all unrighteous wars, all oppression, and all slavery, whether it be of body or of mind; that your duty to suppress all sources of intemperance, and all evil habits that have sprung up since the days of Moses or of Christ; that the offence of neglecting to perform these duties is just as heinous, and that the punishment for such neglect will be just as certain and severe, as though the heavens had been visibly opened and God had audibly spoken, commanding you to do the same right things, or to abstain from the same wrong ones. This does not bring down what you may have been accustomed to consider the higher truth to a level with what you thought to be the lower one; it only elevates the lower to that perfectness of obligation in which you have held the higher.

Let these solemn considerations, my young friends, abide with you through the week and through life; and may we all remember that as God has promised us the highest rewards which our natures are capable of receiving, if we obey His laws; for he that doeth righteousness is righteous, even as God is righteous; so He has assured us that sin is the transgression of the law, and made known to us by ten thousand burning, desolating proofs, that the way of the transgressor is hard.

MEDITATION.

Our Father who art in Heaven, we bow before Thee in reverence and godly fear, and in humility and love we would adore the Infinite perfections of Thy nature. Thou alone art the Creator, Preserver, Ruler, and Final Disposer of all things. We adore Thee for that Infinite Power by which Thou fillest the regions of immensity with planets, and suns, and systems, all, as we believe, the abodes of beings capable of knowing truth, of feeling love, of enjoying happiness — all Thy children, and therefore all our brothers. When we look upward to the stars, may we not look at them as vast masses filled with shining but insensate material, sparkling for an idle show in the azure vault above, but may we look upon them as realms where Thy moral power is manifested even more gloriously than Thy physical. We adore Thee that thou didst create the universe, not only with Infinite power but with Infinite skill, so that as Thy creatures advance in knowledge, they can see more and more of Thy perfections of wisdom, of skill, of knowledge, of the adaptation of all things to all things, creating, to the ear of contemplation, a solemn harmony, an anthem of praise, through all the limitless regions of space. To that grand anthem may we add our hallelujahs. We adore Thee that Thou didst create and dost govern Thy worlds by immutable and uniform laws, so that we, Thy creatures, when we know Thy will, for once, can know it always; so that we have no fear of the caprices, and changeableness, and arbitrary impulses of a vacillating governor. We adore Thee, that Thy laws are all benevolent and holy, made on the great principle that Thy glory and our highest good are identical, so that all our nature can respond to the glorious truth that the law of the Lord is perfect, converting the soul; the statutes of the Lord are right, rejoicing the heart; the commandment of the Lord is free, enlightening the eyes. We thank Thee, Heavenly Father, that Thou hast raised up from time to time, those great and glorious men of intellect and genius, who sought out and discovered the laws by which Thou dost govern the material world, so that we can explain its wonderful phenomena, not by follies and vagaries of superstition, but by the unerring principles of wisdom and truth, so that we can make those laws subservient to our welfare in arts, in mechanics, in agriculture, in using the great forces of nature to minister to our comfort and prosperity. We thank Thee for the men whose genius has developed and laid down those higher rules of social life, of civil law, of equity, of government, of education, by which the interests of great masses of men are promoted and carried into welfare and grandeur. But oh! still more do we praise Thy name for those greater and nobler spirits who have discovered our relations to Thee. * * * * *

TESTIMONY AGAINST EVIL—A DUTY.

V.

TESTIMONY AGAINST EVIL — A DUTY.

My young friends, I have often spoken to you of the great number and variety of human duties. Every relation in life has its peculiar duties. If, therefore, we consider how various, and how numerous, or rather how numberless, are the relations of life, we can have a more adequate idea of how various and how numberless are the duties of life.

Every duty implies a command to fulfil it; so that the moment I become convinced of the existence of any duty belonging to my position, that moment, I hear the voice of God commanding me to perform it. Hence, as I have often said to you before, there are not only Ten Commandments, but ten thousand.

The subject on which I propose to discourse to you at this time, is our duty to offenders, to criminals, and to those who are exposed by any peculiar temptation, internal or external, to become offenders or criminals. Alas! how numerous they are! What distressful throngs of men and women who come into life, not only capable of happiness, but yearning for happiness, have found only disease and sorrow, pain and ignominy, and in sinking at last into an unhallowed grave, have reached the only quiet spot the earth ever gave them! The hopes which nature implanted in their bosoms were never nurtured into blossoming. The curse of unfaithful parents, or of bad associates; the pernicious customs and practices of society, under which they were almost like clay upon the potter's wheel, exasperated their in-born capacities of evil, and plunged them into ruin. The health, and strength, and physical joy of which they were capable, were sacrificed by mismanagement. The mental faculties, hungering and thirsting after knowledge, were never brought into right relations to those objects of knowledge of which the bountiful Author of nature has prepared such a profusion. They were never taught to feel the delights of exercising the moral nature, delights of which a child can have no more conception, without a presentation of opportunities, than he can have an idea of the deliciousness of fruit that he never tasted.

Indeed, people often deny that children have a love of knowledge, merely through their own mistakes in offering knowledge to them. Suppose a mother should buy a vase of the nicest honey for her children, and should pour it on the top of their heads, or the nape of their necks, or into their ears, or on the soles of their feet, instead of putting it into their mouths; and when the children began to fret and cry, and to express the strongest disgust, and strive to run away, she should affirm that children hate honey; she would only do what many teachers do, when they affirm that children do not love knowledge.

Consider, for a moment, what a deplorable perversion of their powers bad men make. Capacitated to do good, they do evil. With powers and faculties to seek out and to perform the right, they seek out and perform the wrong. With health and strength to earn their own living and add to the common wealth, they live by depredating on the property of others. With ingenuity and inventive power to improve the machinery of the useful arts, they pervert their gifts to prepare implements and contrivances for fraud, and robbery, and the coinage of false money. I have witnessed the trials of several offenders, who had showed genius and skill enough in their contrivances to commit crime, to have invented some useful machine that would have made their fortunes. What a different life, and what a different end of life!—to be an inventor and discoverer, like Fulton, or Whitney, or Arkwright, or Franklin, and to bless the world by their talents and study, or to expend talents and study in doing wrong, and end life in the penitentiary! Some of this class of criminals, instead of living by industry, live by blood. To their perverted minds, a little money or an hour of criminal indulgence, was more precious than the life of a fellow-being. Look out upon the broad expanse of society, as upon a map, and you may see the loathsome and hideous vestiges of bad men, marked here and there upon its surface. They go through the community as a tornado cuts its way through a forest, leaving a pathway of desolation, whose ravages it will take a generation to repair. Instead of founding hospitals, they have filled prisons. Those who might have invented and built life-boats which would have saved crews, have become wreckers, waiting on dangerous coasts, to steal, and rob the passengers of shipwrecked vessels. In many cases, those have stood at the bar of criminal tribunals and been sentenced to the jail or the gallows, who, by their native talents and capacities, might have adorned the bench itself, from which their condemnation proceeded. Oh, what a perversion was this of powers and capabilities! What sacrilege committed upon the holiest of God's gifts! It would seem to be enough to satiate the malignity of a fiend, to rob a man of his powers of usefulness, to smite down the arm that would dispense blessings, to stifle the aspiration for worthy deeds. But in bad men the power of doing good is changed into the fact of doing ill. The arm that should dispense blessings showers injuries. The honors within their reach are exchanged for ignominy and shame. Such are bad men, — in eternal discord with all the laws of the moral universe, warring against the divine order of Providence, in a warfare that is certain to bring defeat and destruction upon themselves.

More or less of this class, the thief, the forger, the robber, the libertine, the destroyer of life, or the destroyer of character, within the last month, within the last week, having done their last and worst deeds upon earth, have forcibly quitted the world they tormented. A sad and mournful exit. Are their places to be filled? Are their deeds to be re-enacted? Is the deformity of their characters to be reproduced? Who stand ready to furnish the new recruits for the new campaign of guilt? Can the state afford this desertion from its own numbers to swell the ranks of sin? Suppose the government to be a mere soulless entity, without conscience and without heart, an arch-bailiff, whose only function it is to keep the peace, and provided it does keep the peace, indifferent as to the moral character of the means it uses, — suppose all this, and yet how can the government be indifferent to crime and criminals? If crime were the greatest of earthly luxuries, it is so expensive that it cannot be afforded. The frugality of a Republic protests against so costly an indulgence. If government were intent only on getting rich, shrewdness and far-sighted policy would dictate any expenditure to preserve the morals of the people. If government were a mere jail-keeper and executioner, it could adopt no means of help so effectual for lightening the labor of punishment as the diffusion of intelligence and the cultivation of honesty. Hangman and scourger though it be, it can make a brilliant pecuniary speculation by educating its people aright, and thus saving the expense of halters, chains, prisons. There is no such false economy as in neglecting the proper culture of youth, because of its cost. He is the greatest prodigal and spendthrift who bequeaths money or goods or lands to his children at the expense of their heads and hearts.

But if the state is rich enough to spare a portion of its citizens for the prison and the gallows, where is the parent who stands ready to have the lot fall upon one of his own offspring? If the ranks of guilt are to be replenished for the next generation, as they have been for the last, then it inevitably follows that children and infants, yet in a state of practical innocency, are to imitate the deeds and receive the doom of the ignominious malefactors who have gone before them. An intolerable imagination! In whose arms is that infant now folded, on whose throbbing breast is that babe now reposing, who shall hereafter tenant the felon's cell and fill the felon's grave? One could not see an infant driven to the projecting angle of an edifice by the flames that were consuming it, and vainly stretching out its hands and lifting its voice for succor, without becoming frantic at the spectacle; and yet this would be a gala-scene compared with the sight of one accountable being writhing under those terrible fires of remorse which burn without consuming. What parent has a child that he is willing to have apprenticed and prepared for the terrible work of guilt? Has any one of you, my youthful friends, a little brother or sister whom you are willing to surrender for such a sacrifice?

But if crime be so terrible a calamity, if a criminal be such an utter perversion of the purpose for which man was created, how ought an intelligent and moral community to regard both crime and criminal? When a crime is committed, which party is suffering under the greater misfortune, the party wronged or the wrong-doer? Suppose a man's watch, or coat, or horse to be stolen, or a counterfeit bank-note to be passed upon him, or his name to be forged to a receipt, or a parcel of goods to be obtained from him under false pretences. In either of the cases supposed, there is no actual destruction of property; the aggregate amount of the wealth in the state or country remains the same. There has only been an attempted or a successful transfer of money or of some article of value from one man to another, against the rights of ownership. This is the outward fact, and this is the extent of the wrong done to the loser. Doubtless it is often a serious one. But the individual defrauded or robbed may have, and indeed generally has, other watches, or coats, or horses, or, at least, the means of procuring them. Even if redress can never be had, it very seldom happens that the sufferer is obliged to eat, or drink, or sleep the less, or to forego any of the common comforts or conveniences of life, on account of the loss. This is the measure of harm on the side of the loser. But who can measure the magnitude of the evil suffered by the offender himself? He has outraged and profaned that part of his nature which should have been kept inviolate and sacred. He has written a terrible chapter in his own history that no detergent can ever efface, no alchemy can ever transmute into whiteness — a page that will endure forever as a part of his own living consciousness and memory. Pardon may save him from some of the consequences of the deed, but not even pardon, however bounteous and overflowing, can ever annihilate the fact that guilt was perpetrated, and that he was its author. The very idea of pardon, indeed, must always suggest the idea of offence, and the idea of having offended must forever make deductions from the happiness of a pure nature. Perhaps the offender, previous to his offence, was pressing forward in a course of virtue and honor, which, so far, is always a course of inward happiness; but when he violated his allegiance to truth and deserted her banner, he turned by a right angle and entered the pathway to ruin. The offence, then, was a violation of the great principles on which his moral nature was constructed; it was the sacrifice of honor and duty; it was the exchange of peace of mind for anxiety and the goadings of remorse; it was placing himself in opposition to heaven and in discordance with the whole moral universe. When a man, before innocent, commits crime, he passes, by a sudden transition, into a new world. The change in himself changes the significance of all objects around him; the laws of association in his own mind are changed; a viper is born in his breast which stings and goads him; sounds that he never heard before ring in his ears; a violated conscience turns avenger and scourger, — the foe is within him. Were it merely an external enemy that he had to contend with, he might be fled from, might be resisted, bribed, or would at last remit his inflictions through very weariness of tormenting. But not so with one's own consciousness of wrong. While the soul is alive, that consciousness is alive, for it is a function of the soul. It will not sleep, nor tire, nor relent. Hear what the heathen poet, Juvenal, says:

"From virtue's ways when vicious men depart,
The first avenger is the culprit's heart."

Such is the awful measure of harm on the side of the offender. Contrast, then, the losses of the respective parties, — the offender and the offended. Though the injured party has been despoiled of the last cent of his wealth, though the last morsel has been snatched from his famishing lips, though his shelter has been burned over his head, and himself sent forth naked and penniless into the world, still, after all this, his loss is infinitely less than that of the criminal who inflicted it. Which of these parties, then, needs the greatest sympathy, succor, and assistance? Surely the fate of the criminal is infinitely the most to be deplored. He is the party most demanding sympathy. But what *kind* of sympathy does he require? Does he require that kind of sympathy which pardons, or that kind of sympathy which reforms? Is he to be saved from the consequences of having offended, or to be saved from the disposition to offend? Is he to be rescued from outward and temporary evils, or from inward and indefinitely long ones? A wise sympathy seeks out the source of the calamity and removes that; a foolish sympathy cuts off the twig or shoot of mischief, or pain, but leaves the root in the ground.

There is another aspect of this case. When a family

or a circle of friends is thrown into consternation by the exposure of some offence, committed by one of its members, which is it that a false public sentiment most laments, the breach of the moral and divine law, or the worldly disgrace that follows detection? If the public disgrace and scandal inflict a deeper wound, or cause more regret than the guilty deed itself, it must be because there is a greater reverence for public opinion than for the laws of God. If conscience had a higher homage than the community, then we should lament the wrong in and of itself, more than the shame attending it. A recognition of this truth would prevent men from ever committing a second offence in order to conceal a first. Indeed, if experience did not disprove it, we should be ready to affirm that no man of common sense could ever venture upon the fatal enterprise of defending one offence by the commission of another. For, if the first offence needs the protection of a second, surely the first two will need twice as much the protection of a third, the first three, three times as much the protection of a fourth, and so on, in progression. He who commits a subsequent offence, in order to conceal a preceding one, is striving to get a cover large enough to cover itself.

If crime, then, is so terrible an evil, let us consider how the criminal should be treated. His case should always be treated with great solemnity. A depraved custom prevails in some civilized communities; and it is patronized and rewarded by some educated people, — of using the crimes and distresses of the poor and the wicked as a fund for ridicule and jocularity. In our courts, there is often a body of professional reporters who attend when criminals are arraigned for trial, and who find in their depravity, their ignorance, their fears, and their passions, materials for ridicule and merriment. The degradation of the human soul is turned into sport. Laughter grows wanton over the blighting of domestic affections. Wit is pampered at the expense of all parental ties or filial enjoyments. A human being, fallen from his high estate, eclipsed in all his shining faculties, lost to himself, to his family, and the world, — the saddest spectacle that the pitying eye of heaven ever looks down upon, is made, by a profligate wit, the pastime of beings calling themselves rational and Christian. Men of high intellectual endowments and education, — of a certain sort, — weave romances from human crimes. This mine of human misery and guilt, deep and terrible as Tartarus, is entered and worked as men work mines in California, for pecuniary profit, or worse than this, for the diabolical pleasure of contemplating sin. Did Christian sentiments pervade our hearts and control our actions, the precincts of a criminal court would be besieged by troops of men and women, gathered there to rescue or ransom these fallen brothers and sisters of the race. Men would gather around the fatal spot, where the guilty are brought to be tried and condemned, as eagerly as they gather along the shore of the sea, when a storm is dashing a brave ship on the rocks. The shame and remorse of a criminal ought to send out a cry more piercing than the shrieks of drowning mariners. To be lost in the abysses of guilt, would be regarded as a fate ten thousand times more dreadful than to be sunk in the depths of the ocean. The loss of character and of innocence would be deemed to be, as it truly is, infinitely greater than the loss of all worldly goods, ay, of life itself. To die is but a small calamity; to do wrong is a great one. By what efforts then can we save; by what kindness can we solace; by what generosity can we ransom and restore? — these things ought to task the wisdom and benevolence of men and of society.

We have now seen how men ought to regard crime. They ought to regard it as they regard a conflagration that makes a city houseless. They ought to regard it as they regard unjust war, which, without any recompense, fills a nation with mourning, and lamentation, and woe. They ought to regard it as they regard a pestilence, that consigns youth, and beauty, and strength, to a common grave. They ought to regard it as they regard insanity, which leaves a being without mind, in a world where every step and every act requires mind. They ought to regard it with fear, and deprecation, and horror, and with an undying resolve to exterminate it, for it is a greater calamity than any I have named, or than all put together.

But, more particularly, how ought men to regard crime as it affects themselves? All innocent men feel a common interest to arrest the career of guilty men. All guilty men feel a common interest that all should be honest except themselves and their accomplices; nay, that even an accomplice should be honest, towards themselves. Even those who combine together for the defence and protection of any social vice, and for trampling under foot the law that forbids it, are nevertheless, sturdy defenders of the good laws in which they have an interest. The manufacturer or seller of ardent spirits will go to the death against horse-thieves. Hear the keeper of a gaming-house talk about the villany of burglars, and you would think he was a saint. The trader who increases his profits by adulterating his goods, will curse the man who sells to him by short measure or weight. So that through all the relations of society, even rogues are interested in having every body else honest. Honest men are interested in having the whole world honest, in suppressing all fraud, violence, and wrong.

But honesty cannot prevail, unless the guilty are brought to justice. Hence it is alike the interest and the duty of all honest men to furnish whatever aid they can in bringing the guilty to justice. The man who strives to protect or screen a guilty party, deserts the cause of truth, and allies himself, so far, with the cause of guilt. Who will bring the guilty to justice, if honest men will not? Will they volunteer to accuse themselves? Will the murderer go and ask the sheriff to execute him? Will the robber go to the penitentiary and ask the keeper to imprison him for life or for twenty years? No. Unless therefore, honest men bring rogues to justice, villany will be triumphant and universal. According to the old narrative, ten righteous men could have saved Sodom, and that is true, not only of the ancient Sodom, but of New Orleans or Glasgow. And it is no less true, that if ten wicked men were to be protected and screened from the retributions of justice, because persons cognizant of their guilt would not accuse them, or because grand jurors would not indict them, or because witnesses would perjure themselves by withholding evidence or falsifying evidence on their trial, — these ten wicked men could go over the world, like ten demons of wrath, and leave not a virtuous thing, nor a beautiful thing, nor an innocent thing in all its realms. Not only, then, is the guilty man a common enemy of mankind, but the man who strives to protect, defend, or rescue the guilty man, is the common enemy of mankind.

Having considered the manner in which the guilty ought to be treated, in reference to the good of mankind, let us consider the manner in which they ought to be treated in reference to their own good.

Every one knows the tendency of all human propensities or instincts to grow. The body of the child grows, but not a thousandth part as fast as his habits and dispositions. The good man grows in virtue, and the bad man grows in sin. From the youthful benevolence that rejoices to see an animal happy, one grows up into a world-wide benefactor, into the healer of diseases, the restorer of sight to the blind, the giver of a tongue to the dumb, the founder of hospitals; and his life leaves a shining track along the realms of history, which will not fade away to the end of time; but when the sun of time sets, will shine forth all the brighter, as the stars, unseen before, come forth in their glory when the day is done. Another grows from cruelty to animals, to being a kidnapper, and enslaver, and seller of men, women, and children; from stealing an egg, or robbing a garden or an orchard, to highway robbery or piracy; from using those contemptible vulgarisms in language, sometimes called "baby oaths," to practising all the dreadful dialects of profane language, to blasphemy, and at length to perjury. Through this force of habit, the life of the good man becomes better and better, brighter and brighter, until its glorious close is splendid, and brilliant, and rich as an Oriental caravan of white elephants, with housings inwrought with gems and gold, with sacred banners flying, vocal with song and instrumental harmonies, nearing the Holy City with many worshippers and many offerings. The life of a bad man is like a company of East Indian Thugs, setting forth on a horrid journey, not only to commit plunder, robbery, and assassination themselves, but to teach and train children to commit them, and after making their murderous circuit, returning to their dreary home with bloody spoils only in their bloody hands, with fiendish faces and more fiendish hearts — heralded everywhere by the echoes of the death-groans they have caused.

In view of this growth of all the sentiments and passions of men, the earlier you can check any tendency to wrong, the earlier you can arrest a career in wrong, the greater good you do. He who crushes one poisonous seed, not only destroys the poisonous plant that would have grown from it, but all the progeny of poisonous plants which it would have produced forever. He who crushes one viper's egg, not only destroys the viper that was in it, but all the lineage of vipers to which that one would have given birth. So he who reforms one bad youth, has saved the world from all the lengthening and deepening catalogue of crimes his manhood was competent to commit. To arrest an offender, then, at the earliest possible stage, is the highest and the divinest benevolence, the most heavenly sympathy, save only that which would take him at a still earlier period, and forestall the evil altogether.

I have spoken of the relations of the great world to crime and to criminals. Every college is a miniature world. Here are enacted on a small scale, the same deeds which in the magnified reproduction of after life, make histories immortal. He who will drink ardent spirits here has that in him, which, if not checked, will make him the drunken father of a family. He who will play cards here, if not arrested, is likely to keep a gaming-house in after life. The student who will tell an untruth, if unrepentant, will, as a man, swear to false invoices, and commit perjury in court. Do you say there is a vast interval between these college offences and the world's enormities? I reply, there is no greater difference than there is between a youth and a man. The lower class of offences is as great for a boy or a girl as the higher is for a man or a woman. A rattlesnake is no less a rattlesnake because his rattles have not yet grown. The rattlesnake nature is in him, and in due time its deadly jaw and poison will come out.

But how can the offences of fellow-students be prevented; how can their bad habits be reformed?

I answer, in the first place, by the creation of a public sentiment in favor of order and propriety and against indecorum and misrule. There is a public sentiment in every college as much as there is in New York or Boston; in Wall Street or in State Street. To that public sentiment, students will conform, especially will all new comers conform. Once established, whether for good or evil, it will descend from class to class, that is, from generation to generation. Hence, at the opening of a college, an especial duty is imposed upon all lovers of good order to establish a public sentiment in favor of good order.

Another way to prevent wrong-doing and to arrest wrong-doers, is to remonstrate with them for their offences, and if they will persist after due warning, to expose them to some authority that can remonstrate with them in a more energetic way.

I am aware that I am here treading on what some think very delicate ground. But however delicate it may be, I mean to put my foot down with emphasis, and make you see that it is firm ground. I begin with a concession. I acknowledge, at the outset, that a mere tell-tale student, an eaves-dropper, a Paul Pry, who goes around listening at key-holes or peeping through door-cracks, to find some peccadillo that he may report, is not only dishonorable himself, but must presume upon a dishonorable government, if he supposes they would reward him, or even listen to him with any complacency. What I am about to advocate as laudable and honorable in a student is diametrically opposite to this. Suppose one student sees another drinking or card-playing, or engaging in any of that whole series of nondescript and unaccountable nonsense called college-boy pranks, — engaging in anything which, if all should engage in the same (for this is the test), would lead to disorder or mutiny, — and should first remonstrate with the offender, and if the remonstrance were unavailing, should then frankly but explicitly announce to him that if he persisted in contemning good advice, he would present him in a quarter where was kept something stronger than friendly remonstrance — who dares to say that it would then be dishonorable, if the offence were persevered in on the one side, for the information to be persevered in on the other?

No, my young friends, it is wholly a false code of honor which prevents any one, student or citizen, from preventing wrong-doing. It is false as the code of duelling at the South; false as the code of revenge among the Arabs or the North American Indians. It is wholly a false idea of sympathy which would suffer a wrong to be done without interference, but would then interfere to ward off the just consequences of the wrong. True sympathy, by timely interference, would save, at once, both wrong and consequences. It is the falsest of sympathy that would permit the offence to be committed, then screen the offender, and by such screening, encourage him and others to a repetition of the same offence, and thereby to the perpetration of more aggravated ones.

I ask you to notice this fact, and see if it does not happen with a uniformity too complete to be the effect of chance. Are not those students who are most reluctant to speak to the College Government against a fellow-student, most prompt to speak to fellow-students, and to the whole world, against the College Government or any of its members? As soon as the subject is changed from student to teacher, then this lockjaw silence ceases; the tongue-tied become voluble, and make atonement for screening guilt by arraigning innocence.

Let us take a single instance in the melancholy cases which have just happened. Ardent spirits were procured and brought into a student's room, and invitations were given to other students to come and partake of them. Suppose the first person invited, immediately on entering the room, had said in a firm but kindly way, "Do you not think this is wrong? What will be the effect upon the habits of the students, upon the reputation of the college, upon yourself, even, in after life? What would be the consequence if we should all do so? if every room should become a bar-room; and if one may, surely all may? Now destroy bottle and poison together, or I will report to the President." He adds,

"I say nothing of what has been done so far, but beware of going further."

Would not that bottle and poison have been destroyed? Would not four young men have been saved infinite mortification and sorrow? Would not relatives, the aged father and mother of one, the affectionate brothers and sisters of others, have been saved bitter tears, deep-piercing and long-enduring sorrow of heart?

But suppose the guest so invited takes the other course, — drinks, and when called upon, shuffles, evades, squirms through all the slimy depths of prevarication, adds the offence of falsehood to the offence of drinking, and after all fails to rescue the offenders from punishment. Now, according to this false code of honor, the student whose course might have saved the whole calamity, the whole immediate wrong, and the whole retinue of wrongs that must follow in its train, all present and all future pain and mortification to offender, parents and friends, — he is the one whose conduct is to be denounced as mean and despicable; who is to be held up as the object of scoffs, jeers, and contempt; but by virtue of the same code, the student who would countenance the offence, take part in it, and then sacrifice his frankness and his sincerity by holding up the base shield of prevarication and shuffling in order to screen the offence and encourage the commission of future offences, he is the honorable man, the true and brave man, to be caressed, honored, rewarded! There is only one reason why horse-thieves would not be ashamed of such a code of honor as that: — It is because they are horse-thieves.

But who, in society and in colleges, are the authors of such a code as this? for you may sometimes judge of the moral qualities of a system by knowing who were its framers and its advocates. Do good men or good students ever enact such laws? Certainly not. Good men have enacted the opposite for the protection of society, and good students, having no use, no occasion for any such laws, uniformly acknowledge the falseness of the code. Doing nothing wrong, they have nothing to conceal. Deserving no punishment, they fear none. They have the perpetual consciousness of security and peace, and that consciousness, by force of natural and moral, and not by arbitrary laws, gives joy. No! bad men and bad pupils alone have occasion for any such rules of conduct.

Were you to see a fellow creature sinking in the flood, would it be your duty to help him out or to thrust him in? Infinitely more is it your duty, when you see your fellow-being sinking into any vicious habit, or wading into the stream that conceals its depths, ay, even wetting the soles of his feet in its fatal waters, to rescue him from his peril.

Let me present a consideration to confederates, to accomplices themselves. Conspirators to do wrong can never be faithful to one another. They have no ground of mutual confidence, and can have none. When they make an agreement with each other to be false to mankind or false towards rightful authority, that very agreement contains the germ of being false to each other. Traitors to duty cannot be true to friendship. How can that be a noble code whose very basis is falsehood and prevarication? When traitors to duty yield to a temptation to betray the interests of society, they virtually give notice to each other, on the spot, that if the temptation changes they will betray one another.

Traitors to duty cannot be true to vows. Accomplices may bind themselves by vows and oaths; there is no strength in the vow, there is no strength in the oath, the dry-rot of immorality has taken all validity out of them. There is no aphorism more universally true, there is no axiom in geometry more certain, than that confederates to do wrong can never safely put trust in each other. Such obligations rest upon morality, and in regard to morality, traitors to duty are dead men.

Christ's law of love covers this subject. "Do unto others as ye would that others do unto you." In our best moments, who would not wish to be saved from sin or any of those subtle approaches to it which make sin easy? There is not one amongst you, my young friends, who would not, in his best moments, be grateful to the friend who would save him from his lowest moments, and would not acknowledge him to be his best friend, if he knew it to be done in the spirit of friendship. Each one of you would do it for his younger brother whom he tenderly loves. Then regard each one as your brother, as Christ bids you do. He died to save sinners, not by substituting his suffering for theirs, he was too wise and far-seeing for such folly as that, but by his example of fidelity to truth. He drove the money-changers from the temple. The voice of love is sometimes the voice of thunder. He could warn and he could denounce. Imitate him in this his noblest mission, to save sinners, for each one of you can save sinners as truly as Christ did, and by the same means. My children, love one another. That is all the law and the prophets.

MEDITATION.

Thou adorable and transcendent One, to whom belongs all power, from whom proceeds all blessedness, and unto whom we must render account for all the deeds done in the body; we thank Thee for our existence in this favored land. As those who have gone before us have improved it, and made it a better inheritance for us than it would otherwise have been, may we see how clearly it is our duty to expand and multiply and magnify those improvements for all who in Thy Providence shall succeed us. We thank Thee that we are not beclouded with that intellectual and moral darkness, which rests upon so vast a portion ot our fellow men in other parts of the world. May we exert ourselves to the utmost to secure to all others the social, political and religious privileges which we enjoy, and may we never forget that higher advantages bind us to the performance of higher duties; that we must give an account of our stewardship, according to the talents committed to our hands. We thank Thee for dear friends and relatives, and for all the endearments of social and domestic relations. May our friendships and sympathies be extended in an ever-enlarging circle, so that our several joys may be mutually reflected from each to each, thus increasing the number and intensity of all. We thank Thee for this day of rest. May it be a day of rest to the laborer wasted and worn by the toils of the week; may it be a day of rest to the bondman groaning under his life of servitude and unrequited toil, and a day of rest to the sinner suffering and weighed down by the heavier burden of sin. May this be a day of anxious and solemn reflection to each one of us, what we shall do to make the world wiser and better than it is, what we shall do to make ourselves wiser and better than we are, and a day also of firm, invincible, undying determination that wrong and misery shall cease where we can cause them to cease, that right and truth and the joy of right and truth shall prevail wherever we can cause them to prevail. May we begin at home, in our own hearts and lives, and reform there whatever is not in accordance with Thy Holy Law. Gently and kindly if it can be, but sternly if it must, may we reform those who are within the sphere of our influence, or under our guardianship; and if we would save the life of a fellow-being sinking into the engulfing waters, may we still more save him when perishing in the more terrible perdition of sin.

THE PRODIGAL SON.

VI.

THE PRODIGAL SON.

LUKE xv : 11 et seq.

CHRIST often taught by parables. For such a people as inhabited the East, the parable was far more impressive and instructive than plain, literal narrative. The Orientals were imaginative rather than reflective. They viewed things under concrete forms, rather than in the abstract. With them, not only the creatures of the irrational world conversed like men, but trees and plants had the power of speech. Hence they tended to poetic ideas rather than philosophic ones; and while their poetry was very grand, their natural philosophy was very contemptible. They endued everything with life and consciousness; they adorned it with gorgeous hues, and inspired it with graceful motions; but they had no power to reject a beautiful association because it did not belong to the subject, or to compass and comprehend all the relations that gave to any subject completeness. Hence their rhetoric was splendid, but their logic often mean.

Jesus availed himself of this peculiarity in the Oriental mind. He threw the technical and heartless dogmas of the Rabbis to the winds. They made the question of religion turn on rites and ceremonies; — on the kinds of pigeons they should sacrifice, on the shape of the pots and utensils they should use in their worship, and on the cut and ornaments of the garments the priests should wear. Christ went from form to substance, from the external act to the internal motive, prompting it from the outside of the body to the centre of the soul. He spoke directly to the great heart of the people, and addressed all the good common sense the priests had left in them. And often did he utter such brief, pertinent, and pungent rebukes, that the Doctors of the Jewish law came unanimously to the conclusion, that the world would be much better off if he and his pestilent heresies were out of it.

One of the most comprehensive and penetrating of all Christ's parables, is that of the Prodigal Son. No other one, to my mind, has such force, such pathos, such sweetness, such universality of application. I invite your attention to day, while I attempt to expound some portions of its wisdom and its beauty.

Let me first, however, premise a word as to the Scriptural distinction between a Parable and an Allegory. A Parable is a *supposed* history; an Allegory is a figurative description of a real history. Christ chose the Parable. This enabled him to invent his whole story. He could put in any incident or circumstance, or leave it out. Had he chosen the Allegory, and attempted to describe real facts in a figurative way, the Scribes and Pharisees might have attempted to parry his arguments by alleging that he had added something or omitted something belonging to historic truth. But the Parable was all his own, and if he gave it verisimilitude — a likeness to truth — no one had a right to complain. Not being hampered, therefore, by any historical details, Christ put into this Parable of the Prodigal Son, just as much as he chose, left out of it whatever he chose, and so adapted it to represent universal and eternal truth.

"A certain man had two sons. And the younger of them said to his father, Father, give me the portion of goods that falleth to me. And the father divided unto them his living."

What a rebuke to the Jews! Christ introduces this earthly father as representative of the Heavenly Father. The earthly father has children; so has the Heavenly Father. The earthly father has provided favors for each of his children, and he distributes those favors to them. "He divided unto them his living." On the contrary, the Jews held that though God had created many sons, that is, many nations, yet, that he loved only one of them; and that He had arranged all the events of His Providence to build up, aggrandize, and glorify that one nation, whatever became of the rest. According to their belief, God had not made the other nations for their own sake, nor even for His sake, but for the Jews' sake. Such was their bigoted and supercilious theory of Creation and Providence. They had been selected to be God's favorites, foreordained from eternity to be rulers and lawgivers upon the earth, to go where they pleased, and take what they liked, to rob adjacent nations of their lands for wealth, of their children for slaves, of their wives for concubines. Through pride they thought themselves better than other people, and that very thought made them worse. They thought God would disinherit the rest of the world, and make them his only heirs. They counted upon His perpetual favor and defence, as though such favor and defence were a part of His eternal decrees, and that very arrogance forfeited the blessings they would otherwise have received. Their downfall was the outcome of their principles. False principles will just as certainly lead a nation to ruin, as false steerage will dash a ship on the rocks. They were conquered, they were scattered, aud for eighteen hundred years they have been a scoff and a by-word among the nations of the earth. Sanguine hopes are entertained of their restoration, of a reinstatement of them in their pristine power and glory. When their principles and motives are altered, this may come to pass; that it should come to pass before is impossible. Still another great principle lies folded in the statement, "He divided unto them his living."

He assented to the young man's demand. If, as we may readily suppose, the good father foresaw the ruin which his son would bring upon himself, why did he not deny his claim, and compulsorily withhold him from temptation, by withholding the means to gratify it? He did not, and this illustrates the common order of Providence. To what purpose would God give us free agency in the general, if he were perpetually restraining us in the particular use of it? God gives us strength, health, opportunities, means. He lets us use them as we please. He gives us the talents. He suffers us to get interest from them, or to fold them in napkins. So the father, in the parable, left his son to the consequences of his own rashness and folly.

The insolent manner of the young man towards his father is not unworthy of notice. "Father, give me the portion of goods that falleth to me." It was not a petition, a request, but a command, — the language of a superior to an inferior, — not of the most gentlemanly superior either, for true gentility rarely uses the imperative mood.

"And not many days after, the younger son gathered all together, and took his journey into a far country, and there wasted his substance in riotous living."

What a spectacle! A mere lad, a boy, exiling himself from the securities and guardianship of home, for the uncertainties and perils of a "far country." Mistrusting father and mother, and elder brother and friends, but trusting to the indifference of strangers, and to his own rashness. "He gathered all together." This occupied him for some time, perhaps for days. What think you, were his manner and bearing while making preparations for departure? Self-satisfied, presumptuous, insolent! Did any one seek to deter him from the commission of so great a folly; he contemned the friendly counsel, and sneered at the counsellor. "Do not I know what I am about?" he would say; "when you see me return in a chariot and four, clad in costly apparel, you will know who is wisest." With playmates and neighbors who remonstrate at his recklessness, he banters and jeers; with his own family, who plead with him by their disconsolate looks, and with the silence of hearts too full of emotion for utterance, he sulks. But the morning of his departure comes. He bids the family a careless farewell; their eyes stream, but his are dry; and with a defiant heart he crosses the paternal threshold, and braves an inhospitable world. Can you not see him, as he wends his way along the road, stifling all natural emotions, putting on proud and swelling airs, forcing up his courage by a swaggering mien, and drawing upon that self-esteem and arrogance which he has never known to fail him? "Now I am my own man. Who has so much money in his pocket as I? Now I am beginning to live. This is life!"

Alas young man! your plan is to enjoy life by *indulging* your appetites, not by *subduing* them! you know not how soon your patrimony will be squandered! You have not learnt the immortal truth, that health lies at the bottom of all physical enjoyment, and that morality and religious affections lie at the bottom of all that is worthy to be called happiness even in this life. There he goes, his form waning and lessening in the distance; every step out of light into darkness; from home, towards perdition; he goes to shame, to dishonor, to ruin; he goes to filth and nakedness; to loneliness and desertion; to hunger, and even the intolerable gnawings of famine, and to remorse sharper than famine. On the top of that hill that bounds my vision, I see him. Now, *now*, while the form of the hapless young man is yet visible as a speck in the distant horizon, who of you will volunteer to pursue him, and woo and win him back to security, honor, peace? Alas! we cannot overtake him. He is gone!

Yes! the young man has gone! Sorrow settles down in blackest cloud over the parental home. He is no longer at the fire-side circle. His place at the table is vacant. He is remembered, but not spoken of. The mention of his name would strike the dart of pain too deep into the heart.

But where now is he, the cause of all these sorrows? The text I have quoted, tells us where he is; common sense tells us where he is; the laws of human nature tell us where he is. *He is wasting his substance with riotous living.*

As he travelled on and on, he at last reached a "far country," where the manners of the people were new and their entertainments attractive. There he stops —

not to apply himself to any honorable business, but to revel in what he calls enjoyment. Amongst addle-headed young roysterers, it is called *having a good time.* Now he dresses, he gormandizes, he plays, he drinks, he revels, he associates with immoral men and with impure women. I need not describe the course of his rapid downfall. The forms of ruin are different in different nations and ages; but the substance is always the same. It is the undue gratification of those appetites and passions which God gave us for servants, not for masters. It is suffering them to govern us, instead of our governing them. It is eating, drinking, gaming, revelling, late nights, foul companions. In great cities, these temptations put on all forms that can attract the senses, arouse the imagination, whet the appetite, debauch the conscience. The "gaming hells" are fitted up like palaces, with every adornment and luxury. Drinking saloons charm you with the choicest music and paintings, and flowers festoon the steps that lead to the chambers of death. But all this gorgeousness and splendor are unnecessary. The means of perdition may be found in the vile drunkeries and subterranean gaming holes of the meanest village. Nay, a student in a college may make a trap-door out of his own sleeping-room into hell. The worm that dieth not, and the fire that is not quenched, are in our own hearts; and whether we go into palaces or dungeons, they go with us. There is no grosser fallacy or folly, than to suppose we could have resisted the temptation under which *another* man fell, when we do not resist our *own* temptations.

Contrast the conduct of this young rake, not with a fabulous character, but with a real one; — with that of the American boy, Benjamin Franklin. When, at seventeen years of age, he removed from Boston to Philadelphia, did he put up at the most costly hotel, equip himself at the most fashionable tailor's, and then strut up the street with a filthy cigar in his mouth? No, he was hungry, and he bought a roll of bread, and, while eating it, started off on the errand on which he was bent. He began life at zero, and rose from that point, to the lofty height, where he will be visible, conspicuous, refulgent, to all nations, and all times. There is somewhere in Philadelphia, an instructive series of four paintings illustrative of his ascending course. In the first picture, he appears as the Boston tallow-chandler's son, — a mere boy, working in his father's shop, his shirt-sleeves rolled up to his elbows, and his hands and arms buried in the grease. In the next, he is drawing down lightnings from the heaven, and making his own name as radiant as the lightning he commanded. In the third, he is signing the Declaration of American Independence. In the fourth, he is standing among the kings and mighty men of Europe, concluding that treaty of peace which recognized the freedom and independence of the United States of America, and fulfilling that saying of the Hebrew sage: "Seest thou a man diligent in business? he shall stand before kings; he shall not stand before mean men."

Young man! young woman! whom, of the two, do you most resemble? the youthful prodigal, or the youthful sage? Ask yourselves, whether on the one hand, you obey your appetites and passions, or on the other, your reason and conscience, and you have your answer. The story of the young wanderer's descent to ruin is quickly told. After a few days or weeks' dissipation, his bottles and his pockets are empty, his clothes are soiled or tattered, his credit is run out, his witticisms and obscenities have become stale, his fair-weather friends have deserted him, and he finds himself houseless, homeless, penniless, friendless, naked and hungry, in a strange land; his means are wasted away, just in proportion to his enjoyments, which were not the needed recreations from honorable toil, and elevated and exhausting studies, but the revels of a debauchee. Virtuous resources never fail, vicious ones perish. He flashed and exploded; he swelled and collapsed. What shall he now do? He is naked, hungry, athirst, and without a friend; for those who would have been his friends have seen his pride and folly, and now rather rejoice than mourn over his shame. Perhaps he tries begging, but there is now "a famine in the land," and the benevolent have enough to do in providing for their own families and helping the meritorious poor, whom, perhaps, just such sons or brothers have impoverished. All expedients fail, and, at last, the pangs of hunger and cold force him to hire himself out to a citizen of that country, who sends him into his fields to feed swine.

Feeding swine in the East, was the most despised of all vocations. It was so considered not only among the Jews, but, as we learn from Herodotus, among the Egyptians also. The Roman poet, Martial, confirms this. It was very different from tending sheep. Jacob and Moses and David tended sheep. That was an honorable occupation, and a man's distinction was often estimated by the numbers of his flocks. But the Orientals had a proverb: "Cursed is he who feeds swine." It was held in very different estimation from what it is in Kentucky and Ohio. It was the meanest of all employments; and this young man, lately so gay and flush of money, with his head bridled back in pride before men, and before the women whom his flatteries had insulted — fed swine!

"And he would fain have filled himself with the husks which the swine did eat." Botanically, these "husks" were the fruit of the Ceratonia or carob tree, common in the East, and still eaten by swine, and by the poorer sort of people. It was not the husk (or glume) of our Indian corn, as some have supposed. Indeed, that plant was not known in the East at that time.

How long this errant youth bore his lot of shame and humiliation; how long he envied even the swine he fed; how long he wrestled with pride, and braved the pangs of remorse, no intimations are given. But at last the crisis came. His proud and rebellious heart surrendered, or in the language of the narrative, so full of pathos and sublimity, "He came to himself." My young friends, in all the books I have ever read, sacred or profane, poetry or prose; in all the startling energies of genius, or the inspirations of the tragic muse, I have never seen any combination of words so potent, so touching, as these; "He came to himself." What a glorious deed do these glorious words declare!

The writer of the same gospel tells us of a man who called his name "Legion," who, after the exorcism of his evil spirit, was found "sitting and in his right mind." But he was a maniac, not a criminal. He had a distempered intellect only, not a distempered heart. It was an occasion of rejoicing when he recovered possession of his reason; but an infinitely greater occasion for joy when the Prodigal recovered possession of his conscience. Of the maniac, it is said that he had his dwelling, not in any house, but among the tombs; that no man could bind him with fetters or with chains, for he plucked asunder the chains and broke the fetters in pieces; in fine, that he was untamable, roaming by night and by day among the mountains and tombs, crying and cutting himself with stones. But the Prodigal Son had a fiercer and more terrible madness upon him than this. His lunacy was worse than that of an unsound mind; it was a profligate heart. He had been bound by the silken cords of a father's love, and he plucked *them* asunder and cast them away; the social endearments, the moral securities of home, should have been fetters to prevent him from wandering, but he broke them in pieces and fled to moral exile. He hied himself to drearier spots than lone mountains or tombs whose air is suffocated with the skeletons of the dead; for he sought foul and wicked companions *who were alive;* and instead of barren mountains, he dwelt in those jungles of society where all the vices grew and grew luxuriantly. He, too, was untamable, until length and intensity of suffering overcame him, and brought him round his aphelion curve.

Out of the agony of his soul the outcast exclaimed, "I will arise and go to my father, and will say unto him, Father, I have sinned against heaven and before thee, and am no more worthy to be called thy son; make me as one of thy hired servants."

The remainder of the story is short. "And he arose and came to his father." Neglect not, I beseech you, the all-important implication contained in these words — "He *came* to his father." It was as far back as it was out. He was not carried home in a balloon, or wafted thither on the soft bosom of a cloud, or borne there by any other agency, miraculous or non-miraculous. He had to travel it. He had to travel it barefoot, in all his rags and squalor; reeking with the odor of his late companions, the swine; which odor, pungent as it was, was not strong enough to sheathe the viler fetor of his late dissolute companions. I repeat; neglect not the implication contained in the words, "He CAME TO his father." So much as a man consents to descend, he has to struggle to ascend. The elevation must be equal to the degradation, — else how can he ever reach even the point where he began to fall? Conversion, or reformation, means that all the bad old habits are overcome; — that the intemperate has become temperate; the fraudulent man honest; the selfish man benevolent. The further any one departs from duty, therefore, so much the further he has to travel back, — mile for mile, league for league, — before he is reformed or converted.

But there are two points in this Parable whose importance stands forth in bold relief, pre-eminent and bright-shining; — like a mountain towering from a plain, like the sun blazing in the sky.

As I said before, Christ selected the form of the Parable instead of the Allegory, because it allowed him to put in any circumstance, or to leave out any circumstance, without reference to historical exactness. He framed the Parable just as he pleased, — to suit his case, — unembarrassed by extraneous facts. These two main points are, the fall and the recovery of the Prodigal. And how has he stated these points, upon which the whole power and pathos of the Parable turns?

"And the younger of them said to his father, Father, give me the portion of goods that falleth to me." Can language make anything more positive and explicit than this. "*He said to his father, Father, give me.*" *He* did this. No one else did it for him. It is not even hinted that the devil tempted him to do it. We all of us have devils enough in our own hearts to make the office of any other devil a sinecure. The Prodigal could offer no such lying apology as that he was seduced by an evil spirit. He was not overborne by persuasion, by intimidation, or by force. He was conscious of the truth of what James so emphatically says: "Let no man say when he is tempted, I am tempted of God, for God cannot be tempted with evil, neither tempteth He any man. But every man is tempted when he is drawn away of his own lust and enticed." It was the Prodigal himself, who abandoned his father, who committed self-exile from his parental home, and who spent his substance in wicked indulgences and with infamous associates. It was by yielding when he should have resisted; it was by giving the rein to his own inordinate propensities that he did this thing, and he would have done the same had there been no devil in the universe. And as *he* committed the sin, so must *he* bear the remorse; for it is impossible for any but the sinner to feel remorse for his sin. How does this Parable smite with a force strong enough to destroy ten thousand lives, that ethical and religious monstrosity, vicarious punishment!

The other bold and radiant point of this Parable is stated in the same precise and unmistakable language. It was the Prodigal Son himself who sinned, and it was he who turned from his sin. *He* said, "*I* will arise and go to my father, and will say unto him, Father, I have sinned against heaven and before thee." In that lone pasture; in that forlorn and desolate condition; with swine for his only companions; agonized with remorse; the black cloud of the future shutting down upon him and leaving no spot of light from horizon to zenith, *he* came to himself. Prostrate upon the earth, groaning, sobbing, he put forth the glorious and sovereign resolve that brought him erect upon his feet, and with invincible force and tenfold emphasis, he exclaimed, *I will go to my father.* According to the narrative, he fell without a tempter. According to the same narrative, without friend, adviser, or counsellor, *he came to himself.* He repented. He recovered. He went home. He did it all. There was no machinery of dreams or ghosts, of gods or demi-gods. There was no un-Holy Ghost that made him sin; there was no Holy Ghost that made him repent. As his was all the remorse of the sinning, so all the joy of the reformation was his.

What a glorious sun of hope arises from these facts for every erring, wandering child of earth. If the Prodigal Son could repent and reform, — and Christ says he did repent and reform, then we too, all of us, when we have strayed from the path of duty, can return to that path. In this Parable, one of the most difficult of cases was presented, and yet virtue triumphed. It assures us, therefore, that however far we have wandered, we may go back; however low we may have sunk, we may ascend; however black we may have stained ourselves with guilt, we may purify ourselves into the whiteness of innocence.

See, too, what rewards follow repenting and returning.

See how the narrative is all aglow with proofs of parental love. "When he was yet a great way off, his father saw him, and had compassion, and ran (observe the haste) and fell on his neck and kissed him." What eagerness to welcome! What tokens of endearment! The son began to make his confession and his promises. But the father broke him short off in the midst. Knowing his sincerity, he did not wish to hear his wailings. He did not wait for him to say, "Make me as one of thy hired servants." And what did the father do for this reformed boy? He came home in rags. The father adorned him, not merely with a coat, but with a robe, — the garment of princes, — the best robe that the house afforded. He put a ring upon his finger. Only opulent men wore rings. He came barefoot. The father ordered shoes for his feet. He not only "fed," but "feasted" him.

So it is with every one who abandons vice and returns to duty. For rags, he gets comely garments; for husks, he gets healthful nourishment; for the companionship of swine, he is introduced to the society of sages and saints. Sin is a mean idol, and her votaries must fare meanly; but Virtue is an adorable and puissant goddess, and the only limit to her giving is our capacity of receiving.

My young friends, let me ask you a few questions. Do you not believe that God is the Creator and Father of this universe? Do you not believe that he so framed every one of its laws, that obedience to them will yield happiness, and disobedience, misery? Choose ye, then, to-day, whether you will live in obedience to those laws, or in defiance of them. If you would avoid the shame and pain of the Prodigal Son, follow not his example.

Remain in your father's house; that is, remain in the ways of duty. If, unhappily, you have deserted your father's house, and wandered to a far country, and are feeding any portion of the swine that sin forces its votaries to feed, and are living upon those husks with which sin spreads the table of her followers; now, this moment, before you leave these seats, put forth an energetic and sovereign resolve, and say, "I will arise and go to my Father."

MEDITATION.

Our Father who art in Heaven, we thank Thee for the blessings which surround us wherever we are. We know that Thou hast given us power to enjoy these blessings; we know that Thou hast given us power to abuse them; and we would look to Thy law for guidance, so that we may know how to use — as not abusing them. We would look to Thy law to know how to use the elements, and the mighty forces of nature, which Thou hast stationed like sentinels in every part of the earth, ready to do our bidding. The winds that sweep over the sea, we may employ to bear the implements of death and destruction around the globe, to ravage and destroy, to rob property, or to steal men; or we may employ them to waft civilization, knowledge, science, and the Gospel of Jesus Christ to the darkest heathen lands. May we employ these agencies as means wherewith to do good, and not to work evil to our fellowmen. The stone in the quarry, the clay in the pit, the iron in the mine, the wood in the forests, we can convert into prisons and dungeons, into the gibbet and the gallows tree, and the flaming fagot, wherewith to persecute, and torture, and exterminate our fellow-beings, who do not think as we think, or believe as we believe; or we can use them to build edifices for science, or altars and temples for Thy worship. Oh, may we use all these inanimate forces and substances of nature for Thy honor, and for the welfare and happiness of our fellow-men. The very organs of our bodies may be used like those of a brute, or like those proper to a man; as they would be used by a fiend, or as they would be used by an angel. Our feet can make haste to shed innocent blood, or they may run swiftly and sweeten the earth as they go, to carry succor to the distressed, to reclaim the wandering, to guide the ignorant. Our hands may wound, or they may heal. Our lips may overflow with the honey of wisdom, of truth, of consolation; or with the poison of slander, of falsehood, and of cruelty. Oh, may we never suffer these organs to be enlisted in the service of sin; may we keep them as bright and holy armor wherewith to fight the battles of truth and righteousness, wherewith to beat back ignorance, to subdue error, to extinguish superstition, and to make men more and more like the Divine Teacher, Jesus Christ. Thou hast given us mental adaptations to this world in which we are placed,— appetite for food and for drink, that we may meet the wants of the body, and be invigorated for the duties of life; a desire for the goodwill of our fellow-men, that the path of life may be strewn with the flowers of their approval, and not with the thorns of their dislike; Thou hast given us a sense of self-respect, of self-worthiness, which, if not forfeited by misconduct of our own, tends to uphold us under trials. Oh, our Father, may these and other propensities never rise to overmastering excess. May we control them by the higher law of justice, of equity, of conscience, of benevolence, of veneration of Thee, and admiration of the character of Thy Son Jesus Christ, who was in all points tempted as we are, yet was without sin. * * *

THE PRODIGAL SON.

(CONTINUED.)

VII.

THE PRODIGAL SON.

In this morning's Discourse, we considered the Parable of the Prodigal Son, — a Parable so beautiful in its conception, so pathetic in the tragic mournfulness of its beginning, so inspiring to every repentant man in the moral triumph and jubilee of its close! Of all the Parables spoken by the Saviour, this seems the most impressive, the most touching to the universal heart of mankind; and could such an account be taken, I presume it would be found that more persons remember this Parable than any other part of the New Testament.

All the Parables of Christ are full of knowledge and wisdom, but this is full of genius. Had the idea of it been elaborated by Shakspeare, he would have expanded it into a drama of five acts; if by Milton, he would have spread it over an epic poem of twelve books; while in the simple conception of Christ, both story and moral are contained in about twenty verses.

The two grand points which are brought out by the Parable, are, 1st, the exceeding liability of men to fall from virtue; and, 2d, their power of returning to it. The great object of the Saviour in devising and announcing it, seems to have been to impress mankind with a sense of their awful exposure to sin, their power of ceasing to sin whenever they will, and the rewards for repentance and reformation. Christ says, as explicitly and emphatically as he can say it, that it was the young man who sinned, — he himself, and not any one else for him; — and he affirms, just as explicitly and emphatically, that it was the young man, — he himself, and not any one else for him, — who repented and returned to his father. Indeed, if he himself did not sin, why was he punished with all that mournful and shameful series of experiences? and if he himself did not recover himself, why was he rewarded with all parental endearments, — with the robe, and the ring, and the shoes, and the feast? On the supposition that he himself did not both fall and rise, the swine themselves might, with as much moral propriety as he, have been first starved, and then feasted.

This parable is especially addressed to young persons. Youth are exposed to peculiar dangers. With them, hope strews all the pit-falls in their pathway with flowers, and throws a rain-bow of promise, not only over the past, but over the coming storm. The young lack experience also, and they are too prone to disregard the instructions of those who have gone before them. How can a traveller know the dangers of a road he has never travelled, or a navigator the perils of a sea whose reefs have never been laid down in a chart, nor whose shallows have ever been sounded? If traveller and navigator will contemn the admonitions of wisdom and experience, what other fate can they expect but wreck and ruin?

All innocent youth, therefore, should heed this parable in order to escape the experiences of the Prodigal Son, and all guilty youth should take it to heart, that, like him, they may put forth the supreme and invincible resolve: "I will arise, and go to my father."

Striking as this parable is, and generally as it has impressed itself upon the minds of men, I fear its full significance is not ordinarily comprehended. Is it not a fact that it is generally understood as applying to spendthrift vices; to the squandering of patrimonies or estates by reckless young heirs; to rakes and profligates in their hideous varieties, and to these only? Any such view bereaves the parable of much of its significance and power. Not only houses, and lands, and moneys, are gifts of God which can be squandered and lavished upon appetite and passion, but all the rest of God's blessings can be dissipated and lost in the same way, — health, strength, length of days, ability to acquire knowledge, honor, renown, capacities of doing good to our fellow-men, the calm and peaceful joy of loving to contemplate the character and perfections of God. All these are to be numbered among the "goods" that God divides between his children, and any one who squanders or dissipates any of these, is, *so far*, a Prodigal Son.

Hence, it is not at all necessary that a young man, or a young woman, should spend their father's money at the saloon for drink, or at the fancy stores for superfluous dress, or at the jeweller's for excessive ornament, in order to be a Prodigal Son, or a Prodigal Daughter. Whether sons or daughters, they may be as great prodigals of health, strength, and longevity; of talent, genius, and the power to acquire knowledge; of purity, benevolence, and religion, — I say they may be as great prodigals of all these, as they could be of bank notes or of California gold.

Look at a healthy, well-organized child; what a magazine of capabilities he is! What incalculable forces are folded up in him! His steps are short, but he can yet go round the world. The toys he plays with are light, but in him is the power of rending mountains asunder for his pathway. He is not amphibious, yet he can swim all the oceans. His outstretched arm does not reach far, but he can seize the lightning the moment it leaps from the cloud, and bring it harmless to his feet. His vision is less sharp than the eagle's, but he can see stars whose light has been myriads of years in coming to our earth. Now, to be a prodigal and spendthrift of all these powers, is as easy as for water to run down hill. Drink whiskey, shatter the nerves by opium or coffee, or that vilest, foulest, unhealthiest of all weeds, — tobacco; seal yourselves up hermetically in a coffin or in a room, — it matters not which, — from the fresh air; at the command of fashion, wear those thin shoes and dresses, for which Consumption might have taken out a patent; commit all, or any considerable part of these enormities, and the most vigorous and promising young man or woman, can, in the course of a few short years, spend the substance of all his glorious powers of body, mind, and heart, and exhibit another instance of a Prodigal child. Nay, by some single act of indulgence, — by gluttony, by lacerating the stomach with fierce condiments, or with excessive quantities of even healthful food, any one can extemporize cholera or colic, and extinguish himself in twenty-four hours, — with all the appropriate and becoming agonies of a violent death. Is he not a Prodigal Son, is she not a Prodigal Daughter, who is guilty of these things, or of such things? If any of us find ourselves to have been guilty of any of these offences, let us say, to-day, "I will arise, and go to my father," that is, I will hereafter obey God's laws.

Take the intemperate man; he is the slave of an appetite. The seat of that appetite is a little spot in the inside of his mouth not two inches square. Yet for the gratification of that little spot, all out of sight as it is, see what he sacrifices. He has glorious faculties, — imagination, genius, wit. He can understand art, science, literature, — can, perhaps, make discoveries and originate inventions. He has a moral nature by which he can ascend to the upper realms of emotion, of sentiment, of ecstatic joy. He has friends, kindred, family. He can deserve and win the friendship, esteem, love of mankind. All these he sacrifices, — all the sources of bliss within and bliss without, — for the sake of a few titillations on a spot, — not two inches square, — inside his mouth. Nay, he sacrifices all the natural and legitimate pleasures of that spot itself. Once all the productions of the earth, — the sweets of the vegetable kingdom from the temperate, or from the tropical zone; the rich flavors of all that the huntsman seeks in the forest, or the fisherman draws from the waters, were a zest and a joy to his palate. These delicacies, these luxuries, are all squandered. He has but one taste left, and that is a burning desire for burning alcohol. The problem which the drunkard is trying to solve, may be thus stated; he drank hell-fire, and it burned him. He drank more to put out the first fire, and it burned him worse. At first, it burnt mouth, throat, and stomach only. To stop that flame, he drank more, which burned liver, heart and brain; and now blood, eyes, nose and face, are all on fire. What he has done to extinguish the flame, has made it rage more fiercely. What he did to quench it topically, in one spot, has caused a general combustion. And now, the drunkard's problem I say, is this: How long must he pour hell-fire into hell-fire, to put it out? The only solver of this problem is Death. Is not the intemperate man, then, a Prodigal Son, — prodigal of peace, health, happiness, renown; of the love of man, and the love of God? Oh, young man, the first draught of intoxicating beverage you take, *because you like it*, is the first step *from* your father's house.

The Parable says of the young man, "And when he had spent all, there arose a mighty famine in that land." *And when he had spent all.* That he would spend his all, is spoken of here as a matter of course; it is rather assumed than asserted. And it *is* a matter of course. Every prodigal, at some time, will have spent his all. No matter in what his prodigality may consist; no matter how vast his possessions of any kind may be, — that prodigality will find the end of that wealth. He may be rich as Crœsus, but not a dollar of that wealth will remain. He may be strong as Samson, but that strength will be wasted. He may have the endurance and perseverance of Julius Cæsar, and yet die ignobly as Cæsar did. He may have the cunning and craft of Benedict Arnold, or any other traitor to his country; but his name shall become the synonyme of folly. The prodigal spends all; and then it always happens that of that particular good of which he was a spendthrift, and became a pauper, there arises a mighty famine in the land, so that the sorest want of his appetites falls on the hardest of times.

I might follow out this analogical reasoning in regard to the miser, the libertine, or the political demagogue, who would sacrifice the fame of a nation, or the happiness of a race, for office. But this must suffice.

The Parable, literally understood, refers to a young man; and I fear that those who read it, after having passed the period of youth, think it has no relation to themselves. But in its legitimate scope and spirit, it applies to the man or woman of sixty not less than to the youth of sixteen. Middle life and age have their blessings, their prerogatives, their goods, not less than childhood, and adolescence. Whenever, therefore, we acquire a new power, by which we can encourage good, or prevent evil; whenever we are placed in a new position, where our influence and our example can promote the right, or repress the wrong, — in every such case God has divided amongst us another portion of His goods, and we can use them for His glory, or His dishonor; for our own welfare, or our own ruin; we can use them as His obedient, or as His prodigal children.

Perhaps there is no one of us, who is not, in some respect, in some one thing, a prodigal. We spend some possession, power, faculty, attainment, or opportunity, less usefully than we might have done. Suppose, then, we have been tempted, and have yielded, and have thus gone, to a greater or less distance, into the "far country" of disobedience to God's laws. Suppose this, and the all-important practical question arises, *how long shall we remain there?* Shall we make our resolve, and start back on the homeward-bound journey to-day, now; or shall we wait till next month, or next year, with all the chances that such waiting may prove to be *forever!* However long we may wander in a devious course, we are always sure of one thing: the longer we wander, the farther we go astray, — the farther we have to travel back before reaching our father's house. Whatever vice we cherish, whatever wickedness we practice, we are on the prodigal's down-hill course towards privation, destitution, and ruin. Whatever vice we indulge, whatever wickedness we practice, then, in regard to that vice or that wickedness, first comes poverty (literally or figuratively), then rags, then hunger, then beggary, then the feeding of swine, with their husks for our food, and their company for our recreation. Such is the course, and such the end of every Prodigal Son or Daughter, no matter in what respect they may have been prodigal. All wrong-doing ends in misery, and it comes inevitably to this at last; husks for breakfast, husks for dinner, husks for supper; swine for our companions in the morning, swine at noon, swine at night.

I do not say that every prodigal child is in this condition *at the present time*. Some may have just left their father's house; some may have just reached the "far country," and may be now wasting their substance there in feasting, drinking, and revelling; but what I mean to say is, that every vicious course, not repented of, or abandoned, ends in the most painful of privations, and the most shameful and meanest of conditions.

Do you smile incredulous at this abhorrent and disgusting termination of the career of a Prodigal Son, or a Prodigal Daughter — in whatever respect they may play the prodigal? If so, that incredulous smile is the summit and sum of all folly. Do you think that God, with His infinite ingenuity, and His infinite power, made this universe such a miserable botch, such an ill-contrived and misgoing machine, that it will reward guilt, and punish innocence, so that any prodigal who abandons his father's house and home, can come to anything at last better than the companionship and husks of swine? Woe to him who yields to such delusion! But peace, and joy, and everlasting exultation to him who has never wandered from his father's house; to him, also, who, though he has wandered, hastens back to receive his father's benediction and bounties.

My young friends, will you hearken to a parting thought? The ship is governed by the helm. If the ship is steering for the rocks, and the helmsman will not change her course, all must be lost! But if the helmsman knows and does his duty, he avoids ledge and shallow, and reaches his destined port in security and joy.

Now, my young friends, our thoughts, our intents, our desires, are the helm of our life. If our thoughts, our intents, our desires, are wrong, and remain unchanged, our wreck is inevitable; a wreck complete and overwhelming of our worldly interests, and our immortal hopes. Towards what point of the moral compass are our thoughts, intents, desires, now steering the vessel of our lives?—*from* or *upon* the rocks?—FROM OR UPON THE ROCKS? Be entreated before you leave this house, so to adjust the helm of life, that it will conduct you to the haven of everlasting peace.

MEDITATION.

Our Father who art in Heaven, hallowed be Thy name. On this day of rest from the toils of the body, and those cares and anxieties of the mind with which our pilgrimage here upon earth is encumbered, we would go to that source of strength, without which life is weakness; we would go to that fountain of light, without which this world is darkness; and to that Author of all goodness, without whom the universe would be a waste and desolation. Our Father, we thank Thee for our existence, and that that existence has not been made necessarily wretched and miserable; that with life thou hast bestowed upon us the means of abundant enjoyment. May we possess the power to use these means diligently and wisely. Thou hast given us bodies, constructed throughout with wonderful skill and aptitude, endowed with senses by which we can become acquainted with objects near and remote, with the minuteness, with the vastness, and with the splendors of Thy works. But may we remember that these bodies are but for temporary use; that they have grown, and that they will decay; that dust they are, and to dust they shall return. May we preserve them in health by avoiding indolence and torpidity on the one hand, and all undue labor, and exposure, and indulgence, on the other; may we secure the long life for which they are adapted, by duly strengthening and never unduly exhausting their powers; and may we keep them a fit temple for Thy

Spirit, by rejecting and putting far away every noxious, and offensive, and impure thing. May we remember that these bodies are soon to sleep in the grave, and may we therefore hold them subordinate to the lofty and exalted powers of the mind. Our Father, may we wisely discriminate between these powers of the mind Thou hast bestowed, some of them for the acquisition of knowledge — a knowledge of nature and of Thyself some for the enjoyment of society, some for personal pleasure, and many for the good of others. May we think more of that knowledge which is eternal, than of those enjoyments which are temporary, and may we enlarge and exalt these intellectual powers, by thinking of the life which is to come, as well as the life that now is; by thinking of the millions of our fellow-mortals more than of ourselves, and always subjecting all our endeavors to the Supreme and Perfect Law. But those nobler and sublimer capacities which belong to the soul, which never can decay, which must live near to Thy presence, in light, or far from it, in darkness; which must enjoy Thee and all pure and holy spirits forever, or feel the intolerable burden and discord of a nature at war with truth, and duty, and goodness, blind amid the splendors of holiness which none but those whose eyes are pure can see, and dumb amid the exulting hallelujahs, which none save those who love Thee can utter — may we improve this day to elevate, and adorn, and exalt.

* * * * *

TEMPTATION.

VIII.

TEMPTATION.

MATTHEW VI., part of 13th v. — " And lead us not into temptation, but deliver us from evil."

" LEAD us not into temptation," — the wisest prayer ever made, for it is full both of religion and philosophy.

" Temptation " signifies allurement or enticement to evil. Good men are tempted to become bad ; bad men are tempted to become worse.

The word " temptation " is never properly used in a good sense. It implies an evil agency. It implies susceptibility to evil. If a temptation prevails, it implies descent, degradation, abasement ; it implies loss, fall, ruin, perdition. Hence, one who is totally bad, who cannot be worse than he is, cannot be tempted. He has already touched bottom, reached his nethermost. There is no more room for him to fall or grow down wards. " Christ," says the Apostle, " was tempted in all points, like as we are." Men are tempted. Hence, if men could not be worse than they are, or less good than they are, all the common forms of language on this subject would be an absurdity. The devil is said to tempt men. St. James says, God does *not* tempt them. Hence, temptation supplies a susceptibility in men, to evil, or an evil agency, operating within them, or upon them, and tending or striving to make them bad, or at least, less good than they now are.

On this occasion, I wish as far as I am able, to develop the philosophy of temptation. All moral and religious subjects have a philosophical as well as a spiritual side. No philosophical mind will ever be satisfied with any view or treatment of a moral or religious subject, which does not satisfy his reason as well as his conscience. None ever ought to be. God has reason, intelligence, in an infinite degree; He has infinite holiness also. All His works were created, and His providence governs them under the supervision of both these attributes. His holy affections could have prompted nothing which His intelligence did not ratify, and His intelligence could have devised or superintended nothing whose results were not in harmony with His love. Hence, everything in His creation and in His providence, must have the sanction, approval, benediction, of both His reason and His affections. Our race was created in His image. If we view things as He views them, it is proof positive that we are right. If our view conflicts with His view, it is proof positive that we are wrong. His works and His providence, therefore, must present themselves to us in such an aspect, that our reason and our conscience, as far as we are capable of understanding them, will pronounce them right, — that is, conformable to truth; and good, — that is, conformable to love. If we do not see them in this double light, as commended to both reason and conscience; if our views do not coincide, but conflict with God's views, the presumption is infinitely strong against us.

Temptation is a fearful word. It indicates the beginning of a possible series of infinite evils. It is the ringing of an alarm-bell, whose melancholy sounds may reverberate through eternity. Like the sudden, sharp cry of "Fire" under our windows by night, it should rouse us to instantaneous action, and brace every muscle to its highest tension. Nay, it is like the cry of "Fire" at sea, rather than by land, where, if we suffer the flames to spread, our only alternative is death by the fire, or death by the water. To escape death, we must leap into the jaws of death. What blindness, then, what fool-hardiness, what insanity, voluntarily to expose yourselves to a seductive, incomputable peril, to defy certain temptation, and trust to chance for escape, to walk unshod over burning ploughshares, without antidote or remedy, to play with fireworks over a magazine of gunpowder, in a madman's hope that when your folly meets the Laws of Nature, on God's highway, they will turn aside, and make obeisance, as you pass by.

Temptation is a word of horrid import. It is obvious that the word would lose all its force and be dropped out of the language, if evil never resulted from it. But while temptations exist; while the word retains its significancy, nothing is more fatally sure than that there will be a certain per-centage of falls, of victims. We cannot tell with certainty, where, or on whom the thunderbolt will strike; but yet we do know that about so many will strike every year, blasting and consuming whatever or whoever stands in their way.

That is a wonderful law, and yet as certain as it is wonderful, which is most uncertain if predicated of the individual, but becomes most certain when predicated of masses or communities. The French statistician will tell you within a few units how many men will commit suicide in Paris, next year, and in what proportions these suicides will be distributed among the months of the year; but he cannot select or designate the individuals who will do it. So the British statistician will foretell, almost with the precision with which an astronomer predicts an eclipse, how many murders, robberies, and burglaries will be committed in England next year, though he cannot designate either perpetrator or victim. While there is a felonious element in society, somewhere, at sometime, that element will work itself out into felonious deeds; and somebody, in his property, his character or his life, will feel it. Until mankind, then, are lifted out of the sphere of temptation, that is, while temptations continue and exist, there will be a certain per-centage of acquiescences,* falls, and perditions.

Temptation, then, I say, as it necessarily imports a certain number or proportion of yieldings, falls, perditions, is a word of horrid import. As I hold it up and gaze on it, it is transformed into a ghastly and terrible spectre. Lurid fires shoot from its eyes. Demoniac words burst from its lips, in volleys swift and fearful as cannonading. Every muscle writhes in agony. Its feet have waded through gore. And what a retinue of sorrows and agonies, — of sounds that affright the ear, and of spectacles that blast the eye, — stretch behind it, beyond where the eye, beyond where the imagination can reach.

But by what means does this gigantic enemy of man get interior possession of his victim? Under what disguises does a monster so frightful in the end, beguile

* Hence, that saying of John P. Hale, — as philosophical as it was witty, — that of all essences the devil likes acquiescence best.

us so easily in the beginning? Under what contractions of size does he insinuate himself at first, to grow into such hugeness afterwards, by nutriment, too, sucked from ourselves. It is, my young friends, by processes as obvious as those by which the acorns, of which I can hold twenty in one hand, become oaks, each one of which could crush all of us by its fall.

We have senses, every one of which has its corresponding objects in the natural world, and of these objects we may take too much or too little; we have natural desires for food, for drink, for wealth, for self-display, for pride, for power, each one of which we may indulge to excess. Our moral, mental, and bodily endowments, have an order of precedence, of authority, of rank; we may reverse that order; we may enthrone the subject appetite above the sovereign conscience. On that which should have but a tithe or a hundredth part of our care, we may squander the whole. Hence it is easy to see that every one of our various appetites, propensities, and passions, is an avenue through which temptation may enter. We are a citadel filled with the richest of all God's treasures, but having gates which open towards every point of the compass, through which the beleaguering hordes of temptation may enter and subdue us.

Men will never rescue themselves, nor be rescued from temptation, until its nature and workings are better understood, any more than a physician will cure his patients, while ignorant of both disease and remedy.

Let us try, then, to understand what temptation is, and how it overcomes us.

In all discussions on this subject, perpetual reference is made to the heart. It is averred by the great majority in Christendom, that the natural heart of man is always wrong, wicked, depraved, totally depraved. Some, however, taking the opposite extreme, maintain, or at least assert, that the heart of man is naturally right, but that ignorance, evil example, custom, training, pervert it, debauch it, satanize it. There is an old Latin and legal maxim, which says, "*Error versatur in generalibus.*" Error lurks under generalities of expression. If we look at all the crimes which have made earth an Aceldama for the innocent and virtuous, and scattered Golgothas of youth and beauty over its surface; if we listen to those groans and shrieks that make it re-echo with lamentation, and mourning, and woe, — so fearfully loud and strong, that they must continue to reverberate through the galleries of time for ages to come; and if we say that all these are but the out-birth and out-growth of the natural heart of man, then the phrase "total depravity" becomes stupidly inadequate, and we want some word expressive of a hundred-Satan power, — some fulminating word, which, when sent into the human brain, will explode there, in the presence of all the faculties, and make each one of them understand it with all its might.

But if, on the other hand, you contemplate the Divine sentiments, and the God-like deeds which have emanated even from heathen, — from persons on whom no ray of the Divine light of the Gospel ever fell, — the piety of Socrates, the fidelity of Regulus, the continence of Scipio, the sublime devotion of idolaters who sacrifice, not Jewish beasts, nor even their own Pagan children, but themselves, to their gods, — if you contemplate their loyalty to their best ideas of truth, their fidelity to their best knowledge, poor as that knowledge was, — for we must remember that being true to imperfect knowledge demonstrates higher merit than being true to more perfect knowledge — the merit being in the inverse ratio of the knowledge, and, if we say that these heathen aspirations and elevations of soul came from a natural, that is, a totally depraved heart, then we are sorely tempted to wish that we might honestly exchange some hearts amongst us, self-boastful of their second birth, for some of the natural ones of the heathen, and that the stream of missionaries might sometimes flow the other way.

To see how easy it is to fall into error in using so general and indefinite a term as the heart, reflect upon an analogous case. Suppose, in contemplating some act of moral heroism, some Christ-like self-sacrifice, I should exclaim, "Man is the noblest work of God," the idea would be applauded to the echo. But suppose, on the other hand, after the narration of some deed of ineffable meanness, I should cry out, "Man is the meanest creature on the footstool;" the same company would say "Amen." So, under different circumstances, I might say, without being criticised, "Man is wise;" or, "he is a fool;" or, "he is *sophos-moros*," that is, half and half. Standing before the builder of the Leviathan steamship, or the foreteller of eclipses, or the founder of a State, who would contradict me, should I declare man is great? Seeing the Egyptians worship an ape, who would contradict me should I say, man is little? So you see that I may affirm man to be God-like, or Satan-like, noble or mean, great, or contemptible, a Titan, or a worm, and the people will shout *Amen*. And this is equally true when we combine the grandest and the meanest attributes, and assert them as the predicate of our subject, as when Ralph Waldo Emerson called Napoleon the First, a Scamp-Jupiter. It is just so when men talk about the heart, meaning thereby to include the whole of our passional, emotional, and affectional, nature. When, therefore, you hear a man begin to talk about the heart, and to build an argument upon it, watch him, and see if he does not use the word in one sense in his premises, and in another sense in his conclusion. In the sense in which the word is commonly used in religious writing or speech, all men have at least half a dozen hearts, and it is essential to know which of them is meant.

This is the case; God has created men with various and somewhat numerous organs and faculties, adapting them to the external world, whether material or spiritual; — our eye to light, our ear to sound, our senses of taste and smell, to savors and odors, our nerves of touch to different degrees of density, — solids, fluids, gases. So for self-preservation, we have a feeling of hunger and of thirst, which yield us a large amount, though not the highest kind, of pleasure, which torment and agonize us, when, through shipwreck or famine, they are not obeyed. For the same purpose of self-preservation, we have a sentiment of cautiousness, which foretells danger, and bids us beware of it. When danger actually confronts us, and we must look it in the eye, then we have a feeling or propensity called Combativeness, which bids us to resist, repel, drive it away, and if this is insufficient, we have another propensity called Destructiveness, which aims, not only at the removal of its object, but at its extermination, — a propensity whose whole logical power is confined to this one syllogism; If my enemy is dead, he can do me no harm.

On a somewhat higher plane, but still indispensable to the same purpose of self-preservation, is the desire of property. If a fair day made no provision for a stormy one, nor summer for winter, nor youth for old age, nor parents for children, then no second winter, no second generation would come to mankind. The race would die out, not leaving a historian.

And all these wonderful laws of nature, — the organic, the chemical, the vital, — these thoughts of God materialized throughout universal nature, so countless, so wise, so sublime, what would they be to us if we had not an intellect by which they can be discovered, rousing a veneration by which their author is adored. But with the adaptation between those laws and our capacity to understand them, sweeter are they than honey to the taste. Every one sustains more or less of the domestic relations, parental, filial, fraternal, sororal, and what a group of domestic affections are implanted in the most sensitive parts of our nature, to meet the demands and give us the joys of all these relationships. How a father loves son or daugher, the mother still more ; and what delights, endearments, ecstasies, hold perpetual jubileee in a happy family ; whereas, if there were no child, the fountain of parental love would never be unsealed ; if there were no parental or household love, infants, instead of being regarded as fresh visitants from on high, would be classed under the head of vermin. So Conscience, which finds its expression in what is degradingly called the Golden Rule, as if it was not infinitely more precious than gold, Conscience gives us, in a single sentence, more than is contained in all statutes and law libraries ; *Do as you would be done by.*

Benevolence is queen in the realm where Conscience is king. Love is the bride of Duty. When Justice must punish, Mercy follows him with healing and fragrant solaces, and by her divine art, abolishes the punishment by taking away the evil disposition that merited it. Benevolence must dwell forever at the right hand of God.

Another sentiment of the soul is Reverence, veneration for the Power which presides over the universe, and yet folds an infant in the arms of love; which wheels the orbs of heaven, and yet watches the throbbings of the human breast, and cares for the lowliest of mortals. Our conceptions of this Infinite Father may be dim, or clouded, or deformed, but no race of men has ever yet been discovered which had not some faith, more or less shadowy or radiant, of this Infinite One. In the Christian philosopher, or the philosophic Christian (let temperament decide which), how these attributes gather and glow into exhaustless power, and unspeakable wisdom, and the adorable effulgence of holiness.

Now each one of these functional, passional, emotional attributes of our nature, may be and is called *the heart.* What extent and variety, and amidst this extent and variety, what danger both of misapprehension in ourselves and of misleading others. Abstinence, or over-indulgence in food and beverage, that is, temperance on the one side, and gluttony and drunkenness on the other; continence or its suicidal opposite; honesty or dishonesty in the market place; generosity or selfishness in all social relationships; morality or immorality before men; piety or impiety towards God; — all these, a hundred times every day, are said to proceed out of the heart, and to manifest what it is.

As I said before, then, every man has a dozen hearts, and though there is a strong natural tendency in all these hearts to go together for the right or for the wrong, yet instances of the contrary are not infrequent. History relates instances of atheists who have braved death in defence of *their* religious belief, so to call it.

In a case where generosity was to be appealed to in behalf of suffering, I would far sooner go to the profligate in morals than to the bigot in religion. In a life of nearly forty years spent in trying to reform the common vices of men, some of the toughest cases I have ever met with have been cases of generally honest, good, pious, godly men, who had some sweet pet indulgence they *could not part with.* They could renounce all other sins easily enough, but not this darling one. They could say, "Vain pomp and glory of the world, I hate ye," but tobacco, or a night-cap of toddy, how could they surrender? "Sorrowing Jacobs, ye have taken Joseph, and ye may have the other ten, but will ye take Benjamin also? Must you divide asunder the joints and marrow in this way? Leave me at least my brandied coffee to assuage my gout, or the sceptre and the thunder with which I make the menials of my household tremble. Cannot the good God leave here and there a loop-hole in His law through which we can sometimes creep out for an hour and play truant?" No, no; proclaim it with the voice of seven thunders, there is no loop-hole in God's laws. Every one must be obeyed, and at all times. All these hearts, be they more or less, must be converted, must come, not into enforced, but into loving, exulting conformity to God's laws, — into such a state that if God had made no

15

such laws for our guidance as He has, we should make them.

It is the same in our spirits as in our bodies. As we needed about two hundred and fifty bones in our framework; as we needed some five hundred and twenty-seven muscles for the performance of necessary motions, God has given us these numbers. So as we needed the whole range and compass of our faculties, from the lowest basilar to the highest coronal, God has given us these, no more, no less, and to say that we have supernumerary ones, to say that we are destitute of essential ones, is to impeach our Creator.

Whence, then, comes the evil of the world, the wrong in men; for that there is evil in the world and terrible wrong in men, none can dispute. The groans of sin-caused suffering assail us from every part of the earth; their echoes reach from every point in the long track of time. There are many epochs when it seems as though the whole human race had set itself in battle array against Jehovah.

Now these terrible evils and wrongs which men commit and suffer, come not from the possession of any one of our powers and faculties, nor from the legitimate and normal use of them, but from their abuse, from the too much, or from the too little; from using them at wrong times, from not using them at right times. I am no more responsible for the number of the faculties with which God endued my spirit, be they more or less, than I am for the number of bones or muscles which He put into my body, be they more or less. Over neither had I any control. Respecting neither was opinion or consent of mine asked or given. I had no free agency then and there; for I did not pre-exist to give direction or counsel how I should be originally made. But now, respecting the manner in which I use my powers, respecting the special uses to which I put them ; whether they shall wane and perish through my neglect, or tyrannize and ruin through my indulgence ; for these things I am accountable ; respecting these I have free agency. These things do not happen without my counsel and direction.

Here, then, temptation begins its terrible work. Here it lies in ambush, steals upon us unawares, solicits, fascinates, commands, enslaves, damns.

The imagination of man has led him to personify temptation, to regard it as an evil agency external to ourselves, to embody it, and call it a Devil. Gloomy poets, and painters, and oftentimes religious teachers, represent this devil as a huge, stalking monster, marvellous in bulk, terrific in aspect, a roaring lion. How amazingly untrue. The devil, when he first approaches and besieges us, always comes in the guise of beauty or pleasure. He shows us hope, and promises that it shall be enjoyed. He shows us fear, and offers to avert it. Instead of being an Anak whose shadow darkens the sun, he dwarfs himself almost to invisibility, spiritualizes himself so that the outward organ cannot discern him. He may come in the form of some feeling, improper in kind or in degree to be indulged, some pleasure or advantage to be gained. In the little child, hiding behind the door to do a forbidden thing ; in childish games, cheating in the play or in the count, in order to win ; in the student, taking one unlawful peep into his text-book to make up for the ten minutes he had unlawfully squandered at play ; at the table or elsewhere, eating to gratify the taste, after the demands of health are satisfied, or in drinking for the pleasure of a spot in the inside of the mouth not two inches square, after all the rest of the body, heart, stomach, lungs, brain, has said "enough;" in the privacy of our rooms, doing what we know would disgrace us if door and window were suddenly opened and the world should look in; in trade, the first, smallest fraud in weight, or measure, or account; in the young lawyer, espousing a cause he knows to be unjust, because he cannot wait for an honest fee; in the young minister, subscribing to a creed he does not believe, to get an elegible settlement; in politics, espousing an unrighteous cause, by voice or vote, in hopes of preferment; in society at large, refusing to vindicate the cause of truth, because it may make one unpopular, or, which is quite as bad, refusing to expose offenders through the mean dread of being called an informer, the very name of which we ought to be emulous, when we look upon it as a means of abating evil in the world. It is in these ways, and in ten thousand ways like these, subtle, insinuating, stealthy, under the guise of some form of delight, or wealth, or fame, or power, that the devil first enters into child or man. He never comes to us as a huge, portentous, towering Colossus, vast as though he had been carved from Mount Athos, but attenuated and gay, rallying us upon our fears, piquing our pride, entering the soul through the eye among the rays of light, when we look upon forbidden objects to lust after them; entering it through the ear, with the vibrations of the air, when we voluntarily listen to obscene song or profane words. It is after we have allowed him entrance, and residence, and hospitality, it is after we have warmed, and nourished, and cherished what seemed at first so pleasant, or at least so harmless, that he starts up into gigantic proportions and aggrandizes himself with power, and usurps the throne of reason and conscience, and puts on the gorgon head, and shakes terrors from his snaky locks, and scourges every limb of the body and every faculty of the mind to do his accursed bidding. Then the affrighted soul shrieks out its alarms, obtests heaven and earth for deliverance in a voice betokening unspeakable agony, but Apollyon has vanquished the angel, and in the victim's inner ear howls out his triumph.

Do you think that when Temptation first came to Herod, it came to him in the proposal to kill all the children in Bethlehem and in all the coasts thereof, under two years of age; or that when Temptation first came to Judas, it came in the shape of betraying his master for thirty bits of money, an act as mean and contemptible as it was wicked; or when it first came to the Church, it came in the form of the ten great persecutions, or of wheels to wrench and tear the body limb from limb, or of fagot fires, or of St. Bartholemew massacres? I tell you nay. It came in the guise of some pleasure, advantage, profit; and here are the exact words it said; "Only this once; you are a fool if you can't try it this once;" and the victim, instead of scornfully replying; "I'm a fool if I do," tried it and fell, and ages of ignominy and remorse may not yet have atoned for the fall.

But when the devil or evil (for it makes not a pin's practical difference whether we affix the d or omit it), has once effected a lodgement in a man through his appetites, propensities, or passions, then his next step is to tamper with and debase his moral nature. We have reason which not only sees what is right, and just, and true, in common cases, as it sees the truth of the Multiplication Table, but when trained and practised, it dissolves the most refractory compounds of truth and error, brings out the pure, crystalline truth, and sluices away the foul, fetid error. We have conscience, which, so far as its power goes, not only speaks with the voice of God, but sees with the eye of God.

What a thought! You carry a compass within you, and you sail the ocean, you traverse the wilderness, in storm, in darkness you descend to subterranean caves; you consult this organism in which God expresses one of His perfections, and you know north, south, east, west, home. Conscience is the magnet of the soul. It has a Divine polarity. Amid the tempests of passion, in dark hours of trial, that only lie just this side of despair, when a host of fierce temptations beleaguer, then consult this Divine monitor, and though its tiny needle may tremble amid the attractions of earth, yet, if uncorrupted, its pole-star will be the throne of God.

As I said before, temptation allures, in order to obtain foothold within us; having obtained it, it commands. It says, omit this duty, though it be but the speaking of a word; invade this right, though it be but stealing an apple from a rich man's orchard; obtain that prize or honor, it will cost you only a falsehood; gratify that animal passion, the victim is too feeble to call you to account. And so, after the sensual and passional nature is inflamed, the moral nature succumbs, abdicates, retires, and sin is left sole monarch of the realm.

It may aid our conceptions of this subject, to consider the different degrees of guilt attaching to different persons for yielding to the same temptation. It is obvious that the same bodily act, or mental desire, may have different degrees of culpability or blame-worthiness, according to the differing conditions of the author. A deed very venial in a child, may be very criminal in a man. A deed which might be a mere peccadillo in a heathen, may be heinously offensive in one living under the light of the Gospel. To a man famishing with hunger, and perishing with cold, the theft of food, or of a garment, would be a very different thing from what the same act would be if the thief were surrounded with luxuries and wardrobes. Even in persons of the same class, where the temptation is light, and the knowledge of duty plain, and the time for deliberation ample, the offence bears a complexion of guilt immensely different from what it would if the light of knowledge were dim, and the assault of temptation vehement and sudden. Hence this *formula* in expressing the magnitude of an offender's guilt; *that it is directly as the knowledge of duty, and inversely as the strength of the assault.* Wicked as Sodom and Gomorrah were, it will be more tolerable for them than for Jerusalem, in the days of the Saviour; and better for Jerusalem than for us, if we repeat their deeds. That is, a man's guilt rises in heinousness, with the enlargement of his opportunities to know more and do better. Hence nations may be more wicked now, than they ever could be in ancient times; and our nation more wicked than any other. Drunkenness, and the manufacturing and trafficking in intoxicating drinks, are far greater crimes now, than they were fifty years ago. The man to whom the beautiful and benign laws of Human Physiology have been taught, is an immensely greater offender when he over-indulges his appetites, or takes what is injurious either in quality or quantity, than if he had always been taught that health is the result of chance, or of arbitrary, though Divine appointment. Under wise and Christian training, breathed upon by elevating and spiritual influences, with avenues to honor and duty opened on every side, the backslider and the apostate may become terribly, gigantically criminal. God knows our opportunities for light, and the stress of the temptation that beset us, and He will judge us. Even if He did not know it, our own nature is a self-registering machine, and keeps the tally, and sooner or later will be avenged.

The most formidable attribute of temptation, is its increasing power, its accelerating ratio of velocity. Every act of repetition increases power, diminishes resistance. It is like the letting out of waters, — where a drop can go, a river can go. Whoever yields to temptation, subjects himself to the law of falling bodies. Look at the drunkard, the gambler, the libertine. Do you need any Atwood's machine to prove that in their fall, the velocity is as the squares of the times? Look into the Police Courts of our great cities, and see the young men ; alas, the young women, not going to perdition, but gone! They all said they could yield once, a few times, and then resist. That is, standing on the brink of a precipice, they said they could plunge over, and stop half-way. Incredible delusion! Amazing folly, idiocy! No man who yields to temptation, comes out as he went in. Here is his besotted delusion. He says, I shall meet the second as I do the first. Impossible! When he meets the second, after having yielded to the first, he is a changed man. Desire is increased. Power of resistance has decreased. With a force of twenty he yielded to a force of ten; flattering himself that afterwards, with a force of ten, he can vanquish a force of twenty. When a man crosses the river above the Falls of Niagara, in a frail skiff, does not the first dimple of a whirlpool in the stream, or the tiniest bubble on its surface, shout to him of the swifter flow, of the rapids, the verge, the plunge, the watery Tartarus beneath, whence living man never emerged? Why, in God's name, does not the tempted man see, behind, the smiling, dallying, gay deceiver, that sports, and wantons, and charms, with music's sweetest strains, another of sterner mien, and behind them the whole retinue of infernals, with Abaddon in the rear, and Gehenna at his back. The young men before me, who have been, week after week, to that rum-hole, — why is it that they cannot see the bottomless pit beneath it, without taking up the floor?

The inquiry, "When is a crime complete?" belongs to this subject. In the progress of crime to its consummation, there are three degrees.

1. Evil imaginations voluntarily entertained. I have no right to hang licentious pictures around the chambers of my brain. Not even in thought have I a right to indulge in forbidden pleasures. All such indulgences debase the mind, pollute it, prepare us to realize in our conduct, the wicked imagination or conception. For are such pictures, such impressions upon the tablets of the soul ever effaced? Moral chemistry has no neutralizer that will wholly extract the stain. No graver's tool can ever wholly abrade it; for it is like the image upon the shield of Phidias, graven so deep that whatever would remove it, would annihilate the soul itself. It may be covered up, and thus hidden from the common eye, but a reagent will detect and expose it.

In ancient times, when paper or parchment for writing was in great demand, professional clerks or scriveners used to take old volumes of classics or histories, and wash out or efface the writing upon them, and then record, upon the same roll, what they considered more valuable. The parchments so effaced and re-written, are called "Palimpsests." Many of these palimpsests have been discovered in modern times from which the last writing has been chemically removed and the old writing restored in full. The human soul is a palimpsest. What has been written on it ever will remain on it forever. That is its law. Hence all evil imaginations are recorded crimes.

The sinner reaches the second stage of guilt when, after having luxuriated in the fancied pleasures of a crime, or in the profits or honors of its commission, he at first harbors his thoughts, and then ventures upon the terrible resolution to commit it. This second stage is the natural outgrowth of the first. The imagination gloats over illicit joys. A law of repetition exists in the mind, and every repetition inflames the desire. The temptation grows into form, compacts itself into substance, assumes body, vitality, energy. It says, I must, I can, I will; then prepares its plans and watches for its hour. This is the direful purpose, the resolve.

But dreadful as this is; — this standing with the body half bent over the precipice, below which blaze the eternal fires; this poising and balancing where one inch of voluntary advance will change the centre of gravity, and precipitate to Tartarean depths, even this is not quite all. The consummation of guilt is in the deed. Until this acme is reached, there is a place for repentance, a chance for hope. Conscience may yet shriek out a more terrible alarm. Reason may discern some new and fearful revelation of consequences. The religious faculties, repulsed and driven from the field, may rally and rush back to the rescue. Some mother's words, dropped in the ear long years ago, — blessed angel-words of sainted mother now sleeping in her grave, — unheeded while she lived, but now by magic association, bursting up through layers of impious forgetfulness and wicked pleasures, may thrill and vibrate through the soul, and rescue the *almost* victim from perdition.

I know it is sometimes said that the guilt is complete when the guilty act is resolved on. Is virtue complete when a virtuous deed is resolved on? Certainly not. The fulness of virtue is not in the intention, but in the *execution. The same law governs both virtue and* vice.

But when the consummating deed is done; when the torch is touched to the magazine; when the dagger is struck to the heart; when the orgasm of passion is reached, then all the remonstrant faculties of the soul have been subdued, then all the conspirator faculties have triumphed. Then temptation has consummated itself in crime.

I have spoken of temptation and fall. It may not be amiss in closing to say a word about repentance, about that which alone, so far as it can be done, reinstates the offender.

Repentance is sorrow for wrong-doing, — sorrow, sometimes rising to remorse. This feeling is *toto cœlo* different from another kind of sorrow, — sorrow for being found out. Yet how often is sorrow for being discovered, mistaken for sorrow for being guilty.

A crime is committed, — no matter what. All good men, for the common safety, seek to find out the offender. Weeks, months pass, but no clue is discovered. The shrewdest conjectures are baulked. Suspicions exist, but confirmation of them fails. By and by, a sagacious man, gathering all the scattered rays of light into a focus, throws its blaze into the very face of the offender, and he stands exposed, revealed, proclaimed. Then see how suddenly he begins to profess sorrow for what he has done. Oh, he now says, how I lament the deed! What anxious days! What sleepless nights! Oh, what would I not give, do, suffer, to recall the guilty act! Ah, self-deluded mortal! If you felt any godly sorrow for it, why did you not confess it, make reparation for it, before? Those weeks, those months, when all good men were searching for the offender, and you knew who he was, but acted all the time as though you did not know who he was, carved and shaped your continuing life into a continuing lie, if you were truly sorry for the wrong, why did you not then confess it, express contrition for it, make reparation for it. Your sorrow started up, not when the deed was done, but when the discovery was made.

Would God that I could illuminate this truth with such a strong light that moral blindness could not help but see it. The very constitution of human nature is such, that if a violator of law truly repents, he can find no rest till he has acknowledged his guilt, and made all the atonement for it in his power. If he has stolen money or a watch, he will restore it. What should we think of thief or robber who should protest to the person robbed or despoiled, what agony of remorse he feels for the crime, with the plunder all the time secreted in his pocket. It is just so if one has stolen a man's good name, or injured the family, or the company, or the institution to which he belongs. True repentance necessitates confession. The concealed crime is fire in the offender's bosom. If he flees across the sea, it will scourge him home. If he holds the fatal secret in his heart during life, the death-bed will wrench it from him. Wrung with torture, he is driven to suicide, and "suicide," it has been well said, "is confession." Bad as Judas was, he could not help the involuntary confession of suicide.

And look upon this other fact, and tremble. When a man sins against God, and repents, he must confess that sin to God before peace of mind becomes possible. Why must he confess to God? Does not the All-knowing know it already? Can the offender's lips inform the searcher of hearts? No, not for God's sake, but for his own sake he must avow the fact. He must stand in the presence of the Omniscient, and in the presence of his crime, and say, *I did it*, or peace cannot visit his bosom.

What did the Prodigal Son say, "I will arise and go to my father, and will say, Father, I have sinned against heaven and before thee." And when he met his father, his first utterance was, "Father, I have sinned against heaven and in thy sight." Did his father need anything but inspection to inform him of the Prodigal's career? His tattered garments, but half covering his diseased person; his unshod feet, after that dreadful journey home; his ghastly face, emaciated by famine; his hollow eye, red with weeping; his voice choked with unutterable shame; did the father need any description of his condition, any history of his profligacy but these? Yet he could as well have suppressed the winds or the tides, as to have choked down this articulate proclamation of his guilt.

This was true repentance. This was repentance not needing to be repented of. This was sorrow for the *deed* and not for the *discovery*. All other sorrow is futile and vain; and if men are silly enough to be blinded by it, God is, never.

MEDITATION.

Our Father, Thou who art near to every one of us, we would at this time draw near to Thee. We would banish all selfish and worldly thoughts from our bosoms; we would contemplate Thee in the immaculate purity and holiness of Thy nature, in the adorableness of Thy attributes, in the immensity of Thy works, and in the wisdom and love and mercy in which Thou hast made them all. Oh our Father in Heaven, we would not debase our natures before Thee. Ignorance and sin alone can debase them. We would not exalt ourselves above those who lived in former ages of the world, or who are now our contemporaries in other quarters of the globe. They had not the blessed Gospel in their hands; they had not the clear inspiring of the Truth into their souls. Of us, to whom much is given, shall much be required. We would not boastingly thank Thee that we are not as other men are; but if others in any respect are inferior to ourselves, we would strive for the spirit and the benevolence that will not rest until they are reformed, improved, and made partakers with us in all Thy goodness. May we think of the noble men who have gone before us, prophets, saints, martyrs, apostles, who encountered temptation and resisted it; whose souls rose to the glorious region of magnanimity and self-sacrifice; who, through tribulation, fought the good fight and came off conquerors, and have gone to their eternal reward. Let us ask ourselves, if we had been in their places, whether we should have imitated their deeds; if the toil and struggle of an ascension to the heights of virtue had been set before us, whether we should have scorned the appetites of the flesh, and held down the wayward propensities of our nature, and preferred the honor of God to the plaudits of men; or borne imprisonment, and scourging and death rather than prove treacherous or neglectful in the holy cause of duty. Oh let us never fall into the delusion and fallacy that we have done our duty, at the time or in the place of any other man, unless we can do it now, in our own time and in our own place. And may we never delude ourselves with the fallacious belief that we should not have done as the wickedest of men have done in all parts and ages of the world, that we should not have fallen as they fell; that we should not have become tyrants and oppressors and persecutors and wrong-doers in the innumerable relations of life, unless we can now refrain from the offences, whatever they may be, which we are tempted to commit; unless we can imitate the example of Jesus Christ.

RETRIBUTION.

IX.

RETRIBUTION.

GALATIANS, Ch. vi., part of 7th and 8th verses. "— for whatsoever a man soweth, that shall he also reap. For he that soweth to the flesh, shall of the flesh reap corruption; but he that soweth to the spirit, shall of the spirit reap life everlasting."

II. CORINTHIANS, ix., 6. "But this I say, he which soweth sparingly shall reap also sparingly; and he which soweth bountifully shall reap also bountifully."

HOSEA, viii., 7. "For they have sown the wind and they shall reap the whirlwind."

IN the beautifully planned and skilfully formed universe in which we are placed, great minds have always observed an order in the arrangement of all its bodies, and in the happening of all its events.

First, there is an order in the arrangement of all its bodies. Things are not thrown together promiscuously and at random, piled up in a heap chance-wise, and without beginning, middle or end. That is our idea of chaos. The planets are arranged in a certain order in relation to the sun. The different layers of the crust of the earth have a uniform arrangement which is the same in both hemispheres and in all the continents. Hence, in geology, the primary, secondary, and tertiary formations have such a regularity and uniformity, that when we see the plan of superposition in one part of the world, we expect the same general plan in all other parts. In the human body, why are the arteries which convey the blood outward from the heart bedded deeper down in the flesh than the veins which bring it back from the extremities? Simply because the blood-vessels are liable to be cut and ruptured, and as the arteries always bleed more profusely than the veins, it is best that they should be placed deeper down, where they will be more out of harm's way. If you were to put iron and glass into the same package for transportation, would you not put the glass into the interior of the parcel, where it would be less exposed to blows or any form of rough usage? That is the reason why the arteries are placed nearer the bones, and the veins nearer the skin. The human eye consists of above twenty different parts. In every perfect eye, are not all these parts arranged in the same order? Examine the interior of an egg. Are not the albumen and the yolk always fashioned after the same model? Nay, among animals in other respects most dissimilar, there is still a secret reference to the same general type. The wings of a bird and the fins of a fish represent the arms of a man. The fore-legs of a horse or an ox are only the arms turned down. The mammalia have four limbs; birds have four also, including their wings.

And, secondly, there is an order in events. Events do not occur at hap-hazard. When the sun rises, light is spread abroad. When the sun sets, light is withdrawn. When the sun approaches the tropic of Cancer, the temperature of the whole northern hemisphere rises, and we have the heats of summer; when it recedes to the tropic of Capricorn, the temperature falls, and we have the congelations of winter. You do not see boiling water scald a man one day and freeze him the next. You do not see fire one day burn more fiercely in a blast of oxygen, and do the same thing the next day in a blast of carbonic acid gas. You do not see cork float on water and lead sink at one time, and then see the lead float and the cork sink at another. You never see a man who observes all the laws of health becoming ill; and another who violates all those laws remaining well. The angler baits his hook with curious art for catching fish, unless when he fishes for gudgeons, which bite the naked hook; because among fishes the gudgeons are fools. The devil tempts men through their ambition, their cupidity or their appetite, until he comes to the profane swearer, whom he catches without any reward. The profane swearer bites a hook unbaited even by any seeming good; because among the tempted, like gudgeons among fishes, the profane swearer is a fool.

Now in all these things, Nature, or God acting through nature, is uniform. They never happen one way one year, and another way another year, when the circumstances are the same. They give no sign of being produced by accident or caprice, or by the arbitrary, fitful interference of a superior power; but they proceed onward from age to age, with a solemn, majestic movement, an august procession, that strikes the contemplative beholder with awe, and expands and lifts his soul with indescribable emotions of sublimity and grandeur. We call this the course of Providence; and in the wisdom that planned it, in the power that sustains it, in the benevolence with which it overflows, and in the omniscience which sees the end from the beginning, it is worthy of a God.

We admire the ingenuity of a timepiece-maker, who can construct a chronometer so skilfully, that it can go round the world and not lose or gain more than half a minute. What, then, shall be said of this great horologe in the skies, of this sun and these planets, primary and secondary, which have fulfilled their mighty circuits since their creation and have not lost or gained a moment of time, nor fallen out of repair?

Now, having looked outward, around us, let us for a moment look inward, into our own consciousness. Corresponding with this wonderful order of external nature, this marvellous arrangement of bodies, and this solemn progression of events in the outward world, we have a faculty in our own souls, whose special function it is to take cognizance of the external arrangement and order, and to profit by it; to profit by it in two ways, first, by obtaining more benefits and advantages than we could otherwise do; and secondly, by avoiding more evils.

What a miserable condition we should be in, if the seasons should change places, winter for summer, and spring for autumn, all at random; if the zones should dance about; if the ocean should be sometimes fresh, and the fountains sometimes salt; if the plants which had borne healthful and delicious fruits should produce arid and poisonous ones; if the specific gravity of bodies should change, so that stones would sometimes rise and vapor fall; — in fine, abolish order and adaptation and periodicity from the universe, and the only solace of our miserable lives would be, that they would come speedily to an end.

But mark this: just as well might all these essentials of happiness, and of existence, which are without us, be abolished, as to abolish our power to recognize their existence. It is immaterial whether the sun or the eye be destroyed, vision equally ceases. It is the same whether you destroy outward order, or the inward power of profiting by order; in both cases the advantage is destroyed. Two things, then, are necessary; the order of the external world, and the power of availing ourselves of that order in the mental world.

This sublime external order we call Cause and Effect. It is something more than mere sequence, mere juxtaposition, in point of time. The night always follows the day, and the day the night, but the day is not the cause of the night, nor is the night the cause of the day. But when I throw a rope to a drowning man, or fasten a cable and a cannon ball together, and by means of gunpowder send that ball over a wrecked vessel, I am convinced that there is a *power* in my arm, and in the gunpowder which sent the rope or cable on its benevolent errand. That power we denominate Causation; the faculty within us which recognizes the power we call Causality.

Now the grand order of events in nature, in history, in nations, and in individuals, is nothing but progressive, and often alternating cause and effect. A precedent event is the cause of one or more subsequent events. The subsequent event or events, are the effect of the precedent, and in their turn become the cause of other events, later in time. The first tree produced the first seed, or, changing the priority, the first seed produced the first tree, that tree another seed, that seed another tree, and so on, to all the seeds that exist, and to all the trees that are growing to-day. And so, assuming the bird to have been first created, the first bird produced the first egg, that egg another bird, that bird another egg, and so on, from bird to egg, and from egg to bird, to all the eggs and birds now in being. The direction and forces by which the planets were launched into their orbits, has had a controlling influence on their motions and orbits ever since; and their course and velocity are now so certain, that men can foretell day, hour, and minute, when every eclipse will happen, for a thousand years to come. Fire produces certain effects on iron, and boiling water certain effects on flesh and vegetables, and soft words turn away wrath, and we are assured, through our faculty of causality, that these effects will always be reproduced, whenever the objects to be affected by them are subjected to the same conditions.

Nature, then, is like a vast piece of machinery, contrived by a Being of Omniscience, who could foresee all consequences; wrought out by a Being of Infinite Skill, who could adapt means to ends; worked by a Being of exhaustless Power, who will never be destitute of energy to drive on the process; and administered by a Being of matchless Love, who constantly evolves from it the means of the highest possible good.

In the midst of this wonderful machinery we are placed. If we know its capabilities and their laws, we can regulate their action, producing vast good, averting vast evil. I can rear tares or wheat in all my grounds. I can make bread or alcohol of all my grains. I can sow health or disease, virtue or vice, in all my influences upon men. If I wish to produce given quantities or qualities of manufactured articles, I arrange certain cranks, or wheels, or bands; I arrange the power, whether water or steam, and God turns the wheels, and the result comes forth. I arrange some pieces of glass or burnished metal in a certain order, for a telescope, and lo, God's wonders in the deep firmament [illegible] [illegible]d, rank behind rank, burst upon my adoring vision. If I wish to train up children to greatness of mind, and purity of soul, then I supply the requisite moral and intellectual aliment; and if I have selected my subject judiciously, and have followed principles faithfully in all my course of training, then shall I be rewarded with that most precious of all earthly rewards, a noble character. Causation, then, the operative power in Cause and Effect, is a mighty agency, proceeding from God; and Causality, by which we recognize the law of causation, is a mighty faculty existing in man. It is the mightiest intellectual power bestowed on man. No such intellectual difference exists between men, as between the man who has it, and the man who has it not. The extremes of its presence or its absence, mark the extremes of greatness and of imbecility. Socrates, Lord Bacon, Dr. Franklin, possessed it in a most conspicuous degree. Idiots have but a germ or minimum of it, and hence they are idiots. The great causality, which, on beholding any particular fact or event, can look back and divine the cause that produced it, and look forward and foresee the effects which itself will produce, that makes the great man, — the great writer, the great statesman, the great philosopher. The man who sees events as mere facts, but cannot see in the events, either the causes that led to them, or the effects which in the order of nature, will flow from them, he is the imbecile, the non-witted, the idiotic. He can neither arrange things for the production of good results, nor foresee bad results, and so modify causes as to escape from them. He is a ship without a rudder on the ocean of Time, tossed about at the mercy of every wind or tide of circumstance and chance; and, though there is a possibility that he may be driven to the desired haven, yet the chances are as infinity to one that he will be wrecked. Even if he should be driven where he desires to go, every one will know that it was by no skill of his that he arrived there. But give a man this Causality, and he has a rudder to his ship; and no matter where in the broad ocean, no matter in which ocean he may be; no matter which way the winds may blow, or the tides may sweep, he moves his helm so as to coöperate with, or to antagonize them all; and he doubles capes, sheers from rocks, threads channels, and at last, jubilant with success, he reaches his haven in safety and triumph.

Astronomers saw that Uranus, then supposed to be the outside planet in our solar system, had irregularities in its motions which they could not account for. They calculated the retarding and accelerating forces of all the other bodies in the solar group, but the gravitation of these other bodies did not explain the difficulty. At last, Leverrier, a French astronomer, conceived that the irregularities of Uranus in its orbit might be occasioned by the attracting force of some planet beyond it, though no such planet was known to exist. He set himself, therefore, to examine all the observations that had been made upon Uranus, found that at such a time it was so much in advance of its position, and at such a time so much in the rear of it, and so from revolution to revolution for years and years; and then he calculated that if there were such a planet outside and beyond Uranus, and at a certain supposed and probable distance from it, whereabouts that planet must have been at different times; that is, if Uranus, in making its revolution, began at any point to go farther than it ought to, then the supposed planet must be ahead of it, and so drawing it forward; but if Uranus began to slacken its velocity, and to fall behind what would otherwise be its true position, then the supposed planet must be behind it, and so retarding its motions. At the very first computation (though we can hardly conceive how laborious such a computation must be), he would simply infer that the supposed planet must be in advance or in the rear. At the second, perhaps he might conclude that it was within so many degrees of some fixed point in its orbit. And so, by computation after computation, wrought out by a degree of labor and learning scarcely imaginable by us, he would determine the place of the supposed planet to be within narrower and narrower limits, until he had at last exhausted all his data, or means of information, and could only say, — the new planet is to be looked for between two such points. Leverrier immediately wrote to his friend, the astronomer Gauss, at Berlin, who had charge of a very superior telescope, telling him at what point in the heavens to look for the supposed new world. Gauss pointed his telescope as directed, and the first night discovered the new planet, thus adding another known member to the solar system. Now if causes had not acted uniformly, or if we had no faculty of Causality, how could this discovery ever have been made?

Some traveller has given an account of the troops of monkeys that frequent Gibraltar. The soldiers often go out of their camp to cook their food in the open air, and during cold weather, after they have retired, the monkeys come from their trees and hiding-places, and gather round the fire for warmth. But the fire will soon burn out, and though the monkeys have seen the soldiers, scores of times, go to the piles of wood near by, to replenish the fire, yet they have never associated the two things together, the wood and the fire, — and therefore will remain cold or slink away into their hiding places to suffer, for want of wit enough to know that fuel is necessary to fire.

Now the greatest difference between these two cases, between the discovery of an unknown planet from the aberrations of a known one, and the relation between fuel and fire when the two are placed close together, is a difference in the Causality of the two parties.

This case of the astronomer, and this case of the monkeys, may, perhaps, be regarded as the two extremes. Let me premise a remark or two, and then refer to a few such cases as happen around us continually, and see whether such cases come nearer to the pattern of the astronomer, or to the pattern of the monkeys.

First, then, let me say, that throughout all that part of the creation of God with which we are acquainted, He works by Cause and Effect; He works in such a way that our Causality can understand from what He has done, what He will do. His rules are so uniform and Himself so reliable, that when we see any cause put in operation, we know that cause can never be annihilated. With a single exception, that cause will certainly produce its effect. That exception is this; we may sometimes modify the effect by setting a new cause or set of causes in operation. But it is only through the agency of the new causes that we can escape from the effects of the old; and then, only because God has connected the new causes with *their* effects, indissolubly, just as He had the old ones with theirs. In one class of cases, after having set the cause in action, we can never prevent the effect, even by any new cause that we may put in action; because the effect follows so immediately, so instantaneously upon the cause, that we have no time to get in between them with a new cause; we have no time to thrust a new cause in to modify the effect of the old one. If I hurl a javelin, or shoot an arrow, or fire a ball, at a fellow-being, I can never withdraw the force I have imparted; nor can I leap in between javelin, arrow or ball, and their object. On they go and take the life at which I aimed, and no prayers, or tears, or agonies of mine can arrest them in their course. There is, however, another class of cases, where the interval is so long between the starting of the cause and the consummation of the effect, where so many processes are to be gone through with after the beginning of the cause, and before the completion of the effect, that we can step in between them and modify or intercept the effect. But, observe here, that this must always be done, not by destroying the original force which set the train in motion, but by instituting a new cause or set of causes, which shall produce a new set of effects, superseding the first. One man may design to take the life of another, and may mingle some deadly venom with his food to poison him, or he may resolve to fire his house in the night to consume him; but before the food has been eaten, or the flames have enveloped the sleeping-room, the offender may repent, and remove the food, or give the life-saving alarm and prevent the murder. But here you will observe the prevention is the effect of a new cause; the old cause was not annihilated; the old crime of designing to murder will remain a fact forever, and its scar, at least, if not

17*

its wound, will remain upon the offender's soul forever. When, therefore, we set a cause in motion, it passes out of our jurisdiction. It comes then within God's jurisdiction. With regard to causes, God seems to give us, within a certain limited sphere, a co-ordinate jurisdiction with himself; but with regard to the effects naturally resulting from those causes, He gives us no jurisdiction. These He retains in His own sovereign hand.

Now there is no more common and few more woful errors than those which men commit when they neglect to take care of causes, and then expend their energies or their lamentations upon the effects of those causes. We ought to expend our talents and our toils upon causes, altogether, and then we are certain God will see that the right effects flow from them. But men neglect the causes, and then busy, or burden, or torment themselves about effects, which are no longer within their control.

A merchant is careless about the building of his ship, works defective materials into its structure, appoints a captain who is unlearned or intemperate, and then sends it to sea. A terrific storm arises, and now he can neither eat nor sleep. He would gladly give half the value of ship and cargo to insure the rest. Foolish man! When that vessel was on the stocks, why did you not see that it was well built? Why did you employ that captain when you knew him to be deficient in skill, or intemperate in habits? Then you had the causes all in your own hands. You determined then. God's immutable laws of winds and waves do but execute now what you predestined then, and down she must go. Your ship shall be drift-wood upon the ocean's surface. Your cargo shall lie upon its bottom.

In a fiery drought in midsummer, the farmer becomes most anxious about his crops, mourns, repines, arraigns Providence, perhaps, because the heavens are as brass, and yield no rain, the earth is like an oven, and the corn is scorched as by a slow-consuming fire. But in the spring, when the causes were at his control, why did he not subsoil his land, so that the roots could penetrate down to the moisture and draw up the nourishment which would have given him the luxuriant blade and the full corn in the ear?

The railroad engineer is entrusted with the building of a bridge, high-poised over deep waters. He fails to excavate to the solid foundation, and omits the necessary clamping and bracing and trellis-work. By and by, the newspapers announce that all is *ready*. The Excursion Train takes up the choicest men, the dignitaries of the land, — the skilful, the educated, the worthy, those to whom it is an honor to pay honor. On the company speeds, jubilant, exultant. As the fair-seeming structure comes into view, expectation is too high for utterance, and silence holds every breath for the restrained exclamation of triumph. A crash, a plunge, a shriek! Another plunge, a wilder shriek! And still another, as a third great chariot becomes a coffin, and laden with humanity, entombs itself beneath engulfing waters. Silence reigns again, save here and there

> "The bubbling cry
> Of some strong swimmer in his agony."

So of him who builds a dwelling. If he builds upon a sandy foundation, — if he constructs it of materials which have no strength or cohesion, then he has neglected causes; and he must expect that the flood will undermine it, and the winds overthrow it, and he has no right, nay, it is impiety in him, to ask God to interpose a miracle between his conduct and its natural consequences.

In the filthy and reeking suburbs of a city, from which all cleanliness and decency have been banished, where the earth exhales the miasma that scatters pestilence, where, from holes which the disinfecting sunlight has never shone upon, from crypts and corners which the purifying breezes have never visited, grim Destruction breathes out its poisonous vapors, one lung-full of which is a death-potion, the alarm of cholera is sounded. The residents die by scores. The contagion spreads on all sides. The seeds of death are wafted upon every breeze, and invade districts where purity and cleanliness reside. Virtue and piety fall victims, and in some cases, even the stoutest health succumbs. Now what alarm and consternation, what summoning of councils, municipal and medical, what expenditures, what numbers of men abandoning their business, for flight, with mothers clasping their infants to their breasts, what stupefying terror among those who remain. One twentieth part of the pains and expenditure which it now costs to drive out the plague after its invasion and its work of havoc, would have sufficed to purify the whole region beforehand. But those who had power over the causes neglected to exert that power. They suffered the contagion to be incubated and hatched, and then to rise and shake death from its dark wing over happy and virtuous homes; and the inexorable law of God fulfilled the rest.

A people who enjoy the unspeakably precious prerogative of electing their own rulers, grow indifferent to their high duty, absent themselves from the polls for frivolous reasons, vote from passion or caprice, or a base party spirit, and thus suffer demagogues and profligates to be returned to their legislative halls, there to guide the ship of state, with all its cargoes of happiness, upon whatever courses they will. Soon a crisis comes, a momentous crisis, involving, perhaps, the inextinguishable rights of a race, involving the happiness, prosperity and character of the nation itself, and now those miscreants are treacherous to their duty; the avaricious see a chance for making money, and directly or indirectly, they pocket bribes; the ambitious clutch at power, and thus they sacrifice the dearest interests of millions, yea, of ages of the unconscious unborn, that they may obtain wealth without labor, or possess the insignia of office while conscious that they are destitute of the merits that deserve them. The people, stripped of their earnings, disgraced in character, overwhelmed with shame, are left to mourn the folly and the fatuity that promoted such men to power. But why did not the people make it a matter of conscience to give a vote, and to give that vote for a true man? Then they would have escaped loss and calamity and shame. But they neglected the preparation of causes, and God's laws visit them with the legitimate effects of their conduct.

How strong is the instinct of parental love. Parents suffer no such agony in their own persons as they can suffer through the person of a child. Parents can bear the palpitating heart, the convulsed muscle, the throbbing pulse in themselves; but when the tender organs of a loved child are torn with these agonies, it becomes intolerable. In the aggregate, parents suffer more through the profligacies and criminalities of children than through their own. They may repent of their own and allay the suffering, but when a child's wickedness runs on to ruin and death, then, while life lasts, its torturing fires continue to burn in the parental breast. As a general rule, — I do not deny that there are exceptions, but as a general rule, — children turn out as they might be expected to turn out from the treatment received from parents. What untold agonies, not only in the open day and in the thronged market-place, but in solitude and at midnight, do parents suffer; what soreness of heart, even such that the tenderest sympathy tortures it like fire, does the mother feel for a profligate son, while he, as if urged along by some demon, rushes on to darker shame and a deadlier perdition. Yet the time was when that child's heart was as soft as wax, when his feelings, like an aspen leaf, could have been moved by a breath. Then the mother could have supplied the very moral nutriment that should have been embodied in the growth of its soul, just as the milk from her own breast became a part of its body. Then she sat upon a throne, and weal and woe were ministers ready to do her bidding. Then she was, like a goddess, decreeing the future, originating predestination, telling Fate himself what he should do. But, for some vanity or frivolity of the hour, she forfeited her queenly prerogatives; she was an idiot in Causality, and a lost child and a broken heart are her reward.

But there is one illustration which embraces the essence of all the illustrations I have given; an illustration which shows more strikingly than any other, that if we would make sure of the effects we desire, we must give timely heed to the causes which, according to the ordination of God's providence, will produce them.

Youth is a cause, the condition of manhood and old age is an effect. Time is a seed-field; in youth we sow it with causes; in after life we reap the harvest of effects. God has established no relation more indissoluble than that between youth and age, between the spring-time of causes, and the autumn and winter of consequences. Cause, cause, cause, is stamped all along upon the conduct of youth; effect, effect, effect, is moulded and chiselled in upon the results of that conduct, in age. In youth, the health may be preserved or ruined, to be rejoiced or mourned over through all the remainder of life. The ample, palace-like apartments of the mind may be filled with the precious treasures of knowledge, or they may be left vacant, so that any foot-fall within them, or near them, ever afterwards shall proclaim their emptiness by its hollow-sounding vibrations; or, again, those chambers of the soul, fit for the garnering of grand, and lofty, and refulgent thoughts, and designed by their Maker for the garnering of such thoughts, may be filled with errors of doctrine, and with schemes of criminality, repulsive, contaminating, monstrous, and monster-begetting. In this youthful season of causation, too, the heart may bud and blossom with moral amaranths, which, in after life, will bear the fruits of paradise, of heaven; or it may become rank with noxious habits and impulses, whose very verdure and flower will exhale poison, and whose fruit, in years to come, will be like the Dead Sea apples, full of ashes, and bitterness to the taste. Look at the causes, on one side; look at the effects on the other; look at the adamantine relation which God has established between them; — how one grows out of the other, as the oak grows out of an acorn, or the bird out of an egg.

My young friends, as it respects manhood and old age, you are now in the season of youth, and the preparation of these causes, is, to a great extent, committed to your hands. As it respects another life, we are all in the season of youth, and our destiny, to an inconceivable extent, is in our own hands. God stands ready by His laws, that is, by His providence, to affix the appropriate effects to such causes as we shall put in motion, good or evil. Let us, then, attend to the causes on which our futurity of weal or woe, of greater weal, or of less woe, shall depend. Take care of the causes. He has predetermined the effects of happiness or misery, of honor or shame, which shall flow from them as the stream flows from the fountain.

MEDITATION.

Our Father, we thank Thee for the security of the past night; that during the oblivion of ourselves in sleep, Thou hast not forgotten us; and that, refreshed and reinvigorated by grateful repose, we have risen from our beds, so like a resurrection from the dead, to engage in the duties and the services appropriate to this sacred day. Here, bowing our hearts before Thee, in reverent gratitude, may we present ourselves, in Thy holy presence, as loving children would seek the presence of an earthly father. Wilt Thou, Oh Heavenly Father, stretch forth the hand of mercy towards us, and bid us welcome. Wilt Thou touch our lips with praise; wilt Thou kindle the flame of gratitude in our hearts. May they burn incense to Thee, richer than all the perfumes of the east. By contemplating Thy Power, may we be encouraged to obtain knowledge, by means of which Thou dost invest us with power. By reflecting upon Thy Justice, may we learn to do justice to all our fellowmen;—justice to their interests in all our dealings with them; justice to their characters in all we say or circulate respecting them; justice to the possibilities of good in their natures, in all the influences we exert upon them. And in contemplating Thy Mercy, may we learn to be merciful; may we be merciful to the poor, by helping them, through industry, and sobriety, and intelligence, to obtain a competency and comfort; may we be merciful to the ignorant, by giving them knowledge, and by devising such measures as shall refine that knowledge into wisdom; may we be merciful to those who suffer, by succoring their physical distresses, or by administering the balm of consolation to the deeper sorrows of the heart, and may we be merciful to those who sit in the region and shadow of death, by sending civilization and the Gospel to all the ends of the earth. Oh, Father, may we rise to that highest of all human prerogatives, to that noblest of all earthly dignities, — the prerogative and the dignity of being co-workers with Thee in Thy plans for the welfare, the happiness, the holiness of man. Bless this people and this society, we beseech Thee. May their light so shine before men, that others, seeing their good works, may be led to glorify our Father who is in heaven. Bless him who ministers to them in sacred things. May he grow mighty in the utterance of truth. May he fear God, and not man. May he speak boldly for righteousness, for temperance, for equity, and for the universal brotherhood of the race; and may his labors be blessed in the gathering and strengthening of a noble people, whose blessed influences for peace and for purity, shall reflect the light of heaven into all the paths of the children of men, and whose lives shall be the visible seal that they are true disciples of Thy Son, Jesus Christ.

THE KINGDOM OF HEAVEN.

X.

THE KINGDOM OF HEAVEN.

MATTHEW xix, 24. — And again I say unto you, it is easier for a camel to go through the eye of a needle, than for a rich man to enter into the kingdom of God.

Parallels. Mark x. 25; Luke xviii. 25; Luke xvii 21. — For behold, the kingdom of God is within you. Rom. xiv. 17. — For the kingdom of God is not meat and drink, but righteousness, and peace, and joy in the Holy Ghost. 1 Cor. iv. 20. — For the kingdom of God is not in word, but in power.

1 Cor. xv. 50. — But this I say, brethren, that flesh and blood cannot inherit the kingdom of God.

Gal. v. 19. — Now the works of the flesh are manifest, which are these: Adultery, fornication, uncleanness, lasciviousness,

20. — Idolatry, witchcraft, hatred, variance, emulations, wrath, strife, seditions, heresies,

21. — Envyings, murders, drunkenness, revellings, and such like; of the which I tell you before, as I have also told you in time past, that they who do such things, shall not inherit the kingdom of God.

22. — But the fruit of the spirit is love, joy, peace, long-suffering, gentleness, goodness, faith.

23. — Meekness, temperance. Against such there is no law.

24. — And they that are Christ's have crucified the flesh with the affections and lusts.

Ephesians v. 5. — For this ye know, that no whoremonger, nor unclean person, nor covetous man (who is an idolater), hath any inheritance in the kingdom of Christ or of God.

THE Kingdom of God is the subject of this Discourse.

In considering it, let us first inquire what is meant by the phrase, "The Kingdom of God." We ought to have, not merely an exact theological, but an exact geographical idea of God's kingdom. We must fix its boundaries. We must draw a line of demarcation between God's kingdom and all other kingdoms, so as to include within it whatever does belong to it; and so as to exclude from it whatever does not belong to it.

But you ask; Is not God's kingdom a universal one, an all-comprehending one? does it not, so to speak, reach to the very circumference of infinitude? Can there be anything sheer outside of it? Nay, if we could, according to the bold imagination of the poet, climb those walls

> "Whose battlements look o'er into the vale
> Of non-existence, *Nothing*'s strange abode,"

should we not, even in that solitude, and darkness, and vacuity, still behold God's kingdom?

Certainly, in a physical or dynamical sense, this is true. There *is* no outside to God's power. If immensity were any less, it would not contain all God's energy, for want of room. If eternity were any shorter, some part of the drama of God's providence must be omitted in the performance, for want of time.

But there is another sense, in which these facts are almost reversed. To make this more intelligible, let me resort to etymology and definition. The word *kingdom* is a compound word. Its first syllable, "king," means leader, ruler, sovereign, lord, and the last syllable, "dom," when used as a termination, denotes jurisdiction or property, as in the words, earldom, wisdom, freedom, &c. Earldom is the dominion of an earl; wisdom is the power of the wise; and freedom is the liberty of the free.

If, then, the kingdom of God means, intrinsically, the moral supremacy, the undisputed sway of God's holy law; and, if it means, geographically, the place where that law is supreme, unresisted, unquestioned, then the difficulty will consist rather in finding where God's kingdom is, than where it is not. We shall find trouble in tracing out the circumference or boundary of God's law, not because the included territory is so immensely large, but because it is so microscopically small. Where in the moral world, where in all the realms of mortal free-agency, of human accountability, is God's kingdom, or the reign of God's law, absolute, perfect, perpetual? — not a sin to cloud its cerulean sky, or curse its flowery earth; not a tongue silent, and every voice a concord! Alas, my friends, to find such a kingdom of God as this in our sin-stricken world, we must have some new geographer, some more successful explorer than Captain Parry or Sir John Franklin; we must discover some new region not yet laid down in any atlas, — in any *terra cognita*, or *terra incognita* of human history. For myself, I would sooner undertake to find the Northwest Passage in mid-winter, or to make a Coast Survey around the Antarctic Continent.

If the kingdom of God be "love, joy, peace, long-suffering, gentleness, goodness, faith, meekness, temperance;" if it be to love the Lord our God with all our heart, and our neighbor as ourselves; if it be to do unto others as we would have them do to us; if, in fine, it be to do all these things, and to feel all these things habitually, systematically, spontaneously, to practice them without the compulsion of fear, and to enjoy them without the hope of other reward, then, indeed, there is not a petty prince in Europe, across whose kingdom a horse could leap or an unfledged bird could fly, who has not a wider realm than He, the Author of all.

Was the kingdom of God established in those belligerent nations of Europe, so lately linked together in a death-grapple at each other's throats, wielding not only their own energies, but subsidizing the mighty powers of nature and the earnings of future generations, and aiming their blows at each other's hearts? Is the kingdom of God established in those vast regions of central Asia and Africa, whose deities are stocks and stones, — some fetich, some reptile, some monster; and whose worship even of these base deities consists of baser superstitions? "When the monkey is a God, what must the priest be? What the people under the priest?" Is the kingdom of God established in those self-called civilized nations, whose social condition necessitates great organizations of legislatures, judicial tribunals, executive officers, &c., for the punishment of crime; and even then half the criminals escape? The prison, the gibbet, the gallows, what loud-voiced witnesses are they respecting God's reign upon earth! Where is the community, the college, the academy, the school, in which it is necessary to promulgate no law but the law of God, and where that law is always obeyed? Where is the family in which there is not more or less of discord, of heart-burnings; where there are not many wills and many interests instead of one will and one interest? Oh, where is there an individual, — one man or one woman, — whose heart always points to God as the magnetic needle to its pole, and trembles, ay, quakes with fear, whenever a base attraction warps it, for a moment, from its true meridian?

Where war is, where slavery is, where licentiousness is, where fraud, cruelty, treachery, overreaching are, is the kingdom of God there? These thrust out that. The two cannot co-exist. The earth endured Christ's ministry only three years, — not three weeks after his real character and purposes were generally known.

But salvation for man, in its fullest sense, is only to be found in the kingdom of heaven; that is, it is only to be found in acts and feelings conformed to the will of God. There may, indeed, be a partial salvation. Salvation is not a unit from which nothing can be subtracted, and to which nothing can be added. If I was once a drunkard or a glutton, and afterwards, in view of the calamities and losses of drunkenness and gluttony, I repented, and subjected my life to the laws of sobriety and temperance, then I am so far saved. I am saved from the continued accumulation of the evils of inordinate indulgence; and by a life of rigid abstemiousness, I may from day to day mainly outgrow the consequences of my former folly and sin. So if I were once smitten with the insanity of gambling, and in view of its mischiefs, I disenchanted myself from its strange fascinations, then I am saved from the evils of gambling.

Even the worst men may have a certain quantum of salvation, although it falls far short of being a *quantum sufficit*. What else could Christ have meant when he said it should be more tolerable for Tyre and Sidon, ay, for Sodom and Gomorrah, than for those who had enjoyed his teachings and had contemned them? Salvation, therefore, in the full comprehensiveness of the word, can only be found in putting ourselves, — body, mind and soul, — into entire harmony with the laws of God.

But there is always, in man, the intensest desire for salvation. When the consequences of our wrong-doing overtake us in this life, then we desire to annihilate them; and when we look forward with a foreboding sense of the consequences, in another life, of our misconduct here, then we pray for some antidote, some remedy, some refuge and escape. This grows out of the very constitution of human nature. We are so made that we instinctively desire happiness and dread misery. I think we have an intuitive belief in immortality; that is, when the requisite ideas exist in the mind, the belief springs up spontaneously. Each man for himself says, *I shall live forever.* Education supplies this intuition with arguments, and fortifies and strengthens it into a firm, enduring conviction. Now, that immortality of existence, as it first presents itself to the mind, may be an immortality of happiness, or an immortality of woe — of rapture or of agony. The stronger desire doubtless is to avoid the pain. It is a less strong desire to enjoy the happiness; but both together constitute a motive of transcendent power; and every thoughtful human being means, in some way or another, before leaving this world, to obtain a guaranty of happiness in the next. With a very few anomalous cases, which may perhaps be called cases of insanity, no one means to cross the river of death without securing a blissful haven to land in on the other side. There is the most unaccountable procrastination, there is the grossest superstition in regard to the means; but the intention is unquestionable.

I propose to consider some of the different plans which men lay in order to get into the kingdom of God.

Heaven is commonly conceived of as a place, a locality, — as we conceive of the District of Columbia, or London, or Switzerland. Somewhere in God's universe it is supposed there is a spot where elemental storms never deform the sky; where inward sorrow never cankers the heart. There is rest after labor, peace after conflict, smiles after tears, and such happiness as quenches all fiery memories of former pain; and the common or popular notion is that when good men leave this world, they are translated, that is, transported to heaven, as an aeronaut sails off in a balloon. By what means, then, can men obtain assurance, and insurance, that when they die they will be borne away to the abodes of bliss, and not to the realms of sorrow?

I think there is one grand principle of human nature, which underlies all others and co-operates with all others, for securing a passport and an entrance to heaven. This principle is a selfish one, and it is to get into heaven on the cheapest terms practicable. As in common transactions men wish to buy much by paying little; as in common journeyings or voyagings men desire to get a railroad ticket or a steamboat ticket on the lowest terms; so the sinner, conscious that he deserves punishment and fearing that he shall receive it in some place outside of heaven, strives to obtain a safe passage to the realms of bliss with the least possible sacrifice of what he loves best here; and as the traveller who is about to perform a voyage across the Atlantic, selects the steamship or packet which has the best accommodations, the richest fare, the most comfortable and luxurious berths for his nightly repose, so many of the self-called disciples of Christ desire to worship in the most elegant and luxurious churches, where they can sleep away the tedium of their journey to heaven.

The missionaries to the Caroline Islands found a theology prevailing there, which exempted its believers from all responsibility about their future condition. The natives believed that their going to heaven or to hell, after death, did not depend at all upon their conduct in this life, or upon the state of the soul at death; but they held that after the soul had separated from the body, and while it was on its way to the spirit-land, it was met by companies of good and evil divinities who fought over it and for it, like Greek and Trojan over the dead body of Patroclus; and as one or the other of the combatants prevailed, the soul was borne away to Paradise or to Hades. So little idea had they of virtue, of morality, of duty; so little did they suppose their divinities cared about virtue, morality, and duty, that the soul's eternal destiny was to be decided by brute force, in a hand to hand combat, in which the soul itself was to be a mere looker on; an interested, but a powerless spectator.

So there have been sects in the Christian world, professing to derive their faith from that most eminently virtue-inculcating religion of Jesus Christ, who maintain that man's salvation depends exclusively upon what God does for him, and not at all upon what he does for himself. They believed that man is born in such a state of sin and misery, as ensures his ultimate perdition; that he can no more help himself out of that state, than a lump of lead falling through a vacuum, can unclench gravitation, and stop midway; — nay, to put his perdition beyond possibility of hope from himself, they go back and affirm that he was conceived in sin, and brought forth in iniquity ; — nay, to make his damnation a thousand times inevitable, they construct ramparts of impossibility against his salvation six thousand years off, by saying that he fell when Adam fell, and has been falling ever since ; — nay, again, they affirm that it was decreed by the Omnipotent and Unchangeable God, from all eternity, that human souls should be forever lost ; — so that, if such a man would be saved, he has got this problem to work out literally. He must go back to the time of his birth, and preside over that event, and not be born in a state of sin and misery ; he must go back and prevent his being conceived in sin ; he must go back to the time when Adam fell, and by main strength prevent his falling ; ay, pre-existently, and pre-Adamitically, he must go back into those recesses of eternity when God's decrees in relation to him were made, and make the Unchangeable God reconsider, and make those decrees the other way ; — all these things he must do, as preliminaries, as conditions precedent, before he can begin to do anything about saving himself. After he has prevented the immutable God from making His decrees ; after he has refused successfully to have Adam for his great progenitor, and been born of some outside lineage that exists nowhere ; after he has been present at his own formation, and birth, and compounded the moral elements out of which he should begin to be, then, and not till then, will the impossibilities be removed from his path, so that he can begin to take some measures towards effecting his own salvation. I am not now impugning this faith ; I am only attempting to state it.

But these two cases, — the case of the Caroline Islanders, whose chance of entering heaven depends upon the gladiatorial and pugilistic skill of friendly or adverse divinities; and the case of those Christian sects who believe they are saved without reference to their voluntary actions and affections in this life; — these two cases, I say, are exceptional, and by no means represent the religious faith of the mass of mankind. I know of no other heathen nation that leaves the moral nature and the moral character of man wholly out of account in their estimate of his future condition. All other heathen, all Mohammedans, and most Christians, set too high a value upon man's moral nature, and his virtuous conduct, not to affix future rewards and punishments to his present observance or violation of duty. It is only when some dogma of exclusive grace, or exclusive fatality, or exclusive luck, comes in, that a man's future destiny is supposed to be determined, without reference to his earthly merits or demerits; — that is, wholly independently of his moral character. Indeed, it is the *general* opinion, that if man's evil propensities are subdued wholly by a foreign force, not only without co-operation, but in spite of resistance from himself, that he might as well have been made virtuous by machinery, or gravitation, or steam-power.

If, then, we should for a moment recognize the popular belief that heaven and hell are places, geographical localities, as much so as Ohio and Missouri, how the one appeals to our hopes, how the other rouses our fears. These present transcendent motives for the practice of virtue, for abstinence from vice.

But, on the other hand, when we reflect upon the tremendous energy and vehemence of men's passions and appetites, how in the climax and madness of their paroxysms, they rush to their gratification, forgetful of all restraints, defiant of all consequences, — peril, torture, or death, — the ever revolving wheel of Ixion, the eternal thirst of Tantalus, the gory beak of the vulture of Prometheus, forever plucking at the culprit's heart; — when, I say, we consider all this, how infinite the good to be obtained, how horrible the woe to be avoided, and how fierce and fiery the earthly lusts to be gratified, what wonder is it, if men do try ten thousand schemes, and exhaust all human ingenuity, to obtain that future good, and to avoid that future evil, *both* at the least possible sacrifice of this world's gratifications?

The conqueror, to whom a city turned to ashes, and strewn with the dead, seems more valuable if he can say, "It is mine," than the same city, though vocal with prosperity and joy, if not his own, says: "Can I not indulge my rage for conquest on earth, and still win admission to heaven at last?"

The avaricious man says: "Can I not hoard treasures in this world, and still, near the close of life" — (not too early, because treasures laid up in heaven are unproductive capital) — "financier so shrewdly as to have treasures laid up for me in heaven also?"

The polygamist says; "Can I not have my harem here below, and still find Cyprian chambers among the Houris above?"

The intemperate man says: "Can I not revel in the intoxicating draught while I live upon earth, and then sit down with Jesus Christ to drink wine with the redeemed in the New Jerusalem above?"

The kidnapper says: "Even though I do rob men of the right to their own bodies and their own souls, and women of the right to their children and their virtue, yet, if I repent on my death-bed, will not the Infinite Redeemer give me, too, a passport to heaven; nay, have I not been told all my life long that Christ came from heaven, and died on the Cross to meet just such desperate cases as mine?"

The veteran sinner, his heart concreted of guilt, and his hands clotted with innocent blood, — the cosmopolite in the world of crime, at home everywhere, who can speak all its wicked languages, and is dextrous, ambidextrous, at all its infernal acts, cannot he, too, rely on the mercies of the same Redeemer, and when about to be launched from the gallows into eternity, use these very gallows as his pedestal, and so reach the realms of glory by a shorter flight? Does not much of the doctrine we hear from the pulpit sanction all this?

But selfishness and ignorance have invented even cheaper ways than these of getting to heaven easy. Some people expect to cajole St. Peter, and "run the gate" which leads to everlasting bliss, by tricks and shams, that would not deceive the meanest toll-collector on the meanest bridge or ferry in this world, — the Catholics, by saying prayers in an unknown tongue; the Orientals, by winding off written prayers from one cylinder into another; the Jews, among whom domestic animals were plentiful, by offering sacrifices of lambs, or doves, or bullocks; the Chinese, among whom provisions are scarce, by offering the less costly incense of perfumed paper and contemptible toys? A few years ago, a violent feud sprung up, which split in two a religious sect in Pennsylvania, on the question whether their garments should be fastened by hooks and eyes, or by buttons and button-holes; and in the State of Tennessee, within the last two months, a question was appealed to the Presbytery, whether the bread of the Lord's Supper should be cut or broken! Kneeling or standing in prayer; marrying a deceased wife's sister, &c., &c., are also subjects of difference of opinion. And how universal the practice of seeking heaven by the persecution of others, instead of self-repentance and reformation; of burning heresies out of other men, instead of extinguishing evil passions in ourselves.

Now there is one deep and deplorable falsity, lying at the bottom of all expectations of getting to heaven in any of these ways. That falsity Christ exposes, when he says, "For the kingdom of heaven is *within you.*" Yes, the kingdom of God is *within us*, or *for us*, my friends, or it is nowhere. It is not afar off, in some starry realm; in some distant temple, floored with gold, canopied with glittering gems, adorned with divine arts beyond Phidias and Praxiteles, beyond Raphael, or Wren, — the Vatican, or the Alhambra. The kingdom of heaven is not in any externals of pomp or dominion, of luxury, or of fame. It is in our own hearts, I say, or, for us, it is non-existent. What, then, is this kingdom of heaven, which must exist in our own consciousness, or have no existence? Let me answer in the very words of Holy Writ. It is to fear God, and keep His commandments. Is is to love the Lord our God with all our hearts, and our neighbors as ourselves. It is to do to others as we would be done by. It is righteousness, peace, and joy in the Holy Ghost. We are not, then, to go abroad, exploring after the kingdom of heaven. That kingdom must be inaugurated in ourselves, — in our feelings, thoughts, lives, in all our aspirations for future excellence, in all visions of future bliss, — in what we do when alone, in what we do before our families, our neighbors, the world. All else is fable. One man cannot have this kingdom for another man, — husband for wife, nor wife for husband, father for child, nor child for father, minister for people, nor people for minister. Go round the world, then, and shout it in the ears of all living men; rouse Heathen, Brahmin, Mohammedan, Christian; make the dead hear, — the dead in trespasses and sins, — command them no longer to explore the realms of space, in quest of the kingdom of heaven; no longer to seek for water-carriage, or air-carriage, — for canvas, or for wings by which to sail or soar to some lofty heaven, or seventh heaven, high up in the zenith, or far away beyond Arcturus, or the Pleiades; for know, that the first truth of all truths, and the greatest truth of all truths, is this; that heaven must be in our own thoughts, affections, and conduct, or, for us, there is no heaven anywhere.

> "The mind is its own place,
> And in itself can make a heaven of hell,
> A hell of heaven."

Is not the argument that leads to this conclusion, founded on the primitive rock?

The ancient heathen, the neighbors and contemporaries of the Jews, believed they could propitiate their gods by sacrifices, by human sacrifices, by sacrifices of their own children, whom they made pass through the fire to Moloch. They were conscious of sinning against their gods. They feared their avenging wrath. How could they appease them? By a sacrifice of something they loved. They loved their children, and so, on bloody and on fiery altars the children were offered up. The innocent babe, the noble boy, the beautiful girl; — the priests thrust or hurled them, shrieking, into the flames, as they would cast in billets of wood. See here the iniquity of a wicked heart. They did not offer to the gods that for which they cared nothing. They were not so imbecile, or idiotic, as to suppose that the gods would accept as an atonement, what to them had no moral value in affection, nor any market value in cash. Hence they sacrificed what was really dear to them, their offspring. But they did not sacrifice what to them was dearest of all, — the sin itself. They gave up the child, but held fast to the sin, because the sin was dearer than the child. When mariners find their ship in peril of sinking, they lighten her by throwing the least valuable part of the cargo overboard. So the heathen hurled a darling child into the fire, hugged the more darling sin to his breast. They could give father, or mother, or wife, or child, to God, but could not give Him their heart.

Moses thought he made a great advance, and he did make a great advance, in that dispensation which symbolized repentance and reformation by the sacrifice of animals, — of doves, and pigeons, and goats, and rams, and bullocks, — for the sacrifice of children. There was no inhumanity in this; nothing that makes us shudder and recoil, as we should do, at seeing a beautiful, innocent child tossed into the flames, or into a den of wild and hungry beasts; but the same false idea was liable to be propagated by this dispensation, as by the heathen rite, — the idea, namely, that there is, or with a holy being, can be, any sacrifice or atonement for sin, which can take the place of the repentance and reformation of the sinner himself. Hence, with what eloquent and vehement denunciations did the sages and prophets of the Hebrews inveigh against the substitution of an outward form for inward purity; until Christ came and swept away the old dispensation altogether. Hear the Psalmist; Ps. L. 9, &c., "I will take no bullock out of thy house, nor he-goats out of thy folds. For every beast of the forest is mine, and the cattle upon a thousand hills. I know all the fowls of the mountains; and the wild beasts of the field are mine. If I were hungry, I would not tell thee; for the world is mine, and the fulness thereof. Will I eat the flesh of bulls, or drink the blood of goats?" Here the key-note changes from denunciation to promise,—"Call upon me in the day of trouble, I will deliver thee." "Whoso offereth praise, glorifieth me; *and to him that ordereth his conversation aright*, will I show the salvation of God." In what plaintive, yet indignant tones does Isaiah repel the preposterous supposition that there can be any sacrifice *for* a sin but the sacrifice *of* the sin itself. "To what purpose is the multitude of your sacrifices unto me? saith the Lord; I am full of the burnt-offerings of rams, and the fat of fed beasts; and I delight not in the blood of bullocks, or of lambs, or of he-goats." "Bring no more vain oblations. Incense is an abomination unto me. The new moons and sabbaths, the calling of assemblies, I cannot away with. It is iniquity, even the solemn meeting. Your new moons and your appointed feasts my soul hateth; they are a trouble unto me; I am weary to bear them." Here, again, the key-note changes. "Wash you, make you clean, put away the evil of your doings from before mine eyes; cease to do evil; learn to do well; seek judgment; relieve the oppressed; judge the fatherless; plead for the widow." * But Christ was greater than the

* Isaiah i. 11 &c.

Psalmist, greater than the prophet, and he abolished all this subterfuge of substitution; and the author of the Epistle to the Hebrews condenses the whole philosophy of the thing into a single sentence, when he says; "For it is not possible that the blood of bulls and of goats should take away sins."

What, then, must be done, not to secure us a traveller's passport into some yonder kingdom of heaven, but to introduce, to naturalize, to domesticate the kingdom of heaven in our own hearts? My friends, one thing is certain; — before we can get the kingdom of heaven in, we must get the kingdom of Satan out. All arrogance, all haughtiness, all envy, all malice, all cruelty, all evil concupiscence, of whatever kind, must be rooted out of the soul. We must hunt evil passions out of our bosom, as pioneers hunt out noxious animals from a newly settled territory.

I pass by such gross offences as robbery, bribery, perjury, theft, embezzlement, peculation, &c.; — these, even the blear-eyed goddess of the law denounces, — but if I have an account to settle with a man, and he has forgotten an item of debit, or overstated an item of credit; if he should make an error in my favor in counting money, or in any way is unintentionally about to give me one cent, one mill, one infinitesimal, over and above my honest due, I must swallow arsenic into my stomach, or shoot lead into my brain, sooner than drop that money into my purse. If I have a rival for public honors, and see that the votes are passing over from my side to his side; if I have a neighboring farmer or merchant, and he is making money faster than I; if I have a college mate, or a school mate, whose talent and attainment are eclipsing mine, and their merits are brought into discussion in my presence, I must do them justice, full justice, — such justice as brightens out of justice into generosity, into magnanimity; and then, though I lose the earthly office for the next year, or four, or six years, yet I obtain an office in the celestial kingdom for eternity; instead of California gold, I get treasures that are incomputable, incorruptible, and for college honors, I get a moral diploma that admits me to the society of angels. If I am well-born, as the phrase is, — have parents of respectability, —wealth, education, social standing, and my classmate, neighbor, fellow-citizen, was born of infamous progenitors, for ten generations back, without a single break in the base lineage; — was taken from a Foundling Hospital, or dropped in a sty; was born black, or red, or copper-colored, — all these give me no sanction for one emotion of pride or vanity, on account of my better fortune in these particulars. If it could have been submitted to him and to me beforehand, under what circumstances we should be born, and he had chosen his fortune, and I had chosen mine, then I might have some reason for self-gratulation or complacency. But when such a man looks at me with respect and appreciation, and I look at him with derision and scorn, then it is that we do choose our circumstances; then it is that our souls do determine whether they will be high-born, or low-born; whether they will be bred up in a palace, or in a sty; whether they will be clad in garments of beauty and purity, or in rags of meanness and filth. If I exercise acts of cruelty, and indulge feelings of contempt towards a good black man, because his skin is black, and my skin is white, then my heart is black, and his heart is white, and I carry my black heart about, and show it as a foul beggar shows his sores. It is of comparatively little consequence where a man was born, but it is of infinite consequence what sort of man he is, twenty years after he is born. If my neighbor is unfortunate, and I do not pity and succor his misfortune to the extent of my ability, then it is I who have suffered the greatest misfortune. My want of pity is a greater privation than his want of prosperity. A man had better be burnt out of house and home, than to have all the generosity and nobleness of his nature consumed by pride or envy. The one loss consists in money, stocks, goods. The other loss consists in high thoughts, angelic emotions, god-like deeds, and the everlasting peace of soul that flows therefrom, like the river of life from the throne of God.

But you say the loser does not know his loss, and therefore it is no loss to him. But he will know it, and when he does find out, he will then also find out that his loss has been accumulating at compound interest all the time while he was ignorant of it. It is not pleasant for a man to discover, late in life, that through all his previous years he has been a dunce; that he has been a pauper, when there was an inheritance of wealth he might have had for the claiming. In God's moral universe, the selfish man is the miserablest of all dunces, and all paupers. The selfish man lives on the most nauseous food, when he might regale himself with heavenly repasts. He lives in basement stories, instead of in those chambers where he could look out upon all the glories of nature, and where the purity and freshness of nature could flow in upon him. The selfish man dresses himself in rags, instead of in royal robes, and he is the serf and slave of the hardest master, instead of investing his capital in heavenly treasures, and being admitted as co-worker and co-partner with God.

Now our human passions and propensities are inexpressibly strong, and it is these which keep the selfish man in chains. We have them in common with the brutes, and with an intellect to enlarge their indulgence, which the brutes have not. These passions and propensities are not only strong by nature, but they have been hereditarily inflamed, for generations and centuries past, by ancestral folly and ignorance. Their natural force has been reinforced. They have accumulated momentum in the descent. They are blind. They are atheistic. They mutiny and rebel against all higher law than their own; and they wage the war not only with their own but with ancestral rigor. Owing also to the vicious customs of many households and of society at large, even the hereditary force of passion and propensity which we inherited from our progenitors has been aggravated in our own persons. When, then, at the age of discretion and self-consciousness, we wake up to find the impetuosity and vehemence, the recklessness and defiance of our passional nature, we find that steeds of hell have been harnessed to the chariot of heaven. Conscience, then, must be a puissant charioteer, or the team drives home to its own place, and bears passengers with it.

My friends, I need not speak in metaphor. The solemn and eternal truth is that our appetites and passions must be subjected to the sway of conscience, of benevolence, of a holy reverence for our Creator. We must do justly, love mercy, and walk humbly with God; or, whatever we may say about conversion, or regeneration, or redemption, or even salvation itself, is all fiction and a silly romance. Here comes the conflict. Here the nether and the upper powers battle for their throne in the heart; — the love of God and the love of man, on the one side, fleshly lusts, pride, avarice, ambition, on the other. Here in the moral realm, in the soul itself, are victories to be won or defeats to be sustained, infinitely more glorious or more disastrous than those of Trafalgar or Waterloo. Here, if need be, right hands are to be cut off to destroy the very instrument with which we procure the indulgence of a darling sin; and right eyes plucked out, to close up the avenue by which licentious images invade the soul. In these contests, bloody sweat must flow, like that shed in the garden of Gethsemane. Yes, here the sovereign soul may have to stretch its body upon a cross to be racked with unutterable agonies within, and to bear scorn and mockery from without, for days and for nights; but if the contest be nobly maintained, if, in the language of that beautiful Hebraism, we "unsin the sin that we have sinned," then the kingdom of heaven, ay, heaven's King Himself will be within it, and He will strengthen it with the resources of omnipotence, and illumine it with the splendors of celestial light, and clothe it with that highest of all conceivable beauties, "the Beauty of Holiness."

Listen to me, my young friends, one moment more, while I ask the question: "Who has this kingdom of heaven within him, and who has not? What is the test?" If there are infallible tests by which we distinguish the different races of men from each other — the Caucasian from the African, or the North American Indian from the Malay; if there are obvious tests by which we distinguish the different temperaments of men, — the sanguine from the nervous, &c ; if there are tests by which we know the healthy and the diseased, the consumptive and the dropsical, then there must be tests, *criteria*, still more evident and decisive, by which we can distinguish those in whose hearts the kingdom of God bears its benignant sway from those where the kingdom of Satan holds its direful reign. From the metropolis of the soul, as the centre of these opposite kingdoms, the celestial or the infernal light shines beyond the frontiers. It gleams out through the face, it proclaims itself in language, it demonstrates itself in deeds, in the life. What are these tests? Christ has given us one of them in these words: "The tree is known by its fruit." He has given us another in these words: "Herein is my father glorified, that ye bear much fruit." Most impressively, most sublimely, has he given another of them, — a universal one, — in those immortal words which breathe the music of heaven, — when he identifies himself with the hungry, with the thirsty, with the stranger, with the naked, with the sick, with the imprisoned, and declares that those who have fed and clothed and visited and succored them, in their poverty, their loneliness and their abandonment, have fed and clothed and visited and succored him.

My young friends, who can doubt that the kingdom of heaven was in Christ's bosom? If then we would have that kingdom in our bosoms, let us identify ourselves in spirit and action with him.

MEDITATION.

Our Father who art in Heaven, may Thy kingdom come and Thy will be done on earth, as it is in Heaven. And to effect this great and divine purpose, may all governments be conformed to Thy attributes of justice, and love, and mercy, from the governments of parents in their families, and teachers in their schools, to the governments of states and nations, and to those great principles which govern communities of nations. May parents so wisely administer their parental authority, that they may rear their children in the nurture and admonition of the Lord; may they train them to such habits of wisdom and goodness, that when emancipated from parental control, they will not cease to walk therein. May all teachers, while they instruct their scholars in the elements of worldly knowledge and science, also imbue their minds with that fear of the Lord which is the beginning of wisdom; may they lead them to cast away all evil habits, to keep the tongue pure from profanity and falsehood, and all irreverence towards sacred things; to train them to true manliness of conduct, and to all the virtues and graces of true womanhood. May all governments be established upon the basis of equal laws and equal rights, and may no distinctions be known in their administration but that of merit and demerit, of a desire to do good or a disposition to do evil.

Our Father, we would thank Thee for those events in Thy Providence which have led onward towards the education, the advancement, the freedom of the world; for those noble sentiments of ancient poets and moralists, which still kindle the sacred flame of liberty whenever they fall upon the hearts of the young; for those events which roused the souls of men to demand from their rulers the just and equal rights which Thou dost bestow upon all. We thank Thee that when oppression covered the eastern hemisphere as the waters cover the sea, the cloud which had hung for ages over this western hemisphere was removed, and this vast expanse of lands, with its immense capabilities of supporting human life and ministering to human happiness, was revealed to the knowledge of men. We thank Thee that the Pilgrim Fathers were inspired by a zeal that led them to abandon their native land, to encounter the perils of a wide ocean, and to fix their abode on a soil so ungenial, under a climate so severe, and with surrounding perils of savage beasts and more savage men, so imminent, that ambition, and wealth, and luxury, and the love of power, had no disposition to pursue the fugitives.

Oh, Heavenly Father, may we never repeat the wrongs from which they fled. May we never light the fires of persecution by which they were burned. While the law of the land secures to every one the right to worship Thee according to the dictates of his own conscience, may we carry out that law in its spirit, and may we never visit with revilings, with uncharitableness, or with coldness, any one of all our brethren of the human race, because he does not see Thy paternal love or Thy character as we see it. We thank Thee for all our means of moral, literary and religious instruction, for the school, the college, and the church. Heavenly Father, under Thy providence, and under the auspices of good men, a college has been founded in this place, and a great company of youth, the pride and the hope of the land have been assembled, — the only depositaries into whose hands the mighty interests of the earth for the coming age can be devolved. They left the homes of their childhood, — may they find here another and a more instructive home. Oh, how many fathers, how many mothers are looking hitherward to-day! If any sons, if any daughters of this flock are tempted to wander from the path of duty, may they feel the motherly arm stretched around their neck, may the strong paternal hand be laid upon their breast, holding them back from the way of evil. Oh, may they not wait for the external force, but may the inward law of right, written upon their hearts, restrain them from wrong. And oh, if any of these children are orphans, if father and mother have gone to the better land, and they, left without parental guidance, are tempted to sin, may they see, as it were, a mother's arm stretching down from the realms of bliss, may they feel her celestial cheek laid upon their cheek, while her angel voice whispers into their ears; "My son, my daughter, if sin entice thee, consent thou not;" and may a father's sterner voice send a thrill of horror through them, as he announces the dreadful, the immortal truth; "*The way of the transgressor is hard.*" And oh, Heavenly Father, if they are not melted by a father's or a mother's love, may they be melted by Thy Infinite Love. Heavenly Father, Thy true disciples are already blessed more than tongue of mortal can tell, but bless, we pray Thee, our enemies and those who would persecute us and despitefully use us, and let Thy kingdom come, and Thy will be done on earth as it is in Heaven.

IMMORTALITY.

XI.

IMMORTALITY.

PSALM viii. 5. — "For Thou hast made him a little lower than the angels, and hast crowned him with glory and honor"

6. "Thou madest him to have dominion over the works of Thy hands; Thou hast put all things under his feet."

2 TIMOTHY i. 10. — "Jesus Christ, who hath abolished death, and hath brought life and immortality to light, —"

ECCLESIASTES xii. 7. — "Then shall the dust return to earth as it was, and the spirit shall return unto God who gave it."

ONE of the grandest and most precious doctrines of the Christian religion, is the doctrine of human Immortality. The meaning of this doctrine is, that there is something in us all, which fire cannot consume, nor waters drown, nor death assail; that each one of us has an individuality, an identity, a personality, which is unsusceptible of decay, impregnable to corruption, without possibility of perishing.

Christ taught that we should live after the death of the body; and his disciples reiterated his teachings. Paul, in his Epistle to the Romans, promised "eternal life" to all those who should patiently continue in well-doing. In the 15th chapter of his First Epistle to the Corinthians, he twice declares, in the most explicit manner, that this mortal shall put on Immortality; and, in his Second Epistle to Timothy, he affirms that Christ "abolished death," and "brought life and Immortality to light through the Gospel."

The idea of Immortality differs from that of Eternity. We conceive of Immortality as having a beginning, but no end; but we conceive of Eternity as having neither beginning nor end. Hence it is proper to speak of eternity as the attribute of God; but of immortality as the attribute of man.

This doctrine of Immortality, though under the most various forms, has constituted a prominent item in the faith of almost all religions. It seems, therefore, natural to man. We say that vegetation is natural to the earth, because, whenever the requisite conditions co-exist, there vegetation springs up. So this idea of Immortality, with very few exceptions, seems to have sprung up spontaneously in the human mind. The ideas of the eternity of God, and the immortality of man, go naturally together. As soon as the conception of a Future Existence is once formed, then the sentiments of Hope and Fear fortify and deepen it. Men, too, have a natural expectation of reward for doing well; they have as natural a sentiment of Fear, of Retribution for doing ill; and if they are to be rewarded or punished, this necessitates the idea of a time in which they are to receive their deserts.

Most nations first conceived of the World of Spirits as subterranean. Here we must recollect that in ancient times, and before the globular form of the earth was known, the best geographers supposed the earth to be an extended plane. The firmament was an indefinitely vast space above it; and, of course, there was an indefinitely vast space below, or under it. Some of the ancients supposed that the place of happiness was above, and the place of retribution below. Others, as the Romans, enlightened, or comparatively enlightened as they were, placed both their Paradise and their Hades below. Some nations have but one place, occupied in common by all the dead, though with different fortunes for the good and the evil. Most religions have, at least, two such places. The Persians had seven different regions, adapted, of course, to seven different grades of moral character. The Hindoos had twenty-four, thus making provision for still further discriminations in regard to human deserts. I think the New Testament teaches an indefinite number of degrees, or gradations, in the future condition of mankind; not seven only, not twenty-four only, but just as many grades as there are degrees of merit, or demerit. How else are we to understand what Christ says of its being more tolerable for Tyre and Sidon, and even for Sodom, in the day of judgment, than for the cities where he had preached, and which refused to hear? How otherwise are we to understand his words, "In my Father's house are many mansions?" and the parable of the talents; that those who had been faithful over a few things here on earth, should be promoted to the command of many things hereafter. The inevitable implication is, that our condition hereafter is to have relation to our character here.

Another doctrine which has gained almost universal acceptance throughout Christendom, is closely allied to this parent-doctrine of a Future Life, — namely, the doctrine of the Bodily Resurrection, a belief that the very body which dies, is decomposed, is restored to its original chemical particles, and mingles its solid parts with the solid material of the earth, its gases with the winds, and its fluids with the waters, — shall come together again, atom to atom, bone to bone, fibre to fibre, and reconstruct the body which the spirit left.

The common idea of Christendom has been, that the spirits of all the millions and millions of men who have ever lived, would, at the Judgment Day, by some mysterious affinity, find out the particles of matter from which they had been separated at death, gather them into a body, and then re-enter that body, in order to receive, in the very body which they had inhabited, while upon earth, the rewards or punishments of the Future Life. In Cruden's Concordance, a work in almost universal use as a book of reference, under the word "Resurrection," we find the common belief of the age thus stated:

"The Divine Laws are the rule of duty to the entire man, and not to the soul only; and they are obeyed or violated by the soul and body in conjunction. The soul designs, the body executes. The senses are the open ports to admit temptations. Carnal affections deprave the soul, corrupt the mind, and mislead it. The heart is the fountain of profaneness, and the tongue expresses it. *Thus the members are instruments of iniquity*. And if the body is obedient to the holy soul in doing, or suffering for God, and denies its sensual appetites and satisfactions, in compliance with reason and grace, *the members are instruments of righteousness.* Hence it follows," says he, "that there will be a universal *resurrection*, that the rewarding goodness of God may appear in making the bodies of his servants gloriously happy with their souls, and their souls completely happy in union with their bodies, to which they have a natural inclination; and His revenging justice may be manifest in punishing the bodies of the wicked with eternal torments answerable to their guilt."

This idea continued to prevail even among learned and philosophic divines, until recently; and even now, I suppose, it is held by a great majority of the Christian Church.*

In modern times, however, science has asserted its claims to be heard on this subject, in the same way that, heretofore, it asserted its right to be heard on the questions of Geology, and Astronomy, and Psychology, &c.; and, at last, after almost incredible opposition and obloquy, has made itself heard, and respected.

Science asks such questions as these: Suppose some portions of the world to have been so populous, that, already, some of the identical material which has been incorporated into the bodies of one generation, has decayed, passed into the great laboratory of nature, been used again for the growth of fruit or vegetable, and from these has been re-incorporated into the bodies,

* I have a very vivid recollection that in one of the school books most extensively used in the public schools of New England, when I was a boy, there was a description of the Resurrection, in poetry, in which the air was represented as filled, and the sun as almost darkened, by the parts and fragments of men, — heads, arms, legs, &c., — on their way across continents. and over oceans, to meet and join the bodies to which they respectively belonged. And so deeply did that affect my mind, that I remember distinctly the old school-house in which I was sitting, and all the attendant circumstances, as clearly as if it had been but yesterday. And though I accepted the general statement as true. with childish trustfulness, yet it did puzzle me. even at that tender age, to conceive, if one member had been lost in one country, and another in another; if a soldier or sailor had lost an arm in one battle, and a leg in another, on another continent, or on a distant ocean, how the scattered fragments would know which way to steer to find their fellows!

and made part of the living tissues of another generation. Suppose the world should continue for such a round of ages, that this should be true of all its habitable regions? Or, take the case of the cannibal nations, where neighboring tribes are constantly making war upon each other, and where the universal custom is, and we know not for how many ages, has been, for the victors to banquet on the vanquished; where, among themselves, when a malefactor is put to death under the law, it is a part of his sentence, not only that he shall be executed, but that his body shall be given up to be eaten, as some of our laws give up the body to be dissected; and where, as late British travellers tell us, in regard to the Caroline Islands, female children have been considered so great a delicacy for epicures, as seriously to diminish the number of adult women, and where, therefore, the only method to save them was to pass laws for their protection, as we pass laws for the protection of useful birds. In all these cases, and cases like these, do not the plainest facts of Physiology and growth assure us that the same particles of matter must have successively formed the tissues, the heart, the blood, and the brain, of many different persons? To whom, then, in the resurrection, shall the materials, which constituted a part of so many different bodies, belong? Or, if a devoted missionary, full of that zeal for the spread of Christianity, which bears him, like wings, across continents and oceans, to preach the Gospel to the heathen, shall himself be devoured by the heathen he went to save; and by the common law of assimilation, shall find himself distributed in particles through the substance of the bodies of a dozen maneaters, shall he, at the resurrection, according to the quotation which I read, go with the cannibals to perdition, or they with him to glory?

Suppose a man, like St. Paul before his conversion, goes mad against Jesus Christ and his disciples, assists in the martyrdom of Stephen, drags men and women to prison, punishes them whenever he finds them in the Synagogue, compels them to blaspheme, and persecutes them into strange cities; suppose that while in this rabid and tigerish state of mind, he loses the very right arm with which he is wont to execute his ferocious will; and then, like St. Paul after his conversion, concentrates all the energies of his life for the cause of Christianity, braves the dangers of the sea, and the more formidable dangers of cities on the land; submits to hunger, to imprisonment and stripes, and at last to death, and never shrinks, under any circumstances, from fidelity to truth; in the resurrection shall that sinful right arm be joined to that sainted body; or, according to the doctrine I cited, shall it suffer forever in the future world, because it had been the "instrument of evil" in this?

Besides, if there is a foundation for the common notion that all the particles of a man's body change once in seven years, (and there is no doubt that the greater part of them change much oftener than that), then what is to prevent some of these particles, even in communities not cannibal, from belonging successively to different persons? And of all the sets of particles which have successively belonged to the body of an aged man, with which set shall he re-habilitate himself at the resurrection, — with those of which he was composed in infancy, or in middle life, or in old age? — if he were seventy years old when he died, with which of the seventy sets of which he consisted in the seventy years of his earthly sojourn? If not with the whole, which would be enormous, then there must be a selection; and if a selection, then which shall be taken and which rejected? Is it answered that those particles only of which a man consisted at the moment of death shall be borne by his spirit into the next life? Shall this be literally true in regard to persons who have perished by starvation at sea, or in deserts, or in besieged cities, or by emaciating consumptions, or other wasting disease, which has left nothing but skin as a vesture to nothing but bones? — or would the soul have a choice; and could it select those which had clothed it in its moments of highest virtue?

Shall the smallest infant that dies, in this world, be only an infant in stature at the resurrection, and the largest Anak an Anak by his side?

To meet these and similar objections which will not be silenced, that learned philosopher and divine, Dr. Edward Hitchcock, the late President of Amherst College, Massachusetts, suggested and maintained a perfectly revolutionary idea. He said that every human body is composed of a certain quantity of carbon and nitrogen, mingled with a certain quantity of water, and that to constitute the identity of any individual, — to constitute the same body of the same person, — it was not necessary to have the *same*, but only *so much* of the ingredients of which the body was composed; that is, if a man at the time of his death should weigh one hundred and sixty pounds, and should, therefore, speaking in the language of chemistry, consist of about "fifty pounds of carbon and nitrogen diffused through six pailfuls of water," then, at the resurrection, it would only be necessary to put the same amount of carbon, nitrogen and water into an exactly similar form, no matter where the ingredients came from, in order to make the same man. According to this view, a man might die and leave his body in North America, but at the resurrection, the body of that man might be recreated out of chemical ingredients taken from Australia or the Sandwich Islands, and he would be the same man.

Such is the doctrine, not long since put forth by that eminent evangelical divine and scholar, Dr. Hitchcock, in order to reconcile the current interpretation of the Bible with the present condition of science.

I have been led into this digression, because the idea of the resurrection branched so naturally out of the doctrine of a future life.

It is a curious and somewhat unaccountable fact that the earlier Jews had a less clear, definite and vivid conception of a future state of existence, than other ancient nations. It is the belief of many, perhaps of most theologians, that the Pentateuch, — the five books of Moses, — the first five books of the Old Testament, contain no reference whatever to the doctrine of a Future life. Even in the second commandment of the Decalogue, as it is found in the 20th chapter of Exodus, one of the threats denounced against the fathers for their iniquities, is, that the consequence of those iniquities shall be visited upon their children unto the third and fourth generation, that is, upon children, grandchildren and great-grandchildren, at least; but not that those iniquities should be visited upon the offenders themselves in a future life.

Afterwards, however, the idea cleared up, either into a more positive denial, or a more positive affirmation of the doctrine. The fact seems to be both affirmed and denied in the Book of Job. What can be a stronger negation than when Job says (xiv. 7), "For there is hope of a tree if it be cut down, that it will sprout again, and that the tender branch thereof will not cease. Though the root therefore wax old in the earth, and the stock die in the ground, yet through the scent of water it will bud, and bring forth boughs like a plant. But man dieth and wasteth away; yea, man giveth up the ghost and where is he? As the waters fail from the sea, and the flood decayeth and drieth up; so man lieth down and riseth not; till the heavens be no more, they shall not awake, nor be raised out of their sleep." And again, a little further on; "If a man die, shall he live again?" He may, however, mean, shall he live again *upon this earth?* while he may still have held to the doctrine of a shadowy spirit-land, somewhere outside of this world, or perhaps inside of it. How emphatic is the denial in Ecclesiastes iii. 18 – 22!

"For I said in mine heart concerning the estate of the sons of men, that God might manifest them, and that they might see that they themselves are beasts. For that which befalleth the sons of men befalleth beasts; even one thing befalleth them; as the one dieth, so dieth the other; yea, they all have one breath, so that a man hath no pre-eminence above a beast; for all is vanity. All go into one place; all are of the dust, and all turn to dust again. Who knoweth the spirit of a man that goeth upward, and the spirit of a beast that goeth downward to the earth? Wherefore I perceive that there is nothing better than that a man should rejoice in his own works; for that is his portion;

for who shall bring him to see what shall be after him?"

In the Apocrypha, the idea of Immortality is set forth with great clearness. It seems that the Jews, during the Babylonish captivity, must have become familiar with the views on this subject then prevailing in the East.

But in the New Testament, as was before intimated, the doctrine of Immortality is stated with great emphasis, in the most explicit manner, and with an earnestness and solemnity which shows it to have been one of the principal facts in the consciousness of both speaker and writer. When not expressly affirmed, it is constantly assumed. Every thing, — parable, narrative, doctrine, exhortation, — becomes disproportionate and preposterous, without this. The idea of Immortal life is the grand reconciling idea of the New Testament.

Having now considered the meaning of the doctrine of Immortality, — that it implies the existence of something within us which is indestructible, something that not only *may* live, but *must* live, I proceed to the consideration of the proofs of this doctrine which may be derived from reason and conscience, — from what is appropriately called Natural Religion.

And in the first place, it seems to me that no little weight should be attached to the almost universal instinct, or conscious expectation of Immortality in the human mind. This is nearly or quite universal. Does any one say it is universal, because it has been universally taught? But who taught the first teacher? And what gave this belief such amazing force that it has been able to brave all the repulsive and abhorrent doctrines which have been connected with it, or engrafted upon it, in different ages of the Christian Church? I suppose I should have the concurrence of all the sects in Christendom to the proposition, that there have been times when the prevalent ideas appertaining to this doctrine were so dishonoring to the character of God and so repugnant to the reason of men, that if any plausible pretence for denying it could have been seized upon, it would have been denied. Nay, I can conceive that at some periods of Christian history good men might have been tempted to inculcate a belief in annihilation and to preach annihilation, as a pious fraud, in order to escape the remorseless views of a future life which were then current. Why then has the common instinct of mankind fastened with such tenacity upon the idea of an interminable future for us all, if that was not only an error, but such a repulsive one?

It is an idea now almost universally prevalent among thinking men, that the world without us and the world within us, have, by divine wisdom and skill, been so adapted to each other, that each of them *means*, *signifies*, *implies*, *prefigures* the other; — that our perceptive faculties *import* or *suggest*, so to speak, all their related objects in the properties and qualities of the external world; that our reflective faculties in the same way *imply* the wonderful laws and adaptations of nature; and that our relations to our fellow-men and to God might be *inferred* from our moral and religious nature, by a being of a sufficiently penetrating and comprehensive intellect, in the same way that a man, who should see from day to day and from year to year how a chronometer works, would at length come to the conclusion that it was made to measure time. All wise systems of education are founded upon this principle. For one who fully comprehends the human lungs to deny the existence of air, or who fully comprehends the structure of the human eye to deny the existence of light, is as if a man should deny that he ever had a mother. Now, why should there not be a related object, namely, Immortality, as the correlative, or correspondent, of this general instinct or expectation of Immortality?

It is objected that, though the belief in Immortality is general, yet that this belief has assumed and still advocates the most contradictory forms; and that these forms have been nothing more than an embellishment or exaggeration of the good or ill learned from experience; and therefore, that heaven or hell is nothing more than a Camera Obscura reflection of this world, without any independent existence, and therefore perishing or ceasing to be, as soon as the objects are removed which produced it; — I reply that the Form of the belief, the Concrete of it, is of no consequence. We should expect beforehand that this belief would contain error, more or less. Perhaps all error has not yet been eliminated from any one science; but this does not destroy our faith in the sciences. So neither should the absurdity, preposterousness, or monstrosity of the notions associated with the belief in a futurity impair our faith in the doctrine; nay, the historical argument becomes stronger, when we consider how men have clung to it, in spite of all the enormities associated with it.

Without the Love of Life, or Vitativeness, as Phrenologists call it, man would not be fitted for a world like this. The accumulation, at certain points, in personal experience, of disappointments, pains, or calamities, would be too strong for us (for the link once broken could not be restored), and therefore the world would be depopulated by suicide, were we not fastened to it by a special instinct. And this Love of Life was given to us to carry us over those dangerous places where neither present nor prospective enjoyment could counterbalance the pressure and vehemence of present ills. Now, as this Love of Life implies the fact of Old Age, (unless some foreign force intervenes), and as Old Age, when it comes, quietly relaxes and unclasps this Love of Life, while it increases the hope of future existence, (if the life has been worthily spent), why, I say, by parity of reasoning, does not this instinct of Immortality imply, nay, why, in logic, does it not *necessitate* Immortality? I do not see how those who understand and adopt this doctrine of complete and systematic adaptation of one thing to all, and of all to each one, throughout the universe, can bore a hole through the bottom of this argument without scuttling his own ship.

If the theory of several modern ethnologists should prove to be true; of whom, perhaps, Agassiz is the principal, who is earnestly supported by the traveller, Bayard Taylor, — namely, that the races of men have had a various origin; it seems to me that such a conclusion will add not a little force to the argument in favor of Immortality, which is derived from the common belief of mankind. How did peoples springing from various stocks, all come to concur in this faith? If it might have sprung up by accident in one race, could accident have originated it in all? On what other hypothesis then, than that the sentiment is a natural one, can the existence of it, so nearly, or quite universal, be explained? And if the sentiment be a natural one, and a natural one in all the races of men, how forcible the inference that it will have its corresponding fact in the history of man.

But I proceed to other considerations, which seem to me even more conclusive than this.

We have learned so much of the order of Providence, both in the natural and moral world, that where there are strong analogies in the circumstances, we expect to find analogies in results.

Think, then, for instance, of all the incomputable number of seeds that have ever come to maturity; of the specific principle of life which each contained; of the salient point where that life would begin its work of organization, just as soon as it should be subjected to the requisite conditions of moisture, and warmth, and air; and when the seed is subjected to those conditions, think of the radicle and plumule drawing their nourishment, first from the seed, and then pressing against its rind, or bark, or shell, and ready to burst from its confinement, — the radicle to penetrate into the earth in the form of roots, the plumule to ascend into the air in the form of stalk or trunk; and now what should we suppose if a man should rise up and tell us that every seed which had ever been subjected to these conditions, and had been brought to this point in the processes of germination and growth, should be forthwith annihilated? — that the radicle should never strike into the earth, that the plumule should never ascend into the air; that all should, at this expectant, prophetic point, be obliterated from existence. What should we think of the Contriver of such an order of nature, if he were the Destroyer also?

Think of all the eggs that have been formed by all

the oviparous races, — bird, reptile, or insect, — each egg supplied with the ingredients necessary to the formation of another individual of the same race. Take the egg of a bird; see, after one or two, or two or three days' incubation, according to its kind, a little spot where a heart begins feebly to beat. From this vital centre, see tissues beginning to radiate in all directions. The bones begin to appear. A ganglion of nerves indicates the future brain. The great system of blood-vessels is formed. A dot shows the place of the future eye; a point the place of the future ear. Phosphorus has been deposited in the yolk to yield phosphoric acid, from which to form the bones. Legs and wings at last spring out, supported by the complement of bones, and strung with the requisite muscles, and made sensitive with ten thousand nerves. The embryo bird has now exhausted its supply of food; it has outgrown its narrow limits; its legs are cramped by restraint; its wings struggle for expansion; and now, using its sharp bill as a pick, it begins to make a breach in the walls of its prison; and now it is ready for egress, fitted and equipped to walk on the ground, to swim the water, or to waft itself through the air, according to its kind. In an hour it shall be enlarged, and the horizon and the zenith shall be the only boundaries to its freedom. No, it shall never be enlarged; it shall be annihilated. That curious mechanism, those hollowed bones, fitted to take in the air, and buoy it aloft, that harp-like throat, instinct with song, which the greatest musician that ever lived would give all his fortune if he could call his own; those webbed feet, perhaps all ready, without an hour's apprenticeship, for perfect navigation; or that subtle instinct, by which, through a presentiment of unseen dangers, it can hang its nest away from harm; — all these are only a ridiculous toy, not made to exemplify wisdom and skill, or to confer happiness, but only to gratify whim and caprice, and back to nothingness they must go!

But what seems, to my causality, conclusive upon the subject, is a consideration which I need not enlarge upon before reflecting men. Such men must have thought out the relations of things so fully, that I need do but little more than to place premises and conclusions side by side, and they will see the logical relations between them.

If a human embryo, — the infant before its birth, — could know and comprehend its structure and functions; if it could ask such questions as these: Why have I two hundred and fifty bones (or the beginnings of bones) all articulated and jointed in so curious a way, with bands for strength, with braces against antagonistic force; with hinge-joints in one place, and ball-and-socket-joints in another, &c., &c.; why have I four hundred and fifty muscles, all fastened to these bones, all prospective of motion? why am I fitted with an eye, and so wonderfully arranged as to be capable of producing all the graces of motion, in this darkness where no light comes, or with lungs where there is no air? why have I the rudiments of social organs and loving faculties, when I am here all alone? why have I the faculty of calculation, able, if developed, to weigh planets, and measure the distances of the stars, when I shall never see planet or stars? why have I the sentiment of ideality, where there are no elements of form or color to be combined into beauty? &c., &c., through the whole gamut of physical, intellectual, and moral endowments; — I say, if such questions could be put by an embryo-child, could any other answer be given than that they were all created in mere wanton wastefulness and nonsensicality, or, on the other hand, that the being who had been endowed with them was yet to be ushered into a sphere of light, and air, and motion, and beauty; of friends to be loved, and of a God to be worshipped?

Or suppose the embryo-child were submitted autopsically to a being of so high an order of intelligence, that, at a glance, he could comprehend all its adaptations and significations, to what conclusions must such a beholder come in regard to the aim and purpose, — the final cause, as the logicians say, of existence? Would he, or could he conclude that its then present condition of darkness and circumscription was its final and ultimate condition also; that when its period of gestation should have passed, this being itself, with all its powers and faculties, should perish from animate existence?

On the other hand, would not such a sagacious and far-seeing beholder as I have supposed, look on all these powers and faculties in their ante-natal state, as a prophecy and a promise, yea, a covenant, not made with sign-manual and seal only, but with an oath, that such a being, in some sphere of valleys and hills, of winds and streams, of colors and songs, of natural law, and of moral law, of kindred and friends, of love to man, and love to God, should find "ample room and verge enough" for the ascending struggle, the expansion, the glorification of all its wonderful endowments? And after arriving at such a conclusion, on principles of unmistakable logic, and having his whole emotional and devotional nature set aglow towards the Contriver and Perfecter of such a beautiful work, were he then to be summoned into the august presence of that Contriver and Perfecter, and to be told by Him that the work which had so kindled his admiration, and stimulated his homage, was designed only for a nine months' toy in a prison; that there was an atmosphere, but those lungs should never respire it; that there was a world of pearls and shells, of flowers and fruits, of rainbows and auroras, and a firmament strewed with suns, but those eyes should never see them; that there was a sphere for sacred affections, for holy sympathies and loves, for virtuous ascension along an upward path-way that had no culminating point, but forever rose higher and higher into the zenith of excellence; but that this being, so qualified and equipped for that ascending career, and with its wings already outspread for the flight, should never soar one inch into that upper realm; — suppose, I say, that all this were announced to the before delighted, but now astonished beholder, would he not look upon the wonderful workmanship with pity, but upon its Author with contempt?

Now the display of such wisdom, and skill, and power as were necessary to create the senses, limbs, and faculties of the unborn child, viewed in connection with the extinction of that child's life at the very moment when prepared to enter upon its higher and ampler sphere, seems to me but faintly and remotely to typify the *fatuity*, the *dementia*, of creating such a universe of splendors, and loves, and beatitudes, as we suppose this to be, and of creating human beings capable of enjoying it forever and ever, with more and more adequate comprehension, and with more and more extatic bliss, and then, after an average life of only about thirty years, — and such a life too, — to sweep the whole away into nonentity and oblivion ; — I say the folly of the first is but finite, compared with the infinite folly of the last. Indeed, if the aimlessness of the nine months ante-natal life, without the average thirty years' life to redeem it, would be justly stigmatized as folly, the contemptibleness of man's achievements, and the horribleness of his crimes and sins, during his average thirty years' life, without a subsequent Immortality to justify it, — ay, not merely to justify, but to glorify, and to beatify it, — might justly be stigmatized and derided as idiotic. Is the great God a mere blower of soap-bubbles, that He creates the universe to which we belong, which is supposed to consist of forty millions of visible stars, and has created, as is believed by astronomers, five thousand other universes within the bounds of our imperfect vision, each as large as this, and creates man more wonderful, and more precious, because he can think and feel, than all these universes put together, and gives him a life of but thirty years duration, and then extinguishes him altogether? No! the argument that such a being as man shall live forever, is as much stronger than the argument that the embryo shall live its thirty years, as eternity is grander than our life-time.

To me, the negative facts that the human race, with all their capabilities of achievement, have as yet achieved so little, and with all their susceptibilities of enjoyment, have as yet enjoyed so little, and suffered so much, is a proof that the orbit of our being is not yet filled, that it has not yet reached the goal of its destiny. I should demand, at least, a few centillions of constantly improving ages, to make the plan of our existence reputable to its Author; and after this grant had been meted out and filled up, I think the argument for Immortality would then become so strong, as to preclude all scepticism.

Is there not something almost ludicrously incongruous in this Sadducean creed of the soul's non-existence after death, when we reflect that, if it be true, the works of man live so much longer than the spirit of man, that Moses goes on to this day, not only directing the cut of beards, and the style of cookery, but holding Jesus Christ himself in abeyance, in regard to a numerous body of men scattered over all the earth; that John the Baptist should still go on plunging the converts to the church into deep water, or, more economically, sprinkling them with a few drops; that the names of Leonidas, and Wallace, and Tell, should still ring through the hearts of men, as a clarion rings in their ears; that Alfred and Washington should inspire millions of souls with great ideas of social organisms and ameliorations; that the written words of ancient orator and poet should be re-written upon the minds of each new generation, as new foliage clothes the forest with each returning spring; — that all these things should be done, through such a course of ages, after the authors of them all have passed into non-existence? And is there not a sardonic horribleness in the idea that the magnificent scoundrels of olden or of modern times, the scamp-Jupiters of mankind, who have organized polygamy, or extended slavery, or made intemperance and debauchery fashionable, — that these, I say, should be suffered to skulk and sneak away into nonentity, without either being made better by repentance and reformation, or punished for being so bad?

Let us examine this subject in another of its various aspects. Should I see a man building and filling the most capacious storehouses with food that never was to be consumed, and he knew it; or wardrobes with myriads of nicely wrought garments that were never to be put on, and he knew it; or constructing a city of splendid edifices, fitted with all the comforts and adornments that philosophy or art could prepare, which he all the time predestined that no mortal should ever inhabit; or preparing the most splendid ship, whose keel he had predetermined should never touch water; still, I could call such a man economic, I could call him frugal of resources, I could call him wise and benevolent in his expenditures, compared with a Being who, after having made all these geologic, telluric, pneumatic, astronomic, preparations, which we see about us, and then — after having also made such an intellectual and moral race as we are, and put it in possession of the whole — could then destroy the race, but yet preserve the machinery; could demolish the edifice while he let the staging remain; could annihilate the jewels, but save the casket. Oh! is not the man sordid and material, is he not absorbed and smothered in matter, who can imagine that the heavens will stand, while the souls that inhabit them will die?

Why do we apprentice a child to a trade, but that he may follow it when he becomes a man? Why do we send a child to school, or to college, but that he may be fitted to act in the wider sphere, and to perform the nobler duties of manhood; and why has God placed us in this world of preparation, of probation, if there be no higher life for which we are to be prepared and proved? If the doctrine of Immortality be not true, then, considering the size of the mountain, no mouse so small ever derided a birth-pang.

I can understand why our Heavenly Father should cover the earth with flowers, and then suffer them to wither and decay; why he should strew the bottom of the ocean with pearl and many-colored shells and permit them to radiate all their beauty away in the deep; why He should span the dark cloud with double or triple rainbow, and in an hour melt them into air; why He should shoot up the northern auroras and quench their glittering flames; why all the glories of the sunrise and of the sunset should hold their perpetual circuit around the earth from east to west, all of which are to be swallowed up in the brightening morning or in the darkening night; why, with the annual ascension and declination of the sun a vast wave of beauty and luxuriance should perpetually vibrate between the summer and the winter solstice, between the temperate zones of the north and of the south, to be followed at each extreme by wintry frosts and desolation; — I say, I can understand all this, for these hues and forms of beauty, these grandeurs and splendors of nature, have no *conscious* existence; they did not know they lived, they do not know they die; no song of exultation ushered them into being, no hopes died when they departed from it; and God is so rich that He can afford to cover the firmament from horizon to zenith with the most gorgeous tapestry, and tear it down and replace it with new, every minute while we gaze; He can afford to load every tree in the forest and every tiniest spire in the field with his icy regalia — such as all the monarchs in the world cannot buy — during the night, and then melt them down in the morning, and then produce new charms and wonders from the old. But I cannot understand why our *conscious* being just awakened here into life, and capable of such keen and unending gratification; why our virtues purchased by heroic struggle or endurance, yielding such intense subjective enjoyment and longing for a career of immortality; — I cannot understand why these should be dissipated like the morning cloud, or expire like a vernal flower, by some inherent law of limitation. I cannot explain or conceive why it should be, when, perchance, I have inherited excessive and exorbitant propensities from my ancestors; or find myself, when first awaking to self-consciousness and self-comprehension, already in the grasp of demoniac passions, by reason of some crime in my progenitors or mischance in my organization, or mal-adjustment of my powers; and when, after making myself fully acquainted with the full compass of my heritage of woe, or the full calamity of my unhappy constitution, I address myself, in a life-long struggle to the work of self-recuperation, and one after another I do battle with these fiends of evil dispositions that have been incarnated in my person; I cut off, one after another, the hundred hydra-heads of each monster appetite and passion and lust, and like the hero in the old Grecian myth, I apply a cautery of red-hot iron to the quivering flesh of every wound, though that wound is in my own soul, and hold it there through wildest and fiercest agonies, until the living fibre is crisped and charred too deep to allow life ever to spring from it or visit it again; and when, at last, I have achieved the mighty victory, and stand in majestic and glorious proportions, hero and conqueror over that late domain of sorrow and of sin, and am now ready to enter upon those sublime realms of splendor and beatitude and to wing my celestial course upward, through cycles of time and spirals of ascension all the more vigorously because of the strength wherewith I endued my soul in the aforetime contest with my satanic foes; that there, at the very apex and crown of all my past endeavors and achievements, with my soul purified and rejuvenated, with my heart panting to run the new career, with my aspiring eye fixed upon the zenith, and feeling the grand momentum of progression lifting in every atom of my being; that then, I say, instead of the victor's palm and the triumphal entrance, and the "Well done, good and faithful servant," I must be struck into annihilation, changed into a vacuum, reduced to that idealess, conceptionless state, if such a state ever was or ever could be, anterior to Nothing. Let us exclaim not only "O, what a lame and impotent," but what a contemptible and blasphemous conclusion! The Creator of such a world has made a systematic business of fatuity, and given an eternal organization to infinite folly!

How strong that desire of improvement in the human mind, which is the companion, if it be not the condition of Genius! — that Ideality, I mean, that always runs ahead of Actuality. Achievement is only the eminence whence we survey something better to be achieved. Ideality is only the *Avant-Courier* of the mind, and where that, in a healthy and normal state, goes, I hold it to be a prophecy that realization can follow.

How strong, too, the desire of perfection in the heart of a good man; what grief over error; what delightful anticipations of improvement! These, too, I hold to be prophecy ; just as the embryo lungs prophecied the air, and the embryo eye, the light. Without Immortality, well did Lord Bacon say,

> "The world's a bubble, and the life of man
> Less than a span;
> In his conception wretched, from the womb,
> So to the tomb,
> Curst from the cradle, and brought up to years,
> With care and fears; —
> Who, then, to frail mortality shall trust,
> But limns the water, or but writes in dust."

How pertinently it may be asked

> "Shall Spring the faded world revive?
> Shall waning moons their light renew?
> Again shall setting suns ascend,
> And chase the darkness from our view?"

But

> "In those lone, silent realms of night
> Shall peace and hope no more arise?
> No future morning shed its light,
> No day [illegible] the darksome skies?"

MIRACLES.

XII.

MIRACLES.

MATTHEW vii. 21. — "Not every one that saith unto me, Lord, Lord, shall enter into the kingdom of heaven, but he that doeth the will of my Father who is in heaven."

MATTH. ii. 28, 29, 30, and part of the 31st. — "A certain man had two sons, and he came to the first and said, Son, go, work to-day in my vineyard.

"He answered and said, I will not: but afterwards repented and went.

"And he came to the second and said likewise. And he answered and said, I go, Sir, and went not.

"Whether of the twain did the will of his Father?"

THE texts selected unavoidably suggest the highest ideas of human duty. The highest human duty consists in an intelligent obedience to God's will. I say in an *intelligent* obedience to God's will; for a blind obedience worships God only with a part of our nature, — an intelligent obedience, with the whole of it. All the intimations anywhere or in any manner revealed, assure us that God likes works better than professions, practice better than theory, deeds better than creeds. Christ did not go about throwing written or printed tracts into people's houses which inculcated the Calvinistic Five Points, or the Episcopalian Thirty-nine Articles, or the Universalists' Universalism, or even the brief platform on which we of the Christian Connection profess to stand. He went about "*doing good;*" and all eloquence, and all poetry, may expend themselves forever on eulogy, and all they can do is to unfold and blaze, one after another, upon human eyes, the infinite refulgencies of those two simple words.

Just in proportion as a man becomes good, divine, Christ-like, he passes out of the region of theorizing, of system-building, and hireling service, into the region of beneficent activities. It is well to think well; — it is divine to do well.

How far then can man, — this frail, feeble child of clay, as he is so often called, this worm of the dust, this shadow, this vapor, or by whatever other contemptuous appellations any one may choose to malign or belittle him, — obey God, imitate God; obey and imitate the Divine Christ.

And here, my young friends, I am not about to discuss the softer and tenderer parts of this subject. I shall venture at once upon the toughest, the most indigestible, insoluble portions of it; for I feel like the brave old knight of the tournament, who had such confidence in the justness of his cause, that he gave his adversary the advantage of sun and wind.

How far can we obey God and imitate Christ? which, indeed, is the same thing, for if we imitate Christ, we are sure we shall obey God. We can imitate Christ so far as those outward acts are concerned, by which he ministered to his own personal necessities. He ate, he drank, he slept, as other men. "For John came, neither eating nor drinking, and they say, he hath a devil. The Son of Man came, eating and drinking, and they say, Behold a man, gluttonous and a wine-bibber!" So far, the imitation is not without danger of running into excess. But can we imitate him in his self-denials! In the midst of Oriental luxuries, surrounded by royal magnificence, which he might have made his own by flattery, or even by acquiescence; can we imitate the moral heroism and intrepidity with which he denounced the iniquities of those who had power over him of life and death? Can we imitate, and by some close degree of approximation, too, the miracles he is recorded to have wrought? I say, we can. It has been done, and it can be done again.

Not that I think the excellence and preciousness of Christ's mission are half so well proved by the recorded miracles, as by the spirit of purity and beneficence that governed his whole life; yet I desire, if possible, to suggest a new use to be made of these narratives, and to turn them to practical account in the amelioration of human calamities, and the elevation of men. The mere mechanical power of interrupting the course of nature, — of hushing the rage of storms, of stopping the sun in his course, of turning water into wine (though I think if he were on earth now, the miracle would be the other way, and he would turn wine and all alcoholic drinks back into water), — this dynamical or chemical power, may exist altogether independent of any moral attribute. But to subdue a passion or propensity that my natural organization, or early education, may have planted in my bosom; to subject myself to toil, and privation, and self-sacrifice, for the well-being of others, even of my enemies; and to count it as so much gain to myself, if I can avert calamity from them, — this is divine. To woo a wandering brother back to the path of rectitude, to remove one obstacle that obstructs his return to virtue, I should regard as an infinitely greater achievement than if I could arrest the motive power that wheels the solar system.

Can we not, then, make some better use, or, at least, some further use of Christ's miracles, than has hitherto been made of them? They have been supposed to be inimitable; things to be wondered at, and almost worshipped, but not copied; challenging our admiration as marvels, but not encouraging or stimulating our efforts as examples; — in fine, occupying a sphere of active beneficence inaccessible to man.

But are the recorded miracles of Jesus Christ, these lofty, unapproachable achievements, standing not only far above present actuality, but future possibility, with which, indeed, man's powers are incommensurable? In a word, if Christ did possess miraculous power, and did work his recorded miracles by virtue of that power alone, cannot we, without any miraculous power, produce results partaking of the same divine, beneficent character?

Every one understands what is sometimes called the Doctrine of Compensations. In Mechanics, for instance, in order to produce momentum, velocity may be substituted for weight. That is, a small body moving swiftly, will strike as forcible a blow as a large body moving slowly. One man, by means of tackle and machinery, will exert the equivalent of a hundred men-power. So in the mental realm, mediocre ability, with perseverance, often overtakes and outstrips the most splendid talent; and even our nursery-books told us how the slow-moving snail reached his journey's end before the swift-moving hare with his loitering. Intensity and concentration of thought often effect what neither genius nor intuition can do, as the strokes of the feeble but long-repeating mattock dig deeper than the thunderbolt. Give us time, say the water-drops, and we will bore a hole through your thickest strata of granite. Give us time, say the coral insects, and we will build up another Australasia.

Christ's miracles are sometimes spoken of in a general way, as that he healed all manner of diseases; but the specific instances, the most remarkable illustrations of his recorded power, consist in his enabling the dumb to speak, and the blind to see, and in casting evil spirits out of demoniacs. Here were cases of terrible infliction, or of terrible privation; — the privation of some bodily sense, whose loss subtracts so much from the enjoyments of life, and whose restoration would affect beholders with such wonder and awe. Let us examine, then, some of those narratives, and see how far forth wise and good men may go in imitating them. The desire to do so is the first step, and this is kindled by the example.

One of the earliest accounts describes his quieting the storm on the sea of Galilee. Here he asserted his power over the elements of Nature.

But what was the scene of this demonstration? It was the Sea of Galilee, — sometimes called the Sea of Tiberias, or the Sea of Gennesareth. This body of water was but fourteen miles long, and only seven broad in its widest part. Situated between what were then called mountains, both on the east and the west, it was liable to gusts and squalls; yet it could never experience anything of the elemental violence or commotion which rage in the Atlantic or Indian Oceans. Twice the quantity of water it contained would not be enough to make one respectable, heaving, mid-sea wave of the Atlantic. Whence, then, came their danger? It came from the frailty and insignificant size of the boats which they dignified by the name of ships. The cry was, "Lord, save us, we perish." The peril threatened life.

It is easy to see that the danger is as certainly warded off by increasing the power of the craft to defy or endure the storm, as by parrying the blows of the storm itself. Life is equally saved, the sense of security is equally enjoyed, whether God enables me to sing a lullaby to the tempest, or to fasten my cradle with such moorings that tempests shall only rock, but cannot overturn it.

Would it not at that time have appeared in every way as great a miracle, if, when the sky was overspread with blackness, Christ had looked up into it, and watched it till the moment when a bolt of lightning leaped from its cloudy throne, straight at that boat whose freight was the Christianity of the world, and in an instant, in a thousandth part of an instant, had waved it aside harmless? Yet this is only what every one can do now.

Another instance of man's power over the elements, is exhibited in the Miner's Lamp, the invention of Sir Humphrey Davy. In the mines whence Englishmen draw the fuel which preserves their personal existence, and through which come all those wonders of mechanical production, said to be equal to the labors of six hundred millions of men, — in those mines an explosive gas is exuded, invisible, unremovable, and when ignited, unquenchable, and destructive of all life within its compass. The miners must carry down lights; for how, otherwise, in that solid darkness, could they work?

Here, then, the two laws confront each other, face to face, — the law which necessitates light, and the law by which the flame begets earthquakes. Sir Humphrey Davy, — not by any fiat of power, it is true, but by toilsome study, by sagacious and persevering experiment, found that this explosive gas would not permeate a gauze-wire network, whose meshes were reduced to a certain fineness. He therefore fabricated a gauze covering, lantern shaped, in which to enclose the lamp. This lamp the miners carry into the mines, and destruction, awed and abashed, retires before it. Particles of the gas, it is true, do flow in through the meshes ot the network, but so few, that they only feed the flame, and increase its light. Thus Genius and Power make the very breath of the monster, that stands ready to devour them, contribute to their welfare.

Here, then, are cases where the skill and perseverance of man, working rejoicingly by noble means to noble ends, imitates — I do not say equals — the grandeur and the sublimity of Christ's power, when he laid his hand upon the stormy air, and upon the tempestuous sea, and bade them be still.

Another of Christ's wonderful works is alleged to have consisted in his feeding and satisfying multitudes, — on one occasion five thousand, on another four thousand, besides women and children, with a quantity of food amazingly disproportioned to the company. How beautifully this is paralleled, in a moral sense, by those missionaries who take a few Bibles and books of religious literature and science, and carry them across oceans to heathen lands, where a moral dearth prevails, where the people perish for lack of knowledge; and with these few books, what multitudes do they feed with Divine knowledge; and the greater the numbers they feed, the more overflowing baskets they have left; out of which, not only contemporary multitudes — ay, contemporary nations — may be fed, but of which the teeming millions of posterity may eat and live.

Is it a poor or unworthy imitation of the Saviour, when famine smites a whole people, when among thousands, and tens of thousands, pallor unhumanizes the face; when the fever of famine burns away the body, atom by atom, with its inward fires, and atrophy denudes the frame; when famishing infants perish upon famishing mothers' breasts; when hope dies, and the grave opens; then, to see a sail, a fleet, now on the horizon, now in the offing, at the wharf — and suddenly, as if by some mysterious attraction, food leaps from the crowded hold to the perishing victim; the pulses swell with returning strength, and the reviving heart shouts its hosannas of joy; oh, is not this a splendid imitation of the feeding of the multitudes?

Who shall contradict the saying of Adam Smith, that "he is a public benefactor who makes two blades of grass grow where but one grew before?" This the scientific man does. Wherever the intelligent and industrious man goes, though it be to barren waste, or pestilential morass, health and abundance follow, if any regard for the common weal sanctifies the civilization. Those divinities whom the ancients worshipped, — Ceres, Pomona, and Flora, who strewed and beautified the earth with grain, and fruit, and flower, have in modern times domiciled themselves among men, and have exchanged their Divine titles for plain Professors of Chemistry, and we now call them Agriculturists and Horticulturists.

Another class of Christ's miracles consisted in enabling the dumb to speak. To give the power of speech to one who never had it, or to restore it to one who has lost it, is, indeed, a wonderful work. Can this work of Christ be imitated by common men? We all know that it can. Many of our States, especially the Free States, are beautified and ennobled by Institutions, where the power of communication, of free, large, learned communication, is bestowed upon the victims of such privation.

There are two modes in which this beneficent work is effected. One of them originated in Paris about a century ago, in 1755, under the auspices of the Abbé de l'Epée, one of Christ's true followers. It was copied from France into England, not long after, and into this country in the year 1817, by the Rev. Thomas H. Gallaudet, of Hartford, Connecticut. The method of communicating, almost exclusively used in France and England and in the United States, is by Dactyology, or Finger-speaking, by which certain positions of the fingers become signs of certain letters or words, so that one might say the pupil hears with his eyes.

But in Germany and some other countries of Europe, where language is more phonetic than in France or England, the dumb are really taught to speak, to articulate, to utter words themselves, — perfectly intelligible words too, and they understand those who speak to them by the motions of their lips. Wonderful as is the thought, it is nevertheless proved that there is a language of muscles as truly as of voice.

Peter Ponce, a Spaniard, in the 16th century; Wallis, an Englishman, in about 1660; the Swiss physician, Amman, in 1692 and 1700; The German clergyman, Raphael, in 1715; the Jew, Paveira, in France, in 1780; and the German Cantor (singing-master) Heinicke, at Eppendorf, near Hamburg, the father of all the German deaf and dumb institutions, in 1770, have each and all taught their mute pupils to speak, *each of them in his native tongue.*

The emotions never will grow old in my heart which were called into vivid consciousness, when, for the first time, in Magdeburg, in Prussia, I visited a school where deaf-mute children were taught to speak, — to speak as other children speak. I had heard of this method before; it was a thing outside of me; but here I heard itself, and it became a part of me.

The very phrase "A school for the Deaf and Dumb" awakens in the mind the ideas of a silent, soundless life, of a world voiceless as the grave. In this respect, death has nothing to deprive them of. But here, these privations were supplied. Human benevolence, Christ-like, divine, had achieved the triumph. Friendship, sympathy, and those coöperative joys which so multiply each other by their thousand reflections from heart to heart, — all these lost delights, by this divine art, had been restored. It was a spectacle of the moral sublime. I thought of him, the Saviour, who had raised the dumb out of the grave of silence. I walked forth with those wondering multitudes who followed him into the mountain, "nigh unto the sea of Galilee," to have their sick healed, their dumb made to speak, their deaf to hear. I heard the promises made to his disciples, that if they would cherish his spirit and obey his commands, they too should lay hold on these miraculous gifts. I understood not the law of his power, but I blessed God that it was also in other men, to be developed in more intelligible forms. The spirit of Christ had, for some reason, evaporated from his disciples; the power of succor had been lost for centuries. But, here was it not renewed? or, at least, was there not the closest imitation of it, and in a form to benefit all the sons and daughters of Silence? The dumb spake as in the time of Jesus, but, by this means, not a few in Judea only, but all the deaf and dumb in all the world could be enabled to speak. Thus the delights of social converse, the instructions and the consecrations of private and of public teaching are poured upon

> "The ear sequestrate and the tuneless tongue."

In Germany alone, there are now not less than seventy-five of these deaf and dumb schools where children are taught to *speak*. I commend others to the enjoyment of the thrilling happiness with which I witnessed the wonderful spectacle.

If we are bound to suppose that Christ regarded with joy the few opportunities he had of supplying these privations, with what delight, with what approval he must now look upon all his followers and imitators in this blessed work!

The Gospels describe another field for the display of divine power acting in man, — the restoration of sight to the blind. What Almighty power it was, when all the universe was solid darkness, to call the sun and stars into existence! But the effect is the same on our sources of comfort and of joy, to call into being the human eye without which we could see neither sun nor stars. A sun without an eye, and an eye without a sun, for all human purposes, are the same. The privations of the blind are as different from those of the deaf-mutes in substance as in form. Though the blind are generally objects of greater compassion, from their peculiar dependence, yet the deaf-mute is by far the greater sufferer. A blind person is more immediately dependent upon others for his subsistence, but the deaf-mute is farther removed from knowledge and sympathy. The sight of all objects within the circle of vision is lost to the blind; but how narrow that circle is. By the loss of eyes he loses the sight of all objects within the visible horizon only; but by the possession of hearing, he can become acquainted with all events not only within but without that circle. The ear has no horizon to bound it. And this is true, not only in regard to contemporary matters, but in regard to all history. So that, although the blind man cannot see things immediately around him, yet he can hear things from all lands and times. On the other hand, though the deaf-mute can see the things immediately around him, he cannot hear of things anywhere. The blind can profit by all the wisdom he can hear, the deaf-mute only by the objects he can see. Hence the sight is more necessary to the comfort of the body, hearing is vastly more so to the growth of the soul. The consequence is, that the number of distinguished and learned men among the blind, as compared with those among the deaf and dumb, is fifty to one. The ear has been happily called the "vestibule of the soul."

The systematic instruction of the blind is of very modern date. The author of this noble, I might almost say this divine art, was Valentine Haüy, of Paris. Haüy had become acquainted with the baroness Von Paradis, a blind German lady, who visited Paris as an organist, and performed with great applause. About this time an event took place at the annual fair of St. Ovide, which fully roused his commiseration. An innkeeper there had collected ten poor blind persons, attired them in the most ridiculous manner, garnishing them with asses' ears, peacock's feathers, and spectacles without glasses, to perform a burlesque concert.

What therefore was designed for the thoughtless or wanton amusement of others, only kindled Haüy's benevolence. He resolved to do for the blind, through the sense of touch, what the Abbé de l'Epée had done for the deaf-mute through the medium of sight. Accordingly he founded an Institution for their instruction in Paris, in 1784; and in 1786, public exercises were performed by his pupils, at Versailles, in the presence of the king. This gave the school great *éclat.*

Next to France, institutions were established for the blind in Great Britain; in Liverpool, in 1790; in Edinburgh, in 1791; in London, in 1800; and afterwards in Bristol, Norwich, Dublin, &c. But all these were private institutions, maintained by private endowments and contributions.

After establishing his school in Paris, Haüy was invited to St. Petersburg, and established one there in 1806; and, in the same year, another in Berlin, in Prussia.

The first Institution for the Blind ever established on this Continent, or, indeed, in this Western hemisphere, was the New England Asylum, in Boston, Mass., in 1829. This, now, for twenty-seven years, has been under the care of that distinguished man, Dr. Samuel G. Howe, even then known as the Philhellene, or Lover of Greece; but now, by the broader title of Philanthropist, or Lover of Mankind. Under the superintendence of Dr. Howe, this Institution has made more improvements in the methods and instruments of teaching the blind, than all the other schools in the world added together; and its efforts have been atttended with a proportionate success.

Dr. Howe has also introduced into this country, of late years, the still more difficult instruction of Idiots. The success of this last and most astounding work of benevolence, proves incontestably, that in every human being exists the germs of faculties, and that the divine spirit of Christian love will find the means of discovering and fertilizing them, even when they have been so covered up by the sins of disobedience to God's laws, that the very semblance of humanity is lost. Here, indeed, is the literal fulfilment of Scripture. The sins of the fathers are visited upon the third and the fourth generation. But the blessed law of recuperative force is visible even here.

As Dr. Howe now does, and always will occupy a conspicuous place in the Annals of Benevolence, it will not be inappropriate to give a brief sketch of his life.

There is a large number of men, who, on account of his differences from them in religious views, thrust him out of the pale of Christianity. Passing by his belief, let us see if, in his life, he has not imitated the Saviour as much as they. I have known him long. Perhaps few have known him as intimately. We were in college together, and for twenty years I was officially associated with him in the administration of that Institution with which his name is now imperishably connected. For a great deal of that time, there was scarcely a day in which a personal interview did not give me some new proof of his wisdom and goodness.

At the time when the Greek war of Independence broke out, Dr. Howe was a student of medicine in Boston. Even then, his youthful heart was an altar already loaded with incense. The sight of a brave people struggling for liberty, kindled that incense into a flame; — a flame which has burned uninterruptedly, for Greece, for Poland, for Hungary, for Italy, and for those in this country who are under direr oppression than Greek, or Pole, or Hungarian, or Italian. He flew to Greece, and for six years, a part of the time as a surgeon in the army, or on board the fleet, a part of the time as a volunteer, like Lafayette and Kosciusko, in our Revolutionary war, — he devoted himself to the liberation of that people. He adhered to their cause until he left them free. Then he taught them something of the arts of peace. The first cart made in Greece was made under his superintendence. The old ancestors of that people had made chariots for battle, but not carts for agriculture, and their descendants inherit a sufficient degree of the old organization to shape a graceful boat with a jack-knife, while so little were the useful arts cultivated, that they needed instruction in fabricating the most common utensils of life. The Egyptians had overrun the Peloponnesus, ravaging and destroying all fruit and harvest, and the people were reduced almost to starvation. At that critical moment, Dr. Howe returned to this country, preached a crusade through all New England and New York, raised some sixty thousand dollars in money, and an immense quantity of clothing, with which he relieved the mortal necessities of the Greeks, and sustained them until the final hour of triumph. Twenty years after, when he rode alone into Greece on horseback, one day, an accidental travelling companion was astonished to see him recognized by a peasant woman, who spread the glad intelligence, and he was immediately surrounded and borne into the neighboring city, *nolens volens*, on the shoulders of the people. Such joy was manifested at the sight of him who had founded a village on that spot in the days of stormy trial, that his accidental companion was moved to tears at the spectacle of the enthusiasm, even before he knew the details of the history. At that point of time, the Greeks were just again triumphant over oppression, and his friends ruled the ascendant, and were glad to do him honor. They also sent a Greek newspaper to his friend Charles Sumner, in which the incident was related, or probably we should never have had the pleasure of learning it, for Dr. Howe is never the hero of his own story.

To return to his early history. At the time of his return from his Grecian expedition to Boston, Dr. John D. Fisher, who had just completed his medical studies in Paris, came home to Boston, also, with his great heart filled, brimming, with the project of establishing an Institution for the Blind, like that of the Abbé Haüy, with which he had become familiar in Paris.

In a city so renowned for its charities as Boston, the bricks and mortar for such an establishment could easily be obtained. But where could one find the great, organizing, executive mind to be put at its head, and to be its sensorium?

The most sagacious turned to Dr. Howe as the man above all men for the place, and he was appointed. He accepted, and immediately embarked for Europe, to visit the institutions at Paris and elsewhere.

It was while in Paris, on this mission, that his chivalrous spirit prompted him to accept a trust which well nigh proved fatal, not only to the enterprise in which he was embarked, but to his life. This visit to Paris was during the Polish insurrection of 1830–31. A thrill of enthusiasm in behalf of the Poles, as a few years before in behalf of the Greeks, ran through this country, and large contributions of money and clothing were made in their behalf. These donations were forwarded to General Lafayette in Paris, to be remitted by him to their suffering objects. General Lafayette despatched two agents, a French and a German officer, with the succors. One of them was taken prisoner by the enemy; the other was baulked in his purpose and returned. Who now had the bravery and the skill to carry the needed relief to the perishing army?

It should be stated here that a large, perhaps the largest body of the Polish insurgents, had just been driven across their frontiers into Prussia. Prussia stipulated that if they would surrender their arms and dismiss their officers, she would afford them a refuge. But having, for some reasons of state, changed her policy, and become more friendly to Russia, she surrounded the Poles with a cordon of soldiers, and attempted by starvation on her side of the line, to drive them into the jaws of the Russian bear on the other side. It was at this perilous juncture, when, guarded by Prussian soldiers on one side, and watched by Russian victors on the other, and perishing from want within themselves, that Dr. Howe undertook to carry the needed assistance to this hunted band of patriots. He was then on the point of starting for Berlin, to visit the Blind Institution, established there by the Abbé Huäy, a quarter of a century before, and he accepted this perilous commission as an episode. As soon as wheels could carry him, he stood within the Polish cantonments, ground consecrated by the presence of patriots, desecrated by the rule of tyrants. The Poles had been quartered among the peasants, and they were scattered over a space a dozen miles in extent. By the terms of capitulation, their officers had been removed. One officer, however, having determined to abide the fortunes of his companions, remained; and the more securely to cover his concealment, feigned illness; and from his sick quarters, unknown except by a few trusted ones, all necessary orders were issued. Over this extended space, and among this large number, Dr. Howe began, personally, the distribution of his alms, by travelling from hut to hut, scattering gladness wherever he went. Soon he came to a peasant's rude hut, where, he was told there lay, in an upper loft, a dying Pole. He ascended to the apartment, which bore all the evidences of a sick man's chamber, — the attendants, the silence, the medical paraphernalia; and by the dim light from a darkened window, the form of a man was seen prostrate upon a pallet of straw. Dr. Howe explained his errand, assured him that he came as a friend to help, and not as an enemy to betray. Convinced of this, the feigning sick man sprang upon his feet, and stood before him a tall, gigantic grenadier, ready, as chance might offer, for friendship or for battle, — ready for any thing but to live a slave. It was their commander.

The supplies came at a moment when the Polish army was at the point of despair. They were promptly delivered and joyfully received; and Dr. Howe, having fed the hungry and clothed the naked, started immediately for Berlin, to learn how to give eyes to the blind.

Immediately after arriving at Berlin, he accidently met an American citizen with whom he exchanged cards, giving, most fortunately, the name of the hotel where he lodged. The next morning that citizen called at the hotel and inquired for Dr. Howe, but was told that no such person was, or had been there. Appearances, however, excited suspicion, and by adroit and persevering inquiries, this gentleman found that a body of the police had visited the house during the night; but Dr. Howe, for six weeks, was nowhere to be found by any friendly inquirer; nowhere to be seen by any friendly eye. The facts were, that no sooner had Dr. Howe distributed his succors among the Poles, than they were changed as from dead men to live ones. A new soul had been created within them, and all indications pointed to him as to the Creator. Now let us see what has been the fortune of the moral hero.

In Prussia, every traveller must go from place to place by public conveyance. All public stages are there truly public ones, for they are owned and driven by the government. However urgent one's business may be, whatever emergency may arise, no private man with private horses or private carriage is allowed to help one on one's way. The government, for police purposes, transacts all this business. They register the name of every passenger, note where they take him up, and where they set him down, so that they can tell the outgoing and incoming of every traveller who passes through the kingdom or moves from place to place in it. Hence the blood hounds easily tracked Dr. Howe from the camp of the Poles to his hotel in Berlin; and at midnight, on the first night of his arrival in the city, they knocked at his chamber door. On opening it he saw three men. They were clad in citizen's dress, and at first only asked him the news from the camp, and requested his attendance before some civil commissioners. On his declining to go, he was told he must go; and on his demanding by what authority, the captain of the band unbuttoned and laid open his citizen's coat, and showed the uniform and the badge that has all the thunders of the government at its back. He parleyed; and finally, by promising to attend them in the morning, he gained a respite for a few hours during the residue of the night. Availing himself of this critical period, he selected what valueless and insignificant papers he had which he tore into shreds, shuffled and threw into a basin of water, but all his valuable ones and such as might connect him with the transaction, he hid in the hollow of a bust of the king of Prussia, which is almost universally found in all public rooms and places of resort throughout the realm.

With early dawn reappeared the police, who had watched all night at his door, to conduct him, as they had intimated, to some tribunal or company anxious to hear the news.

Whoever has been in Berlin will remember a vast stone building in one of the most conspicuous streets, nearly in the heart of the city, obtruding its silent horrors upon the sight, and striking with fiercer horrors all the recollections and associations of men. It is the government prison, the Bastile of Prussia. There, in a stone room eight feet by six, without fresh air, without light, Dr. Howe was thrust, and there began a night of darkness, equally impervious to the light of day and the light of hope, and which lasted six weeks. Of all men and their confederates in the underworld, none but the princes of police, and the prince of darkness, knew where he was. No communication by letter or speech was allowed, none save that unseen communication with the great Father of us all, which all good men have, and of which no earthly or infernal foe can rob them.

At the end of two days he was taken before a kind of commission (somewhat, perhaps, like a certain kind of commission in this country, only in that mere despotism, I believe, the base hirelings did not have double the fee for convicting, which they did for acquitting, as is the case in this land of boasted freedom). That tribunal conducted his examination on some atomic or infinitesimal theory; for they read to him not less than three hundred written questions, beginning with the names of his father and mother, and evincing the most extraordinary interest in every event that had happened from the day of his birth, and taking down all his answers in writing. At the end of two days more, he was taken before the same officers again, and the three hundred and more questions were all put to him again, and again were all his answers taken down in writing. At the close of the second examination, he was remanded to his dungeon, too small to welcome friend or comforter, but large enough to hold all the spectres of horror or despair, that can ever visit a good man's heart. There, in utter solitude, within stone walls, hard as though each granule in their structure were a tyrant's heart, as though they had been constructed of tyrant's hearts as coral insects build coral reefs, he remained six weeks, having no expectation of any other home or tomb but that, unless, indeed, he might be surrendered to Russia, and doomed to Siberian mines.

One circumstance which transpired, marks the untiring industry of the Prussian police. At his first examination, he saw that the whole mass of papers which he had torn up and thrown into the water, had been taken out, dried, and readjusted, part to part, as one readjusts the dislocated pieces of a Chinese puzzle. But they did not discover the important papers in the old king's head, — not being Yankees.

At his arrival in Berlin from the Polish camp, as I before mentioned, he met an American gentleman, who made a call of civility upon him at his hotel the next morning. The denial that any such person had been there, and the fact that the police had visited the house during the night, aroused suspicions of foul play. This gentleman, therefore, immediately wrote to Mr. Rives, then American Minister at Paris, communicating his apprehensions. Mr. Rives made inquiry of the Prussian government concerning the matter, and was officially informed that no American had been there, only a Frenchman, a confederate of the Poles, who pretended to be an American. But he persisted, and finally, after six weeks of negotiation, and to avoid a threatened collision with the United States, the Prussian government withdrew its retractile fangs from the flesh of its victim. At night his prison door was opened; he was put into a carriage, and supposed he was doomed to Siberia; but the rising sun reassured him, for he rode in an opposite direction. He was driven six hundred miles without stopping, and tossed across the Prussian frontier with an admonition never to set foot within it again. His trunk and effects were there all restored to him, except forty-two dollars, retained for prison charges, after the manner of South Carolina, when she imprisons northern colored seamen.

When I went to Europe with Dr. Howe, in 1843, his name was found still standing on the proscribed list in all Prussian frontiers, and he was still forbidden to enter the kingdom.

The King of Prussia has since relented, for he sent Dr. Howe a gold medal for his wonderful achievement in educating Laura Bridgman, — the medal being of a class bestowed only upon those who have performed the most distinguished philanthropic services. It is a curious fact that this medal was of precisely the value of the prison fees above mentioned!

I presume you have all heard something of Laura Bridgman. She was a child, blind, deaf, dumb, and almost utterly destitute of the senses of taste and smell. Here was this glorious world, — Nature, Beauty, Love, Humanity, without; there, within, brooded, and slept, and moaned, an immortal soul. What North-west passage, or any other passage, shall be opened to that hidden, spiritual continent, more valuable than any new-discovered continent upon the earth, or any new-discovered star in the heavens? Who shall enter and gather the fruits of this new garden of the Hesperides? What angel shall convey a spark to kindle the incense already laid upon that lovely, but lonely, sequestered altar?

There was but one man who knew how to open that sarcophagus, and bring to life the immortal spirit within it, — and that man was Dr. Howe.

With what deep emotions do we look back to the moments when great events were preparing for their birth, — to Christopher Columbus wooing from Nature the secret of another continent; to Sir Isaac Newton, recognizing the invisible bond of attraction that holds the Universe in its beautiful order, or to Dr. Howe, with Laura Bridgman upon his knee, opening an avenue to her soul, and bringing out the captive into the light of day, and the more precious light of knowledge, — into the truths that pertain to time and to eternity. Then she was a blank, — voiceless, thoughtless, seemingly inaccessible. Now she is learned, sensible, beautiful, and far more intelligent than the average of young ladies, who have had more than her advantages, without suffering any of her privations.

Now, I suppose, Dr. Howe has given an equivalent for the sense of sight to more persons, ten to one, than all the Apostles put together. How nobly has he imitated the miracles!

Although, as Tacitus said of Seneca, "he would make a fit tutor for a prince," yet for more than a quarter of a century he has spent his noble and beneficent life among the blind. His last Annual Report was numbered the twenty-fifth.

Dr. Howe is now in his fifty-fifth year. Naturally of a fibrous, most enduring, and resilient temperament, his health was broken down by exposures while in the army of Greece. He is the best specimen extant, of all that was noble and valiant in the old chevalier, and in their day he would have been as terrible and as generous a warrior as Godfrey, or Amadis de Gaul. He is a man capable of all moods of mind, from the stormiest to the gentlest; with a voice that could shout on a charge of cavalry, or lull a sick infant to sleep. When that ocean of feeling he carries in his breast is calm, the halcyon bird might there build her nest, and brood her young; but when the tempest of a holy indignation rouses it, navies could not survive its fury.

Though devoting himself primarily, and mainly, to his speciality of benevolence, yet, when that work is done, he engages in other philanthropies. To whom is education indebted more than to him? He and Charles Sumner did more than all other men to correct public sentiment on the subject of solitary confinement in prisons. And the same hand that carried succors to the Greeks in 1826, and to the Poles in 1831, carried them to Kansas also, last year.

When any benevolent enterprise is undertaken in Massachusetts, his leadership or counsel is always invoked; and if he be absent in any critical juncture, or desperate emergency, men cry out as the host of Clan Alpine at the battle of Beal an Duinè,

> "One blast upon his bugle horn
> Were worth a thousand men!"

One of the most striking traits in my hero's character, is its simplicity; — not merely an absence of pretension, but a negation of it. Unlike many truly great men, he has no particle of self-show, or self-demonstration; and a stranger might ride with him a thousand miles without being informed that he had ever been anywhere that every body else had not been, or seen anything that every body else had not seen. Like an unpolished diamond, the surface is the only unbrilliant part of him; though dim without, all luminous within. When he writes, or when he fights, the beholder is not dazzled by the sheen of the battle-axe, but the antagonist dies under the weight of the metal, or by the precision of the blow. Like the Arab's sword which had shivered every sword it had ever struck,

> "Ornament it carried none,
> Save the notches on the blade."

Another leading class of cases respecting which the Gospels record displays of miraculous power, refers to demoniacs. I do not propose here to discuss what was the nature or character of this alleged demoniacal possession. One class, and a large class of commentators on the Bible, believe that many of the demoniacs were cases of actual diabolic possession; that a real spirit of evil or devil, one or more, had power to get inside of a man's brain, and take the reins of thought and feeling out of that man's hands into his own hands; dispossess the true owner, and enter into possession himself. They believe that, in some way, the foul spirit got hold of the cerebral ends of the man's nerves, and through them worked the muscles of his arms, legs, tongue, and the rest of his physical machinery, so as to make the body and the organs of the victim obey the spirit of the fiend.

Another class of commentators maintains that all these cases were simple cases of what we call lunacy, insanity, or madness, like those we have now amongst us, so many of which are successfully treated at the hospitals; and experienced physicians say that if you wish to see a case of madness, worse even than that of the man who had his dwelling in the mountains and in the tombs, and whom no man could bind with fetters and chains, — they say if you wish to see a man worse than this man, — you have only to give a drunkard a quart of whiskey, and the devils will need no further invitation, or license, to act "for the public good."

Now what could be more natural for such a tender and compassionate nature as Christ's, than to take pity on these demoniacs, and to exert his highest power for their relief? But from his time, down to a very recent period, this deplorable class of our fellow-beings has been abandoned to their terrible fate. Their case has not been understood by the doctors pathologically, nor by the ministers psychologically, and the almost universal public sentiment has been, that insanity was a direct visitation from heaven, and that he alone who had stricken, could heal. The insane endangered the property and life of others, and, therefore, they must be confined. Those who confined them, regarding their own safety alone, and not the welfare of the victims, have shut them up in garrets and in cellars, in outhouses, or in pits, excavated from the hill side; have disposed of them anywhere, and in any manner, except by outright murder, which would have been merciful when compared to the slow tortures to which heart and brain were doomed by man's selfishness or superstition. In the most exposed places, they have been kept, winter after winter, without fire, and in nakedness; and even those who called themselves physicians, have prescribed scourging, and starvation, and suffocation in water, up to the nearest point this side of drowning, and frights, and pretended visitations of evil spirits! Oh, it is incredible what men have done under the selfish impulse of self-protection, unhumanized by any touch of sympathy for the welfare of others. And this was the universal treatment of the insane, throughout all Christendom, until a very recent period. Three or four sporadic cases are all that can be found, in the history of this wretched class of beings throughout all Europe, where such abhorrent treatment as I have described was not their common lot, until the close of the last century. Human love, God-like by its intensity, has sometimes dared to act from its own impulse to save a beloved friend from the common fate, and if knowledge had come to its aid, a deeper insight into the power Jesus Christ exercised for good might have ameliorated their condition earlier; but how superstition chains the souls of men! What is Christ as an exemplar to man, if his power is regarded as superhuman, rather than as divinely human? Would God require man to do that which man cannot do? — not the God whom I worship!

Esquirol was the first man who made any impression upon the public in favor of better treatment of the Insane. In one place he found some twenty of these supposed demoniacs manacled, caged like wild beasts, furiously mad, nestling in their own filth, deserted by relatives, and by all human kind, agonized by the tortures of a malady whose very nature excluded consolation, and so goaded into hostility to the human race, that the sight of a keeper threw them into paroxysms of rage. Into these dens of despair Esquirol entered. He unfettered their limbs. He led them out into the pure air and light of heaven. He spoke to them such divine words of sympathy as melt ferocity as fire melts iron. His soul transmigrated, as it were, into their bodies, and he proved that if the devil can get possession of a human organism to torture it, an angel also can take possession to bless it.

In this country, Dr. Todd, of Hartford, Connecticut, was the first man who ever treated the insane, on a large scale, on humane principles. He was a charming man, — a man to love at sight, — genial, warm, sunny, the benevolence of his heart shone out through his face, as the light shines through a vase of alabaster.

But the man who made the deepest impression upon

the American mind, in this sphere of benevolence, was his pupil, Dr. Woodward, who, for thirteen years, had the superintendence of the Lunatic Hospital at Worcester, Massachusetts, which was opened in January, 1833.

On this subject, Dr. Woodward gave a new direction to the whole public mind of America; and wherever you now go, the best hospitals, in their organization and management, are but little more than a reproduction of him.

He was a noble man, with an Herculean frame, — a great soul in a great body. I have seen that sinewy hand of his, which could break an iron bar an inch square, wipe the tear from the eye of a hypochondriac, tenderly as a mother caresses an infant. While others would take a company of sane men and turn them into maniacs, he, in the same time, would take a company of maniacs and restore them to sanity. His gigantic frame and his gentle bearing inspired at once both awe and affection. His tremendous physical strength, with his affectionate demeanor, was like an iron hand in a velvet glove. He walked the halls of his asylum like a god. In his presence the most ferocious relented, the most melancholic smiled. As if the all-clasping zone of attraction that binds the stars in their places were broken, and suns and planets should "shoot madly from their spheres," and fly careering through the skies, and some god should emerge upon the scene, and with all-potent voice should arrest their centrifugal flight, and reduce them to their rightful orbits, and send them round again upon their appointed circuits, so he, when reason was dethroned, and each faculty was a maniac, and anarchy raged through the soul, could speak peace to all its troubled elements, and bring the chaotic realm to order.

Dr. Woodward had a right to his loftiness and breadth of stature, and to a body that weighed nearly two hundred pounds, without an ounce of adipose bagging down anywhere; for he was born of healthy parents, and from his birth had been treated and had treated himself physiologically. He ate according to his exercise; he had never tasted ardent spirits; in wine he was a Nazarene, and he hated tobacco with all his heart, and soul, and mind, and strength.

But in this special form of "good will to man," the greatest ornament of human nature the world has yet known, is a woman, — Miss Dorothea L. Dix, who began her career of benevolence about twenty years ago. She was a young lady of Boston, who taught a private school for a livelihood. Being very successful, she accumulated a little competence, which was augmented by the legacy of a relative; and was meditating some enlarged sphere of usefulness. As she was walking home from meeting, one Sunday, after having heard Dr. Channing preach one of those sermons that made the vicious envy the beauty of virtue, and sent men and women into the various spheres where suffering humanity needs aid, whether it be to the prisoner shut up in solitude by his own crimes, or to the destitute who suffer from the crimes of others (and Boston can show many such men and women, so sent and heaven-recorded), she accidentally heard some one describing the suffering condition of some insane people at the jail in the adjoining town of Cambridge. It was a wind-wafted seed, but into what celestial soil did it fall! Her resolve was instantaneously made, in pursuance of which, the next morning she visited the insane in the Cambridge jail, found their condition deplorable, and forthwith began a system of measures for their immediate relief, and, if possible, their ultimate cure. But before this work could be accomplished, she heard of others in a distant part of the same county, in a similar condition. These also she visited and succored. As her thoughts were now flowing in this channel, her ear was quick to hear what otherwise would have passed unnoticed; for we hear and see the things we care about, and but little else. Then her visits extended to a neighboring county; then to another and another, until she had examined every prison, jail, house of correction, poor house, suspicious-looking barn or outhouse in the State, where an insane person was confined. Indeed she penetrated farther; she descended into cellars, knocked at closed arch-ways, opened trap-doors; but when she stood on the borders of the State, here was a limit. She had done what she could for her native State; let others take care of theirs. Not so did she conclude. Her benevolence poured out, like God's, wherever sorrow held out its supplicating hands to receive it. In her heart, the map of the world had no state or national lines. Soon she was accidentally in Newport, R. I., where a lady of her acquaintance took her out shopping. While abroad, she heard the cry of an insane person. She rushed forth to find the victim, and having found him, she never stopped until she had found all the insane in the State. Then she was really abroad on a voyage of discovery, with the whole world before her. She visited State after State as swiftly as the wings of a strong compassion could carry her. She learned the number and inspected the condition of all the insane in their jails, prisons, and other receptacles. She prepared, printed, and circulated memorials at her own expense. She besieged governors and legislatures. She caused committees to be appointed, and wrote the eloquent reports which they read. She kindled sympathy in human hearts; even misers gave of their stores to her importunity. She changed, at least for the hour, politicians into men. She obtained grants for hospitals, selected sites for their location, prepared plans for their structure, found superintendents for them, and set them in motion. Not content with this, she caused them to be embellished with libraries, music rooms, and means of varied employment, so that sane faculties might be worthily employed to disarm the activity of insane faculties. She travelled from one end of the country to the other, taking journeys of a thousand miles alone, supplying knowledge to meet new emergencies, and subduing sinister opposition, until, in the States this side the Mississippi, including one in Canada, she established *nineteen* hospitals for the insane. I say *she* did it. She did it just as much as God made the stars, or Christ worked miracles.

After she had founded all these hospitals, she conceived the grand idea of obtaining a grant of public lands from the government, sufficient to endow them.

Accordingly she took up her residence in Washington, and attempted the great missionary work of converting the members of Congress to humanity and duty. She presented a Memorial, embracing the whole statistics of insanity for the United States, mostly collected by her own indefatigable labors. Then, with infinite perseverance, she began the aggressive, creative work of enlightening the members, especially those of the south, south-west and west, *one by one*, — transferring her thoughts into their minds, and infusing her benevolence into their bosoms. Almost always she could convert the man; oftentimes the politician was intractable, — insoluble by any intensity of heat, unmalleable by any weight of blow. I said she began the *creative* work. It was more. Creation is one, single, sovereign operation. She had an equal preparatory labor to perform in removing old prejudices, political fossil bones, petrifactions of old dogmas with an enamel. Hence, in her case, annihilation of the bad had to precede creation of the good, — a double miracle.

The first session after presenting her Memorial and preparing her Bill, she carried the House of Representatives in its favor, but the Bill failed in the Senate for want of time. The next session, with almost equal labor, she carried the Senate, but failed in the House, for alleged want of time. At the first session of 1853–4, she carried both Senate and House, but the bill was vetoed by the President.

When one considers the moral charm and beauty of the work proposed, the heavenly disinterestedness with which it had been prosecuted, and the ever-renewing fruits of blessedness which would attend its consummation, one could not believe, one would feel authorized to deny, that if the momentous alternative of perfecting or destroying this enterprise could be brought home to any one individual; if any one person could be made to see, what a hell of agonies he could close up, what a heaven of joy he could open, by ratifying that measure, no mortal could be found who would not shut that door of agony, who would not open that door of joy.

The drunkard would set down his intoxicating cup to seize the pen for approval; the miser would stop counting his hoards to give his assent; ay, the pirate would have dropped his tiller in a storm, to give his signature to so blessed a law. But one man *was* found who could nullify, veto that Bill, — and that man was President of the United States.

Failing thus, Miss Dix felt the hopelessness of her case for the remainder of that Presidential term. She therefore went to Europe, and has been travelling in Great Britain and on the Continent, where she has found access to all Institutions of the same nature, pouring out the blessing of her counsel and her consolations on those that were ready to perish. I must not tell her beneficent plans for foreign lands, nor what high places she has beseiged, *nor left till they surrendered* in favor of their own suffering subjects, who were left in groans and bondage till she passed by to succor and to save, — for I might stand in the way of the accomplishment of that for which she labors. When asked in those sad days of trial and disappointment what she should do next about her American Bill, she quietly answered, "try it again every session while I live," — but she was soon convinced that this would be useless. If a beneficent change ever takes place in the administration of our government, from which the very soul of humanity seems to have departed, we will hope, that, whether she lives or dies, the change will be sanctified by the law that she in her Christian love conceived.

What can I say to you, my young friends, to deepen the impression I would leave upon your minds of the character of Miss Dix? Her life is her long, long eulogium. Out of the abundance of the heart not only does the mouth speak, but the hands act. To those who have never seen her, however, I may remark that she is a person of singularly modest and reserved demeanor. It seems to require as great an effort in her to appear before committees, or assemblies of men, as for a soldier to volunteer in a forlorn hope. Again and again have companies of distinguished ladies, her co-operators and admirers, requested her to sit for her picture, or at least for a daguerreotype, but she always declines. Her voice is womanly and low, with deep tones, but never loud ones. An instinct teaches her that a loud-laughing, shouting, screaming lady is as gross a contradiction in terms as a white blackbird, a square circle, or a six-sided triangle. No person has as yet been able to obtain from her any memoranda for a biography, or sketch of her life. So wholly is she devoted to doing, she has no time for displaying. Yet with all this retiring sensitiveness, which recoils from public assemblies, she always addresses prisoners when she can, and she will speak to hundreds of them till the sun goes down, and show them how they can transform the Hades of a penitentiary into a mere stopping-place on their way to glory. In such a time-destroying manner is she importuned with confessions and requests from prisons for advice, that she once wrote and caused to be printed a circular letter which she sent to all the prisons where she had taught and counselled.

In her peregrinations she has always travelled alone, carried often by rude drivers in the night time over unfrequented roads, to reach some special destination at an appointed time. Once in passing through the wards of a prison in Michigan, a young man caught sight of her through the bars of his grate, and made known his wish to speak with her. He asked if she did not remember being taken from such a place to such a place, quite a distance, in an open wagon, by night. On her replying in the affirmative, he said, "I was your driver." "But why are you here?" she asked. "I robbed a man of his money," he replied, "when driving him shortly after." "But I had money at that time," she said, "and a gold watch; why did not you rob me?" "Oh," said he, fetching a deep breath, "I wasn't devil enough for that."

I said she had travelled her tens and her hundreds of thousands of miles without accident and without injury. I might have added, — without insult. In the perfect virtue of woman there is a defensive armor which is villain-proof. It is doubtless a harsh judgment to say that no woman is ever dishonorably approached who has not first signified her permission; that no man ever dares to invade her sanctuary unless he first finds the enclosures down and sees a beckoning hand across the line. Sometimes a heart that knows no guile, an innocence that knows no evil is so far betrayed as to be insulted; but there is plausibility and verisimilitude even in the former postulate. For there is always a battle of spirits fought in the air before a foot approaches or a hand is raised. It is in this preliminary battle of soul with soul, of eye with eye, of the celestial aura and effluvium radiated by virtue against the Tartarian exhalations of vice; — it is this preliminary battle that prophecies the fate of the other. Hence there is a female purity that no villainy can invade, for though its weapons are an etherial essence only, yet they are swift as lightning and solid as porphyry; and whoever dares encounter them, perishes like the Israelite who trod upon the foot of Sinai when Jehovah thundered on its summit. Her sanctity was her shield. She demonstrates how moral beauty eclipses all other beauty. The charms of nature and of art become wearisome and tedious in the presence of such moral glory.

The benedictions of thousands whom she has redeemed from misery descend upon her, like perpetual hymns of joy. Oh, the sin of envy and coveting, if her consciousness were its object, would be transmuted into a virtue. Though her body yet dwells upon earth, yet the soul of such a being must forever walk up and down the streets of the New Jerusalem; and though she declines all worldly honors, however brilliant, yet the light of the seven golden candlesticks forever shines in her face.

Who then shall say that man cannot imitate Christ in his grandest works? All acts of truly disinterested benevolence, however lowly the sphere in which they are exercised, be they but truly self-sacrificing, irrespective of reward, born of the love implanted by the Creator in the soul of man, are real imitations of the miracles of Christ, awakening human sympathies to apprehension of the Infinite. The wild Indian, when made thoroughly to understand that Jesus Christ was willing to suffer that all men might believe his inculcations of duty, lays down his weapons of revenge and ceases to kill except in self-defence. The apostle Eliot made them understand this, for he acted it out; many a devoted Catholic priest who has renounced the world for their benefit, has made them believe it. But it is difficult to make an Indian a bigot, and who can wonder that the work is often undone when they hear the strife of sectarian hate drown the voice of Christian love?

I should rejoice, my young friends, to speak to you of some others of those glorious names that constellate the firmament of benevolence, and to show in what ways they, too, animated by the spirit of Christ, have worked his miracles; of Howard, and Mrs. Fry, of Oberlin, and Felix Neff, of Lord Shaftesbury, and above all, of Florence Nightingale, who outqueens a thousand Victorias, and for the transcendent beauty of whose character God seems to have been willing to pay all the horrors and wretchedness of the Crimean war. But I have spoken of a few whom I know, and I might add such examples as of those who, by the successful experiments of many years, have proved that for every orphan child there is a childless home; of those who have taken prisoners from the hands of the municipal law, and becoming surety for them, have redeemed them from the law of sin itself; of noble spirits who have set the bondsman free, although impoverishing themselves by so doing; who have made the middle passage of the emigrant ship, in order to know and rectify the abuses therein practised. These do the "more wonderful works" which Christ predicted to those who were worshipping his miracles. And they have not done these things merely because Christ pointed the way. They have done them because they, like him, had Divine natures wrapped up in their human natures.

But I will pass to what I deem far more vital imitation of Christ's example, one involving a far higher appreciation of his character; for after all, his alleviation of outward suffering is not to be compared with his removal of spiritual evils. It is true that the amelioration of physical evils does minister to the spiritual needs of man; for while the soul is imprisoned in a useless body, it is often crippled in its ascension to practical virtue.

It is narrated that Christ, by the touch of his hand, could annihilate the heavy afflictions of blindness, deafness, dumbness, insanity, but these were not his greatest achievements, nor his peculiar work. His eye was ever upon the immortal soul. It was *that* he loved above all other things, himself included. This healing of the sick, the maimed, the blind, was but a preliminary work, a by-play, in comparison with what he called "My Father's work." His compassionate heart could not see suffering in any shape without wishing to relieve it; but he would purchase good for the soul at the price of pain to the body, or mortification to the feelings. He could scourge the money-changers from the temple; he could upbraid the Pharisee, as well as cheer and encourage the woman who was taken in the "very act" of crime. He looked to the motive and the hope of reformation. He knew that the woman who bathed his feet with ointment, expressed in so doing a loftier sentiment than those who reproached her for not saving her money for the poor. We are not all so situated that we can perform the great achievements that immortalize a few historic characters, but there is not one of us, not the humblest, who cannot imitate Christ every day in our lives. There is not one of us who has not a brother, or a sister, a friend, or a school-mate, whom we can make better, as well as happier. Every day calls upon us for sacrifices of small selfishness, for forbearance under provocation, and for the subjugation of evil propensities. Drop that stone you were about to throw in retaliation for insult; unclench that fist with which you were about to redress some supposed, perhaps some real wrong; silence that tongue about to utter words which would poison like the venom of asps; expel that wicked imagination that comes into your thoughts, as Satan came into the Garden of Eden, for if you do not drive that out of your Paradise, it will drive you out.

While you are passing these years of study in college halls, you cannot go forth, seeking the maimed, the blind, or the insane, in distant cities, or on the mountain tops. While I am here, I cannot, like Howard, visit all the prisons of the world; or, like Oberlin, plunge into Alpine fastnesses, where the Gospel and the schoolmaster never were heard of, and, beginning with the spade and mattock, as he did, introduce comfort and purity, and set the people forth on their way to everlasting life. But you can watch over yourselves, and over one another; if you see a companion indulging some vicious habit, you can check him, and lead him by the light of your better example; nay, you can spend a week or a month in winning his regards and good will, and then, through friendship and affection, find an avenue to his heart, otherwise never opened. And I, in my sphere, if years have given me any advantage over inexperience, I can watch and warn, and counsel, ay, if need be, reprove, though every word draws a drop of life's-blood from my heart, and thus prepare you for the inevitable trials, the glorious duties, of life. We can thus do as much good in our respective spheres, as if we crossed lands and seas in search of the suffering and ignorant. We have only to follow

Christ's law of life, "Love one another." "Do unto others as you would that others should do unto you." Here is the whole duty of man.

Probably there is not one of the generous, high-souled youth before me, who would not plunge into the water, or rush into the flames, to save his friend, — to save a child, — not necessarily his own, but somebody's child. We feel within ourselves the power to die for others as Christ did. But can we live for others as he did? It is far more difficult, I assure you, to live for the truth than to die for it. I have seen the time when, if that would have answered as well, I could have died for a cause as easily as a babe falls asleep; but to live for it — that is the cutting off of the right hand, that is the plucking out of the right eye. Patient perseverance in well-doing is infinitely harder than a sudden and impulsive self-sacrifice. And hence this "patient continuance" is the brightest jewel in the diadem of Christian virtues.

How infinitely better then, it is, to imitate Christ's miracles than to wrangle about their nature, or the means by which they were wrought. They are not inimitable. He has sympathy for us, and looks upon our humblest efforts approvingly. He was "touched with the feeling of our infirmities." He was "in all points tempted like as we are." He was virtuous, and virtue implies a struggle, a choice between the evil and the good. We are moved to a noble emulation of him by his exercise of moral power, not of supernatural power, for there we cannot follow him. We have seen him taken up of the devil into a high mountain, and we have seen him prostrate in the Garden of Gethsemane. It was Christ himself who said, the "spirit indeed is willing, but the flesh is weak," and it may be that he said it of himself too.

My children, begin early this imitation of Christ. Lose no time. Habit has tremendous power. Good and evil grow in us with animating, with terrifying rapidity. Those tottering feet of infancy shall soon traverse continents, its lisping tongue command senates. The resolve to be virtuous, therefore, to be Christ-like, which your heart makes now and here, — oh, what grandeur and glory may it quickly reach; though feeble now as the wing of unfledged bird, yet from day to day it will gather strength, will learn to wheel in wider and wider circuits, and to essay loftier and loftier flights; — it soars, it soars, — it shoots beyond the stars; — swift and strong as an angel's pinion, I see it cleave the etherial realms; — it passes mid heaven; — it has blessed man, and thereby been sanctified; it has alighted at the throne of God.

THE END.

www.ingramcontent.com/pod-product-compliance
Lightning Source LLC
LaVergne TN
LVHW020237110826
845151LV00003B/944

* 9 7 8 1 4 2 5 5 3 0 4 4 0 *